D1796270

OFFICE OF THE PUBLIC GUARDIAN
HADRIAN HOUSE
CALLENDAR BUSINESS PARK
CALLENDAR ROAD
FALKIRK  FK1 1XR

# THE ELDER CLIENT:

# A PRACTICAL GUIDE

AUSTRALIA
Law Book Co.
Sydney

CANADA and USA
Carswell
Toronto

HONG KONG
Sweet & Maxwell Asia

NEW ZEALAND
Brookers
Wellington

SINGAPORE and MALAYSIA
Sweet & Maxwell Asia
Singapore and Kuala Lumpur

# THE ELDER CLIENT:
# A PRACTICAL GUIDE

Susan M. Duff, LL.B, Dip.L.P,
NP, Solicitor

Fiona F. McDonald, MA (Hons), LL.B,
Dip.L.P, ATT, NP, Solicitor

Published in 2007 by
W. Green & Son Ltd
21 Alva Street
Edinburgh EH2 4PS

www.wgreen.thomson.com

*Typeset by YHT Ltd, London*
*Printed and bound in Great Britain by MPG Books Ltd*

No natural forests were destroyed to make this product;
only farmed timber was used and replanted

A CIP catalogue record for this book is available from
the British Library.

ISBN  978-0-414-01680-4

# FOREWORD

Older people, their families and those who advise them are increasingly challenged by the quagmire of legislation which impacts on Scotland's senior citizens, and which could be of benefit if only it was understood. This practical guide brings together into one place that wide range of legislation in a way which is easy to follow and comprehend, particularly where a number of provisions from different sources can apply at the same time.

While it is very important that solicitors and others who advise older clients are fully aware of current legislation and what it can offer, it is equally important that older people and their families have access to the information presented in this guide to enable them to make their own informed choices and to be aware of their options. This is a well-written publication which demonstrates an understanding of the legal issues affecting older people and it will make a valuable contribution to improving the quality of advice older people are given.

David Manion
Chief Executive
Age Concern Scotland

# FOREWORD

# PREFACE

In this text we have brought together a variety of practical and legal issues specific to the elderly client, accounting for developments up to September 2007. It will be interesting to review the impact of the Adult Support and Protection (Scotland) Act 2007, particularly after the success of the Adults with Incapacity (Scotland) Act 2000 which addressed many fundamental issues.

The financial and tax angles have been addressed with the rates and allowances from the Finance Act 2007. As pensioners will hopefully remain a priority to the government in terms of financial stability and quality of life, it will again be interesting to consider how the figures will change.

With every individual's circumstances being different there is often no correct solution but it is hoped that this book will assist in providing options and highlighting sensible planning opportunities.

Our thanks go to all those at Messrs W. Green & Son Ltd for their support and encouragement with this project.

We would also like to add a dedication from Susan to Fred, Sheila and David; they know who they are and the good things they have done.

September 2007

# CONTENTS

## Contents

# TABLE OF CASES

# TABLE OF STATUTES

# TABLE OF STATUTORY INSTRUMENTS

# CHAPTER 1

# CAPACITY

## INTRODUCTION

Capacity is relevant to all client relationships; does the client have the **1–01** mental power, faculty or legal competency to give instructions? In plain English, does the client understand the situation and is the client able to give meaningful instructions? Legal capacity is required for all the matters a solicitor undertakes for a client (and indeed for any contractual matter carried out by anyone for a customer or patient). Likely examples in the context of a solicitor advising the elderly are buying and selling property, taking loans and equity release plans, granting a power of attorney, making or altering a will, revoking a will, making monetary gifts or gifts of houses, etc.

## PRESUMPTION OF CAPACITY

A dictionary[1] definition of "law" is: **1–02**

> "a rule or system of rules recognised by a country or community as regulating the actions of its members and enforced by the imposition of penalties". A lawyer is "a person who practises or studies law".

Adults are presumed in Scots Law to have legal capacity, i.e. the ability to make decisions for themselves and to manage their own affairs.[2] A person aged 16 or over has legal capacity "to enter into any transaction".[3] The presumption of capacity can be rebutted; the onus of proof being on the person challenging the validity of the decision or deed. Ultimately capacity is a question of law to be decided, if necessary, by a court.

## MEANING OF CAPACITY

The meaning of capacity depends on what the client is instructing the **1–03** solicitor to do. Until recently the law was quite clear in that either a person was capable of making decisions, i.e. *capax*, or was not capable of making decisions, i.e *incapax*. The Adults with Incapacity (Scotland) Act 2000 (AWI (S) Act 2000) introduced some new arrangements for making decisions

---

[1] Compact *Oxford English Dictionary* (OUP).
[2] *Lindsay v Watson* (1843) 5 D 1194.
[3] Age of Legal Capacity (Scotland) Act 1991, s.1.

about personal welfare, managing property and financial affairs for adults whose capacity is impaired. Rather than deciding there is a clear-cut line between being able to make decisions and being unable to make decisions it is recognised that for adults with difficulties there are varying degrees of understanding and ability to make decisions and so the level of restriction on these persons should vary accordingly.

The main distinction between any measure under the AWI (S) Act 2000 and instructing a will (but also other forms of contract) is the ability to retain memory of a decision. To grant a continuing power of attorney one must be able to retain memory of that decision. So, a client with severe short-term memory loss or who only has periods of lucidity could very well make a will which is valid, but would be unable to make a continuing power of attorney even if in a lucid moment at the time the instructions were given.

In relation to preparing a continuing or welfare power of attorney, the following statutory definition of capacity (or rather incapacity) applies:

> "Incapable means incapable of (a) acting; or (b) making decisions; or (c) communicating decisions; or (d) understanding decisions; or (e) retaining memory of decisions as mentioned in any provision of this Act by reason of mental disorder or of inability to communicate because of physical disability; but a person shall not fall within this definition by reason only of a lack or deficiency in a faculty of communication if that lack or deficiency can be made good by human or mechanical aid (whether of an interpretative nature or otherwise); and incapacity is to be construed accordingly".[4]

From a practical viewpoint, where communication with the adult is the problem, the Act clearly requires efforts to be made to facilitate communication, such as the use of interpreters, pointer boards, buzzers, etc. which is apparent from the inclusion of the words "by any means of communication" and the absence of the qualifying wording "insofar as it is reasonable and practical to do so".[5]

Where another form of instruction or a contract is being entered into, then retaining memory of the decision may be less relevant particularly if he or she consistently reaches the same decision given the same facts on each occasion.

For instructing the preparation of a will or a change to a will, any person of sound mind and full age has testamentary capacity. The law states that a person of or over 12 years shall have testamentary capacity, including legal capacity to exercise by testamentary writing any power of appointment.[6] The elderly client will clearly satisfy the age requirement, but does the client have capacity to make, or alter, a will instruction?

---

[4] Adults with Incapacity (Scotland) Act 2000, s.1(6).
[5] Adults with Incapacity (Scotland) Act 2000, s.1(4)(a).
[6] Age of Legal Capacity (Scotland) Act 1991, s.2(2).

The presumption of capacity does not relieve solicitors of the responsibility of ensuring they are satisfied that the client is of sound mind. Being of sound mind can ebb and flow and, unlike matters under the Adults with Incapacity (Scotland) Act 2000, there is no statutory definition, nor a fundamental requirement that the testator retains memory of the decision.[7]

Specifically in relation to will instructions, a useful set of criteria was contained in the Edinburgh Textbook of Psychiatry (Companion to Psychiatric Studies) by Professor Kenneth Macrae.[8]

- Understanding of the nature of the act of making a will and its effects.
- Reasonable knowledge of the extent of his or her property.
- Knowing and appreciating the claims to which he or she ought to give effect.
- Not influenced by abnormal emotional state or by any delusions.

In taking will instructions, most firms will have a style will checklist. In addition to obvious matters such as money laundering details, knowing the client's personal details, status, assets and liabilities and view of tax planning and charity and general take on life, it is prudent to include a notes section and use it to indicate that the interviewer considered capacity and note details of the assessment of the client's ability to give proper instructions.

## THE CONSEQUENCES OF INCAPACITY

Whether a contract is valid, voidable or void because of the capacity, or lack **1–04** thereof, of the person entering the contract will depend on the nature of the contract and the circumstances of the decision. Where there is incapacity to "test", i.e. to make a will, a will is void. However, that same person is legally capable of going into a supermarket and buying a selection of foods and paying for them.

### The consequences for wills

*Domicile and capacity*

According to Anton[9] the question of capacity is generally decided by the **1–05** law of his domicile as at the date of execution of the will. In the case of heritable or immoveable property the law of the country in question may decide the question.

*Facility and circumvention*

A will is voidable, i.e. can be successfully challenged, the onus of proof **1–06** being on the challenger, where there is facility (which is a weakness of mind which does not amount to full mental incapacity) and circumvention (which means pressure by someone seeking to influence the terms of the will,

---

[7] *Nisbet's Trustees v Nisbet* (1871) 9 M. 937.
[8] As quoted in Alan Barr et al, *Drafting Wills in Scotland*, (Edinburgh: Butterworths, Scotland, 1994), para.2–04.
[9] A.E. Anton and P.R. Beaumont, *Private International Law*, 2nd edn (Edinburgh: W. Green, 1990), p.681.

usually for personal gain). Both facility and circumvention must be present for an action to be successful.

These elements have been described as being present where "a person is in such a mental state that he or she is unable to resist pressure, and ... someone else can mould and fashion his conduct as he pleases".[10]

Facility is a matter of degree and can take a number of forms; "A man may be weak and facile from want of judgement or reason ... [or] from mere nervousness and incapacity to resist solicitation".[11]

Other forms of facility may be caused by illness and bereavement[12] or alcoholism.[13]

### Undue influence

1–07    Undue influence is where a person is in a position of trust in relation to the testator and that person has abused the position of trust for personal benefit. A will made in such circumstances may be successfully challenged. There are various relationships in which the doctrine may apply. Some obvious and commonplace situations are:

- a parent and a child i.e. a parent unduly influencing a child[14];
- a child unduly influencing a parent[15];
- a solicitor and a client[16];
- a doctor and a patient.[17]

The class of relationships is in no way limited, e.g. the doctrine was held to apply between an art dealer and customer.[18]

Undue influence does not necessarily require some weakness of mind in the testator whereas facility and circumvention does require some weakness of mind in the testator. In some cases both facility and circumvention and undue influence are present,[19] or at least pleaded,[20] and in some cases the distinction is blurred by the view that all the elements of weakness and facility and circumvention and lesion are interrelated and must be looked at as a whole.[21]

In a recently reported case,[22] undue influence and facility and circumvention were the subject of separate pleas-in-law. Separate averments were made

---

[10] Lord Justice-Clerk Alness in *Gibson's Executors v Anderson*, 1925 S.C. 744 at 790.
[11] Lord Justice-Clerk Inglis in *Morrison v Maclean's Trustees* (1862) 24 D. 625 at 635.
[12] *Munro v Strain* (1874) 1 R. 522.
[13] *Pascoe-Watson v Brock's Executor*, 1998 S.L.T. 40.
[14] *Allan v Allan*, 1961 S.C. 200.
[15] *Grant's Executors v Grant*, 1999 G.W.D. 36–1772.
[16] *Stewart v MacLaren*, 1920 S.C. (H.L.) 148.
[17] *Radcliffe v Price* (1902) 18 T.L.R. 466.
[18] *Honeyman's Executors v Sharp*, 1978 S.C. 223.
[19] *Ross v Gosselin's Executors*, 1926 S.C. 325.
[20] *Gaul v Deerey*, 2000 S.C.L.R. 407.
[21] *Pascoe-Watson v Brock's Executor*, 1998 S.L.T. 40.
[22] *Horne v Whyte*, 2005 G.W.D. 28–525.

and the elements treated separately by the court. The deceased died on July 6, 1998, aged 94. He left a will dated May 2, 1997 which directed his executors to give effect to any subsequent informal writings which were clearly expressive of his intention. On June 19, 1998 he made a codicil which benefited his housekeeper and a typewritten letter dated May 7, 1997 apparently signed by him was found, which also benefited his housekeeper. The averments seem to disclose classic examples of both facility and circumvention and undue influence. Both grounds were upheld and the codicil was reduced. It is important to note that the will and the codicil had been prepared by the deceased's usual solicitor and the codicil was witnessed by his GP but that did not prevent reduction of the codicil.

### Duty of care and wills

Most solicitors will send out a draft will with a covering explanatory letter **1-08** or a summary sheet of the salient provisions of the will. Many also have a practice of placing a copy of the original instruction sheet with any amendments noted with the will.

Until relatively recently the worst a practising solicitor in Scotland could expect from getting the will wrong (and the error only coming to light after the testator is incapacitated or deceased) would be shame and a dreadful tirade from the disappointed meant-to-be-beneficiary. The rationale being that the testator was the client, the meant-to-be-beneficiary is not your client and you only had a duty of care to your client, not to third parties.[23] Those days are gone now. In England, the House of Lords[24] held by a majority verdict that a solicitor was liable to the beneficiary who would have benefited from a will which was drafted by the solicitor on July 19, and remained unsigned on September 14. The liability was for the amount which the beneficiary should have received had the will been executed. And so with many trends, this has migrated north of the border.[25]

It would be prudent to have an office policy regarding time-scales for sending out drafts and a good diary system in place for checking if the client has made the appropriate response at various stages of the procedure.

Extra care must be taken with those in any form of ill health. In practice, a client will have received from the solicitor, whether all in one envelope or over several days, terms and conditions of business (two copies one to be signed and returned), a draft will with an explanatory letter seeking approval or amendments, and asking the client to make an appointment.

This is a lot of information for anyone to process. It is suggested that a follow up reminder letter or a phone call reminder should take place sooner rather than later. If a certain period passes, a letter should be sent politely informing the client that until the new will is completed and signed their

---

[23] *Robertson v Fleming* (1861) 4 Macq. 167; and *MacDougall v Clydesdale Bank Trustees*, 1993 S.C.L.R. 832.
[24] *White v Jones* [1993] 3 All E.R. 481.
[25] *Holmes v Bank of Scotland*, 2002 S.L.T. 544.

instructions will not have any validity and either a previous will would operate or the law would decide the destiny of their worldly goods, which may be at odds with their wishes. Without harassing the client, the solicitor may have to keep pushing client to finalise the process.

**Testator lacking capacity**

*Statutory wills under English law*

**1–09**    If the client lacks legal capacity, he cannot make a will. Compare the situation in England where whilst a person lacking legal capacity cannot make or alter a will of their own it is possible for someone else to apply to the Court of Protection to make a will on behalf of the client. This type of will is known as a statutory will. The rules extend to statutory wills and codicils and gifts, settlements and other similar dealings. Quite often a client will move south to be with family if infirmity sets in and so it should be borne in mind that once living in a new jurisdiction, other possibilities are available for the incapacitated.

*Powers of attorney*

**1–10**    An attorney cannot give will instructions nor sign a will, even if there is a purported power to do so within the power of attorney document itself. This is the situation in Scotland no matter what date the power of attorney has been signed or whether it is continuing or not.

## AGE, HEALTH AND CAPACITY

**1–11**  Having travelled a long distance from one's date of birth does not in itself necessarily affect the ability to process information, but with age can come ill health.

Being in poor health may itself bring a degree of incapacity or may render the client isolated and vulnerable to pressure, well meaning (or not so well meaning), from family and friends.

There are many who "enjoy" poor health and will discuss the details of ailments at length with any captive audience, but it is not this sort of ill health to which the solicitor should be alert.

**World Health Organisation (WHO) definition of "health"[26]**

**1–12**    The word "health" has a proper meaning having been defined in the World Health Organisation Constitution as "a state of complete physical and social well being and not merely the absence of disease or infirmity". The WHO is responsible for a group of documents called international classifications, the full texts and the history of which can be found on their website.

---

[26]  *http://www.who.int* [accessed July 18, 2007].

In 1980 the WHO published "The International Classification of Impairments, Disabilities and Handicaps" (ICDH) which provided a structured approach to health disorders.

In 1993 the WHO proposed a definition of quality of life linked to health; the perception by individuals of their position in life, in the context of the culture and value systems in which they live and in relation to their goals, expectations, standards and concerns.

A second edition of ICDH was endorsed in 2001 giving it the new title of "International Classification of Functioning Disability and Health" (ICF).

According to the classification:

- *impairment* concerns the physical aspects of health;
- *disability* relates to the loss of functional capacity resulting from an impaired organ;
- *handicap* is a measure of the social and cultural consequences of an impairment or disability; and
- *health* related quality of life means health as assessed by the individual concerned, i.e. their own perception of their morbidity.

For many in modern society the signs and effects of ageing are not badges of honour; they can be felt to be signs of shame and indicative of becoming a. less important member of society. Against this background, it is not surprising that many elderly people would describe themselves as having poor health. The fact is that many older clients will have impairments such as hearing loss or sight problems; add arthritis to the mix and most sufferers would then describe themselves as not being in the best of health. Someone with all these problems could certainly be described as impaired, disabled and handicapped, but does that strip the client of legal capacity?

### Possible health issues facing the elderly

*Brain injury*

Has the acting solicitor been informed or ascertained if the client has 1–13 suffered a head injury, stroke or haemorrhage, or developed dementia?

*Dementia*

**Definition:** Dementia[27] is a set of symptoms: 1–14

"evidence of a decline in memory and thinking which is of a degree sufficient to impair functioning in daily living, present for six months or more".

The most common cause in Scotland is Alzheimer's disease but other common causes are Vascular Dementia and Alcohol Related Dementia. The

---

[27] Alzheimer's Society, Press Release April 2007, *http://www.alzheimers.org.uk* [accessed July 18, 2007].

pathology of any form of dementia is that it will damage and kill brain cells meaning that the brain does not work in the way that it could and should.

**1–15  Warning signs:** The usual signs to look for are that the person seems forgetful and may repeat things or may behave in unusual ways. The person may have an insight to their problem and be worried that he is losing control. Some will openly speak of their diagnosis and their fears, e.g. the client who says he is on medication to combat Alzheimers and must sort out his affairs before matters worsen, whilst others may become withdrawn, depressed, agitated or bullish whilst denying there is a problem. They may lose interest in life and find it hard to make day-to-day or future plans and may begin to have problems dealing with finances.

**1–16  Concealment:** These changes may only be noticed by close family and friends and can quite easily be concealed by the person during a half hour interview. Spouses will often support each other to the extent that they cover up very expertly for the other's failings and this can be quite hard to spot especially if, e.g. the husband states that "my wife has always dealt with the finances", etc. Is that so, and therefore he is merely a bit clueless, or is he covering up an increasing inability to comprehend situations?

**1–17  Early stages:** Solicitors should be aware that such illnesses generally begin with small changes in the person, which would not be noticeable to someone during a half hour interview as the person (and the family) are often very adept at compensating by being charming and turning conversations to areas where they feel confident. The progress may be a gradual deterioration and so the illness may have been suffered for some time before anyone would be particularly aware of the problem. The progress of the illness will vary greatly from one person to the next and the problems caused by the dementia can vary in that person from day to day; "he has his good days and his bad". In Scotland it is estimated that the number of people with dementia will increase from 1 in 90 today to 1 in 50 by 2031[28] and so there is a high chance that a solicitor will come across someone in one stage or other of the disease on a regular basis.

**1–18  Progression:** As the illness progresses the changes will become much more noticeable. The memory problems will worsen and the person may forget the names of family or friends, repeat questions over and over, fail to eat properly, neglect personal care, find it hard to comprehend conversations, be unable to follow a book or a film, stop making sense, lose the thread of a sentence, flare up or become upset or start to see and hear things that are not there, need help with handling money and need help with normal day-to day-tasks.

---

[28]  Alzheimer Scotland, *http://www.alzscot.org* [accessed July 18, 2007].

**Later stages:** In later stages of the disease the person will become very **1–19** confused, failing to recognise or recall close family members or be able to maintain any form of conversation and have complete disorientation as to time and place. It will be blindingly obvious that there is a lack of capacity, but what if the client simply seems a bit "off"?

If the client shows an element of confusion or forgetfulness the solicitor should not leap to the conclusion that the person has dementia but should be concerned that capacity may be affected. Many other conditions such as kidney or urinary tract infections, depression or the adverse side affects of prescription drugs, poorly controlled diabetes, etc. can present similar symptoms. Dementia is a medical diagnosis which can only be made by excluding other possible causes of those very symptoms.

Consider the long-term effects of alcohol or strong medication over a whole adult lifetime. This is not to be confused with intoxication and its effect on capacity. Drunkenness is not of itself a reason for not being able to give true consent, unless it has reached a stage where the person no longer knows what he or she is doing. Any contract made in that condition is not void but is voidable, providing the person takes steps to void the contracts as soon as he or she recovers senses (i.e. sobers up) and knows what he or she has done.[29]

### Mental disorder

Mental disorder is defined in the Mental Health (Care and Treatment) **1–20** (Scotland) Act 2003[30] as having a mental illness, personality disorder or learning difficulty. It specifically excludes dependence on/misuse of drugs and alcohol but note that excessive alcohol or drug use can *lead* to a mental illness.

This definition of mental disorder is applied to matters dealt with under the Adults with Incapacity (Scotland) Act 2000.[31] The solicitor should consider if the client has a mental disorder and whether this mental disorder is distorting understanding, communication and behaviour. The client's emotions could be affected and reactions, decisions and behaviour inappropriate or out of proportion.

### Learning disability

Did the person actually have capacity as a younger adult? Many people **1–21** with learning disabilities are living to old age. Learning disabilities are lifelong and are defined by the Scottish Government as:

---

[29] *Pollock v Burns* (1875) 2 R. 497.
[30] Mental Health (Care and Treatment) (Scotland) Act 2003, s.328(1).
[31] Adults with Incapacity (Scotland) Act 2000, s.87(1).

"A significant lifelong condition which has three facets: reduced ability to understand new or complex information or to learn new skills; reduced ability to cope independently; and a condition which started before Adulthood (in this case age 18) with a lasting effect on the individual's development."[32]

A learning disability is not an illness or a disease although it may have been triggered by one, e.g. by meningitis. Adult support and protection is a hot topic in the Scottish Executive and a review of services for people with learning disabilities entitled "The Same as You?" was commissioned and the published report identified a blueprint for the future containing 29 recommendations on the way forward. The very name of the review indicates all adults are to be treated the same and included in society.

*Sensory problems*

**1–22**    Consider if the client has sensory problems. A person can be rendered unable to hear, move, see or speak by a single event such as a severe stroke. The ability to process information and make decisions may or may not have been affected by this event.

**Considerations and indicators relating to health and capacity**

**1–23**    Dealing with the elderly requires patience to allow the client time and space to overcome the difficulties caused by age or infirmity (see Appendix 2: Communication for maximising communication). An open and enquiring mind with an attitude of "all may not be exactly as it seems" will stand the solicitor is good stead. Many elderly clients will want to come in with a family member. However, the solicitor needs to see a client alone to be satisfied that there is nothing sinister about the presence of the other person. However the client may just wish that person there because they always rely on their support and may be flustered without the support. A vicious circle can be turned into a virtuous circle by careful, considerate and polite handling of the situation.

If the client seems confused it may be because he simply cannot hear properly and is embarrassed to admit it. Has the client just taken medication/failed to take medication? Is client dehydrated or simply too hot? Is the client in pain? A recent study by the Picker Institute Europe[33] carried out on behalf of the Patients' Association has found that nearly two out of five of people living in nursing homes are enduring chronic pain. Extreme pain can affect cognitive functioning, cause disturbed sleep and restrict mobility as well as impact negatively on quality of life. Is something else bothering the client? People often dwell on small issues which can then dominate their thoughts and, until they are allowed to get it off their chest, they will not be able to focus and properly discuss the matter in hand.

---

[32] *The same as you? A review of services for people with learning disabilities*, found at *http://www.scotland.gov.uk/ldsr/docs/tsay-12.asp* [accessed September 7, 2007].

[33] Picker Institute Europe; an independent, not for profit research and development institute with charitable status, reported 2007, *http://www.pickereurope.org* [accessed July 18, 2007].

Is the client just eccentric or lacking capacity? It can be very hard for a solicitor to tell where eccentricity ends and incapacity begins. This is a matter ultimately for the courts.[34] A testator, Colonel Alexander MacLean, died aged 80. His will and two codicils directed his estate was to be invested to pay an annuity to his housekeeper and to educate poor boys named MacLean. He left nothing to his relatives and his nearest relative raised an action to have the will reduced on the grounds that Colonel MacLean was insane. A great deal of evidence was led portraying the Colonel as an extremely strange individual prone to obscenity and rambling conversations. He apparently claimed to have no relatives. The court held that there was no insanity despite his eccentricity, even if the will were objectionable to his relatives.

Has the client received any recent unpleasant medical diagnoses? Is the client feeling lonely or vulnerable for that or another reason?

Whilst being aware of these possibilities will make the solicitor a better adviser to a person, if in any doubt about a person's capacity, the solicitor should consult family members, GP and other medical professionals and record this on the file.

## TAKING INSTRUCTIONS FROM AN ELDERLY CLIENT

So the client is an adult who has capacity, unless he doesn't. So how can you **1–24** safely take instructions from the elderly client who has serious health issues: are they such that they strip a person of legal capacity which the law says he is presumed to have?

- Does the client understand the situation and especially the consequences of the decision or instruction?
- Can the client follow the steps?
- If the client has to choose from a range of options, is he able to make an informed and reasoned choice?
- Does the client ask further questions, and ask for other options or relate the information to his own circumstances?
- Does he retain the information for long enough to make a decision?
- Does he ask for time to think or simply say yes quickly to avoid the situation? Is the client able to tell you of his choice or decision?
- Can the client recall the decision later?
- And if not, does the client reach the same decision again if presented with the same facts and options on a later occasion?

### Who decides on capacity?

Ultimately capacity is a question of law to be decided if necessary by a **1–25** court. As with any court action, the procedure is evidence based and the most cogent evidence will be medical evidence (or in certain circumstances psychological evidence). However the courts can and have decided against the medical evidence in reported cases.[35]

---

[34] *Morrison v MacLean's Trustees* (1862) 24 D. 625.
[35] *Rennie v Steven*, 1991 G.W.D. 26–1559.

Solicitors do not judge capacity, but they do have a duty to assess the client and identify situations where capacity might be in question. Being a matter for the courts, medical practitioners do not have the final word, but in practice a solicitor should be alert to problems and consult the medics for an opinion before proceeding to take instructions. The Law Society of Scotland makes this clear.[36]

### Dignity and respect

1–26    When dealing with the elderly client, the solicitor must take care to treat the client in the same way as all his clients are treated. A patronising attitude is not just insulting to the client's feelings but could constitute an infringement of his rights.

### Disability Discrimination Act 1995

1–27    This Act is designed to protect people with disabilities from discrimination in relation to many areas of life but for these discussions the most pertinent is the provision of goods, facilities and services.

In this context disability and disabled person have specific meanings conferred by statute.[37] The definitions include mental and physical impairments if the impairment has a substantial and long-term adverse effect on the person's ability to carry out normal day-to-day activities. Sections 19, 20 and 21 are particularly relevant to the solicitor.

This is not the place for a full discussion of the Disability Discrimination Act 1995 but it is worth remembering that it is unlawful for the provider, in this discussion the solicitor, to discriminate:

(1) by refusing to provide (or deliberately not providing) services which he provides or is prepared to provide to members of the public; or
(2) making it impossible or unreasonably difficult to make use of a service through failure in the duty to make reasonable adjustments; or
(3) in the standard or manner of provision of service; or
(4) in the terms on which the service is provided.[38]

"Discriminate"[39] is treating a disabled person less favourably for a reason which relates to his disability than the provider would treat others to whom the reason does not apply, if the provider cannot show that the treatment in question is justified, or if he fails to make reasonable adjustments and cannot show the failure is justified.[40] One justification for different treatment is if the disabled person is incapable of entering into an enforceable agreement, or of giving an informed consent, and for that reason the treatment is reasonable in that case.[41] In this instance the incapacity must be specific to the particular transaction.

---

[36]    1995, 40 J.L.S.S. 284.
[37]    Disability Discrimination Act 1995, s.1.
[38]    Disability Discrimination Act 1995, s.19(1).
[39]    Disability Discrimination Act 1995, s.20(1).
[40]    Disability Discrimination Act 1995, s.20(2).
[41]    Disability Discrimination Act 1995, s.20(4)(b).

## European Convention of Human Rights

The Human Rights Act 1998 and the Scotland Act 1998 bring many of **1–28** the provisions of the European Convention on Human Rights into Scots law.

## Aids to assist a client

Using aids to get around the impairments a client may have will not only **1–29** ensure a proper service is given to the client; it will strengthen the client/ solicitor relationship. A good example of this would be to follow the RNIB "clear print guidelines".[42] This can allow a partially sighted client to read a document for himself and hence give proper approval and instructions. Use of clear signing blocks or credit card style signature aids can allow the client to sign a large font document affording greater dignity than resorting to what the profession still tends to term a "notarial execution".

## Subscription on behalf of blind granter or granter unable to write

The law relating to notarial executions, namely the Conveyancing **1–30** (Scotland) Act 1924 s.18 and Sch.1, was repealed by Sch.5 to the Requirements of Writing (Scotland) Act 1995, with effect from August 1, 1995. The law on the matter is now contained in s.9 (and Sch.3) of the Requirements of Writing (Scotland) Act 1995. The old law still applies when dealing with a pre August 1, 1995 execution, e.g. if the solicitor is considering if an old document was properly executed or not.

Nothing in this section prevents the granter of a document who is blind from subscribing or signing a document in the normal fashion.[43] This is probably not to be recommended.

The "relevant person" reads the document to the granter, in the presence of one witness, or the granter makes a declaration that he does not wish the "relevant person" to read the document to the granter. Reading should also incorporate describing to the granter a plan, drawing, photograph or similar representation and these provisions also apply to annexations or alterations of documents.[44]

The witness must know the granter, be aged over 16 and be mentally capable of acting as a witness. Subscription by the "relevant person" and the witness must take place in the presence of the granter.[45]

The "relevant person" for such execution, means a solicitor who has in force a current practising certificate, an advocate, a justice of the peace or a sheriff clerk. Outside Scotland, the "relevant person" is a notary public or any other person with official authority under the law of the place of execution to execute documents on behalf of persons who are blind or unable to write.

---

[42] Guidelines available on *http://www.rnib.org* [accessed July 18, 2007].
[43] Requirements of Writing (Scotland) Act 1995, s.9(7).
[44] Requirements of Writing (Scotland) Act 1995, s.9(5).
[45] Requirements of Writing (Scotland) Act 1995, s.9(2).

The form of execution and testing clause are to be in a form governed by regulations.[46] No such regulations exist so most practitioners use the style recommended by the Scottish Law Commission. It should be noted that the testing clause runs from the end of the document and does away with the docquet and testing clause formerly used.

### The Scottish Law Commission recommended styles

**1–31**  *(1) Where the document is read over to the granter*

THIS DOCUMENT [consisting of this and the ... preceding pages] has been read over to the said X by me Y, Solicitor, (address) and is SIGNED by me for and with the authority of, and in the presence of, the said AB, who has declared that he is blind [or unable to write], and WITNESSED as shown below—

..............................                        ..............................
Signature of witness                    Signature on behalf of granter

Name of witness ...................................................................................

Address of witness ................................................................................

Date ......................................................................................................

Place .....................................................................................................

**1–32**  *(2) Where the granter declares that he does not wish the document to be read over to him*

THIS DOCUMENT, [consisting of this and the ... preceding pages] is SIGNED by me Y, Solicitor, (address) for and with authority of, and in the presence of, the said X, who has declared that he is blind [or unable to write], and that he does not wish the document to be read over to him, and WITNESSED as shown below—

..............................                        ..............................
Signature of witness                    Signature on behalf of granter

Name of witness ...................................................................................

Address of witness ................................................................................

Date ......................................................................................................

Place .....................................................................................................

As one would expect, *every page* of a will should be signed by "the relevant person".

---

[46]  Requirements of Writing (Scotland) Act 1995, s.10.

**Disqualification of notary**

A document which confers benefit on the "relevant person" or his spouse, **1–33** son or daughter, shall be invalid but only insofar as it confers benefit on these persons.[47] Contrast the former strict law which voided the whole deed.[48]

The notary should have no form of interest under the will whether as executor, trustee, legatee or beneficiary.

Be especially careful not to be caught out with codicils amending a previous will. In one reported case, a will gave a benefit to a person who later carried out a notarial execution of a codicil. The codicil was held to form part of the original will.[49]

If a will appoints a solicitor as an executor or trustee and permits charging of remuneration by the firm as agents, the notary should not be a partner of the firm,[50] but can be an employee.[51]

Best practice would be to use a relevant person independent to the firm in any document, whether it is a will or power of attorney which appoints one's firm or a partner and allows for charging for acting as such.

## PRACTICALITIES OF DEALING WITH THE FORGETFUL

In a recent case,[52] the deceased had made her own will by handwriting on **1–34** one side of one page disposing of her whole estate. She placed this in an envelope on which she wrote "My will" and signed her full name below but had not signed the deed itself. The First Division held that the envelope and the unsigned document were sufficient to constitute a valid testamentary writing. The costs of such litigation should surely convince members of the public that a fee for a professionally prepared will is a sound investment.

For some odd reason many clients over whom there are no doubts about capacity will fail to sign a will correctly despite being provided with clear signing instructions. The client will sign at the foot of every page of the new will using usual signature and inexplicably on the final page sign his entire name out in full, usually with a great flourish. Many signing meetings will take place at the house so to save a second trip to the house, the experienced solicitor will always take a spare engrossment.

---

[47] Requirements of Writing (Scotland) Act 1995, s.9(4).
[48] *Ferrie v Ferrie's Trustees* (1863) 1 M. 291.
[49] *Crawford's Trustees v Glasgow Royal Infirmary*, 1955 S.C. 367.
[50] *Finlay v Finlay's Trustees*, 1948 S.C. 16.
[51] *Hynd's Trustee v Hynd's Trustees*, 1955 S.C. (H.L.) 1.
[52] *Davidson v Convy*, 2003 S.L.T. 650.

## OFFICE POLICY ON DEALING WITH ISSUES OF CAPACITY

**1–35** It is prudent to have an office policy on dealing with issues of capacity. Having and following a policy should result in better advice to clients and avoid the problems outlined later.

The Scottish Government has recently introduced a resource section on its website and is seeking contributions of good practice in relation to assisting health and social care professionals who are involved in assessing capacity under the 2000 Act. The next step will be for guidance to supplement the various codes of practice. Many of the issues facing practitioners in those professions hold good for the legal profession.

The following is only a suggested office policy.

## OFFICE POLICY GUIDE TO CAPACITY

**1–36** On a daily basis we assess the ability of a client to understand the decision before him. This comes into sharper focus when we are interviewing the client immediately before signing a continuing or welfare power of attorney and even more so when we are meeting new clients regarding continuing powers of attorney.

Capacity affects decision-making. More than one assessment may be required for separate decisions. Capacity is not black and white but is perhaps better described as shades of grey. For example a person with early stage Alzheimers may be able to give informed consent on treatment for a medical condition but may not be able to manage finances. A person with some form of incapacity can often be assisted in making a decision by following a sequence of steps and looking at the pros and cons at each stage at a pace and using language which that person can cope with.

Communication is the basis of our relationship with our clients. Being a poor communicator is not in itself incapacity nor a barrier to receiving legal advice, but a client may need aids to assist both receiving and giving information. Be **very** wary of using "interpreters", particularly those who have an interest in the outcome.

### Understanding

**1–37** It is not always clear if a person has understood us or not. Questioning and cross-referencing is a way to check but can confuse somebody and the following advice is helpful.

- Try and speak at the level and pace of the adult's understanding and processing speed.
- Repeat information more than once.
- Ask the person to repeat information back to you in their own words.
- Avoid jargon.
- Do not overwhelm the adult with too many choices at one time.
- Take account of their literacy.

- Use open questions.
- Observe your own and their body language so as not to threaten the adult.
- Ensure our letter of engagement is signed and understood.
- File note the meeting carefully recording the person's views and questions.

### Memory

Many of our clients will have memory problems and may be able to make **1–38** decisions quite adequately but be unable to recall them later. For many, memory is variable. We all have clients who have their "good days". If a person makes a decision based on information and makes the same decision each time but is unable to remember the decision, it can be argued that they have capacity to make that decision. There should be no automatic assumption that somebody with short-term memory loss is incapable of making a decision. (Except they *cannot* instruct the preparation of a continuing/welfare power of attorney.)

### Duration

Incapacity can be temporary, variable or permanent. In any of these **1–39** states, incapacity is not "all-or-nothing", and will vary from decision to decision.

Remember that if the adult is relaxed and comfortable with you, he or she will be more confident and more likely to be able to make a decision than if stressed.

If in doubt about a person's capacity consult family, GP and other medical professionals and record this on the certificates if you are certifying. In these circumstances try, where possible, to have the Doctor sign the certificate (although this is not foolproof).

### Specific Definition of Incapacity for Powers of Attorney

Defined in the Adults with Incapacity (Scotland) Act 2000[53] as: **1–40**

A person over the age of 16 incapable of:

(1) acting; or
(2) making decisions; or
(3) communicating decisions; or
(4) understanding decisions; or
(5) retaining the memory of decisions,

by reason of mental disorder or inability to communicate because of physical disability. **Even if only one** of these applies a person may be deemed to lack capacity.

---

[53] Adults with Incapacity (Scotland) Act 2000, s.1.

Any assessment of capacity must take this definition into account and also, as with anything relating to the Adults with Incapacity (Scotland) Act 2000, the five principles must be adhered to:

- benefit;
- minimum intervention;
- take account of wishes of adult;
- consultation with relevant others; and
- encourage adult to exercise his skills.

**Warning**

1–41      Be especially careful if one of your clients brings in an elderly relative saying "I think Aunty Betty needs a power of attorney". This will be your first encounter with Aunty Betty and apart from applying all the above rules you should be doubly careful to make sure to see Aunty Betty on her own and if there is any hint that Aunty Betty has any medical condition, be sensible and involve the medics. Another sensible precaution is to minute on the file that although your client brought the adult into the office, you excluded the client from the meeting and made sure that you spoke to Aunty Betty on her own. This file note will save a lot of grief later if there turns out to be a disaffected member of the family who claims undue influence.

The Professional Practice Committee reminds solicitors (1) that a solicitor must have instructions from his or her client; (2) that the client is the granter of the power of attorney; and (3) that solicitors are not the judges of mental capacity. That is for the medical profession from whom advice should be sought if there is any doubt as to a client's capacity. If such advice is taken it should be noted on the certificates in the power of attorney.

# Chapter 2

# WILLS AND TAX PLANNING

The issues of wills and tax planning are topics that need to be addressed by **2–01** all clients not just the elderly. However, the elderly client's family and financial circumstances are likely to be more complex than that of the younger generation and therefore these issues must be addressed with care and the appropriate technical knowledge.

## WILLS

The statistics on the number of individuals who have not made a will are **2–02** worrying[1] and the elderly approaching their twilight years in particular should be encouraged to record their wishes. The reasons for making a will are numerous. Often highlighting the fact to clients that the administration is more straightforward where there is a will and therefore the solicitor's fee lower, is enough encouragement! Bonds of caution (the insurance policy normally required for cases of intestate succession) can also be very expensive, and there is a limited number of suppliers offering the product. Of course, by making a will clients take control of their wishes and the will making process often identifies other tax planning opportunities in addition to those that can be incorporated into the will.

Without a will the laws of intestacy will determine how an estate is to be distributed.[2] These rules provide spouses, children, issue of deceased children, cohabitees and other relatives with certain rights. Where there are no relatives falling within the rules the Crown have the right to inherit as *ultimus haeres*. In intestacy the client will not have dictated the age at which the beneficiaries are to inherit, resulting in the potential for beneficiaries at aged 16 coming into significant wealth.

Using trusts as planning within the will and/or during lifetime can allow for tax planning, as well as providing protection, flexibility and control. Chapter 3 details the opportunities available, tax consequences and issues often peculiar to the elderly client's circumstances in relation to the use of trusts.

---

[1] See SCC research report *Wills and Awareness of Inheritance Rights in Scotland*, September 2006, at *http://www.scotconsumer.org.uk/consumerrights/publications.htm* [accessed August 8, 2007].
[2] See para.15–03.

Will drafting is a subject in itself and it is not the intention of this book to provide styles,[3] however there are some key factors to be considered before the drafting stage.

### Capacity

2–03    As discussed in Ch.1, capacity is paramount in order for clients to record their wishes in the knowledge that they will be carried out. It is important that there is evidence that this issue has been addressed, particularly if the wishes of the client are likely to be viewed controversially at the time of their death by family, friends and disgruntled potential beneficiaries. Files should always be up to date with clear file notes of instructions received, meetings and details of any medical advice sought regarding capacity. Chapter 1 also covers the procedure of notarial execution for blind, partially sighted clients or those who are unable to sign for whatever reason.

If the will is challenged on the death of the testator the onus of proof is on the person seeking to have the testamentary writing reduced.

### Domicile

2–04    It is important to consider the client's domicile before any will is made, particularly in relation to tax planning. Domicile can differ from residency. Generally, domicile is considered to be where the individual has their permanent home, and this is established by looking at facts, circumstances and intention. Domicile is acquired at birth based on that of the individual's father but a new domicile of choice can be acquired as result of a change in circumstances or as a result of a particular action. Domicile is taken into account in looking at tax treatment of lifetime income and gains. However, for IHT purposes the rules are wider, and individuals resident in the UK not less than 17 out of the last 20 years of assessment before death shall be treated as domiciled in the UK.[4] The IHT rules state that those female clients who were married before 1974 are deemed to have acquired their husband's domicile[5] unless express action has been taken to change this.

A UK domicile results in a UK inheritance tax assessment on worldwide assets. Therefore at the time the will is written if there are opportunities for planning matters and activities so as to achieve/not achieve UK domicile the client should be advised appropriately. An expression of domicile within the will can be useful to support the case for arguing one way or another. Additionally, when regularly reviewing the will it should be considered whether the client's domicile has changed or is likely to change, and therefore further planning is required.

---

[3]   For an excellent guide on drafting see Alan R. Barr et al, *Drafting Wills in Scotland*, 2nd edn (Edinburgh: Butterworths Scotland, 2005).

[4]   Inheritance Tax Act 1984, s.267.

[5]   Domicile and Matrimonial Proceedings Act 1973, ss.1, 3, 4.

## Legal rights

For those who are domiciled in Scotland there is the issue of legal rights **2–05** over the net moveable assets of their estate that exist in law regardless of what the will contains. Spouses, civil partners, children and remoter issue of a deceased child all have the right to make a claim. If the individual has entitlement under the will they must select whether to take their entitlement under the will, claim their legal rights or renounce their right to both.

Where a valid will is left spouses and civil partners are entitled to claim one-third of the net moveable estate if descendants survive and one-half where there are no surviving descendants. Children (or their issue where a child has predeceased) can claim one-third of the *legitum* among them where the deceased was married/in a civil partnership and one-half where they were not married/in a civil partnership.

Clients who have separated but have not divorced or had their civil partnership dissolved should ensure that any minute of agreement entered into addresses the issue of legal rights to ensure that both parties have discharged their rights. Where no agreement has been entered into or where a client wishes to provide against a legal rights claim by children, planning should be done to minimise the assets at risk of such a claim. For example, clients can structure their assets, where possible, to ensure that the majority of their estate is made up of heritable assets or consider an interest in possession trust wrapper to remove the assets from their estate for ownership purposes but continue to allow them access (this would not work for tax purposes). In limited circumstances, where a client wishes to provide against children being entitled to claim, there could be merit in dying intestate if the prior rights claim by a spouse/civil partner would exhaust the estate (see para.15–04). However, all the circumstances would need to be looked at and the client would need to have been fully briefed on the risks involved (e.g. if the spouse/civil partner dies the children could end up receiving more than if there was a will which contained fall back provisions).

In addition to legal rights there are other restrictions affecting the client's estate being distributed in accordance with their wishes. If entitlement under a will is illegal, immoral or impossible it will be void.[6] Similarly, provisions which are deemed by the courts to be contrary to public policy will be ineffective. Care must also be taken in drafting wills to ensure that the restraints on accumulations, often peculiar to Scots law, are not breached.

## Title to property

Heritable property in Scotland may be structured such that the title **2–06** includes a survivorship destination whereby on the death of one of the owners the other(s) are automatically deemed to have inherited the deceased owner's share in the property, regardless of any directions under the will. It is therefore essential that on taking instructions for will preparation that the title deeds to any heritable property are checked.

---

[6] D.R. MacDonald, *Succession*, 3rd edn (Edinburgh: W. Green, 2001), p.108.

Evacuation of the survivorship destination can be expressly provided for in the will if it has not been done during lifetime only where the testator was the party who contributed to the proceeds of the house. The Family Law (Scotland) Act 2006 provides that survivorship destinations contained in dispositions between spouses or civil partners are automatically revoked by divorce.[7]

### Location of assets

2–07      It is generally recommended that where assets are located outside the UK a separate will be prepared dealing with these assets only. This will ensure that the foreign will meets the jurisdiction requirements of that country to ensure that the assets can be administered appropriately on death. A foreign will can also minimise any translation issues which could lead to ambiguity in interpretation. In these circumstances the UK will must be restricted to cover UK assets only or there is the potential for conflict. Advice should be sought from a solicitor in the appropriate jurisdiction for the deed to be drafted and for advice on taxes, registration of the deed and any heirship rules. Good practice would be to keep copies of any foreign wills with the UK will and vice versa.

### Identity of client

2–08      In addition to the other factors of consideration it is vital to have the client's identity verified when undertaking such work. The Money Laundering Regulations are such that most solicitors are checking identity as a matter of course but this really is essential for the preparation of wills.

### Content of will

2–09      First and foremost all wills should reflect the testator's wishes. Additionally, where appropriate, tax-planning provisions can be incorporated into the deed, often complemented with lifetime tax planning. The deeds should have contingency plans ensuring that there is minimum risk that any part of the estate would fall into intestacy. Many clients choose to include a charity as an ultimate fallback, and discretion should be given to the executors on what to do with the funds in the event of the charity changing its name, dissolving or amalgamating.

The preparation of a will should be used as an opportunity for clients to review all of their affairs and tax planning. A useful exercise is to prepare a statement of assets that immediately provides an indication of the potential IHT and can be useful in identifying the assets on the executry side of the administration. Family trees with names and dates of birth can also prove invaluable in identifying relationships and again for the executry. Details of any lifetime gifts should also be recorded to correctly evaluate the potential IHT. Funeral wishes can be included, where wished, and any prepaid funeral plans or lair certificates should be stored with the will.

---

[7]  Family Law (Scotland) Act 2006, s.19.

Living wills are entirely different to the traditional will which covers the distribution of assets on death. As discussed in Ch.5 living wills can record clients' wishes in relation to their care and certain welfare matters, although such documents should not be used as substitutes to welfare powers of attorney.

There are so many different factors to consider in providing advice to the client and drafting their will. As the information that needs to be extracted is so personal a solid trustworthy relationship needs to be established. Hopefully at the end of the process the client will be able to recognise the added value that they have received from their solicitor from the drafting exercise. This can be built on further by regularly contacting the client to establish if their will needs to be reviewed either as a result of a change in personal circumstances or as a result of a change in the tax laws.

## TAX PLANNING

Elderly clients, like all clients, have a desire to minimise their tax liabilities, **2–10** to protect their capital and to maximise income. As a result of retirement, elderly clients often have lower income sources and need to ensure that their financial circumstances are set up as tax efficiently as possible. All areas of tax should be addressed and reviewed.

### Inheritance tax

Inheritance tax planning will most likely be looked at with the client when **2–11** drafting or reviewing their will. The current rules provide that on death an individual's estate will be taxed at 40 per cent on the element over the nil rate band amount (£300,000 for the tax year ended April 5, 2008) which does not pass to an exempt beneficiary. The available nil rate band amount will be reduced by lifetime transfers that are treated as chargeable. These include transfers in the seven years before death which were either chargeable at the time they were made or potentially exempt transfers (PETs) and therefore now fall to be treated as chargeable as a result of the death that has occurred. The available nil rate band is assessed on a rolling seven-year period and therefore in assessing the position on death transfers as far back as 14 years ago are taken into account when reviewing the position of the transfers seven years ago.

The legislation states clearly that the following are treated as exempt beneficiaries or are transfers that are not considered to be transfers of value[8]:

- dispositions not intended to confer gratuitous benefit;
- dispositions for maintenance of family;
- dispositions allowable for income tax or conferring retirement benefits[9];
- transfers between spouses or civil partners (restricted to £55,000 if transferor's spouse/civil partner is not domiciled in the UK);

---

[8] Inheritance Tax Act 1984, ss.10, 11, 12, 18, 19, 20, 21, 22, 23, 24, 24A, 25, 26, 27.
[9] Inheritance Tax Act 1984, s.18(2).

- annual exemption—transfers not exceeding £3,000 made in any tax year. If not fully utilised, the part remaining can be carried forward one tax year, although the current year exemption is used to offset any transfers first;
- small gifts to any one person not exceeding £250 per person in any tax year;
- normal expenditure out of income—where it can be shown that it was made as part of the normal expenditure of the transferor, made out of income and the transferor is left with sufficient income to maintain his or her usual standard of living[10];
- gifts in consideration of marriage/civil partnership restricted to £5,000 where transferor is a parent of either party, £2,500 if the transferor is a grandparent or remoter ancestor of either party and £1,000 in any other case. The transferor can only utilise one exemption per marriage/civil partnership and gift must happen prior to the ceremony, not after;
- gifts to registered UK charities;
- gifts to qualifying UK political parties[11];
- gifts to housing associations;
- gifts for national purposes; and
- maintenance funds for historic buildings, etc.

These transfers should therefore be incorporated into an effective tax planning strategy tailored to the individual client's circumstances.

The legislation provides an exemption to IHT over all assets where an individual dies from a wound inflicted, accident occurring or disease contracted while a member of the UK armed forces or auxiliary forces, and the individual was either on active service (or other service involving the same risks) or had previously contracted a disease which was generated by such service.[12] In the case of *Barty-King v Ministry of Defence*[13] a leg wound was inflicted in 1944 at the D-day landings. The death from cancer in 1967 was partly as a result of the wound and therefore the whole estate was held to be exempt. A recent 2007 case has been successful in having the death in active service exemption utilised where the death, a mighty 61 years after the injuries, was able to be sufficiently linked back to the initial injuries.[14]

If clients are bequeathing large sums to charities under their wills, it should be considered whether these should be made during lifetime instead. Obviously it will depend on the donor's financial circumstances, but gifting during lifetime has the added benefit of gift aid relief which can reduce the

---

[10]  It was confirmed in *Bennett v IRC* [1995] S.T.C. 54 that there is not necessarily a minimum period over which the expenditure should occur if the intention to commit to the payments is established.

[11]  Section 24 of the Inheritance Tax Act 1984 provides that a political party qualifies for exemption if at the last general election preceding the transfer of value (1) two members of that party were elected to the House of Commons or (2) one member of that party was elected to the House of Commons and not less than 150,000 votes were given to candidates who were members of that party.

[12]  Inheritance Tax Act 1984, s.154.

[13]  [1979] All. E.R. 80.

[14]  As reported in *Express and Echo*, Thursday May 31, 2007 (a newspaper based in Exeter, Devon).

client's income tax liability for the current tax year (or if elected and made before September 30 the previous tax year).

As stated above it is important to consider the individual's domicile and that of their spouse. If one domicile is considered preferable to another, steps should be taken to ensure that the evidence in favour of that domicile is sufficient to provide, on the death of that individual, that that was their domicile and therefore their estate will be taxed under that jurisdiction.

Transfers made to individuals during lifetime will be treated as PETs. It is assumed that the transferor will survive seven years and therefore no tax is due at the time of transfer. However, the donee should be aware that if the gifts fall to be chargeable the donee is the party that will be primarily liable for the IHT due (whom failing the executors).

Where lifetime gifts, either chargeable at the time they are made or failing PETs, require IHT to be paid as a result of the transferor's death there is taper relief available to reduce the liability.[15] It should be noted that any available nil rate band is used in chronological order, offsetting against lifetime gifts first and the taper relief is only available on transfers where IHT is payable.

### Table I Taper Relief

| | |
|---|---|
| Death within 3 years of gift | Nil % |
| Between 3 and 4 years | 20% |
| Between 4 and 5 years | 40% |
| Between 5 and 6 years | 60% |
| Between 6 and 7 years | 80% |

Additionally, where one individual has inherited and then passes away themselves, quick succession relief is available to minimise any double taxation.[16]

### Table II Quick Succession Relief

| | |
|---|---|
| Period between transfers less than one year | 100% |
| Period between one and two years | 80% |
| Period between two and three years | 60% |
| Period between three and four years | 40% |
| Period between four and five years | 20% |

Before an attorney or guardian undertakes any tax planning on behalf of another individual it is essential to ensure that the power of attorney deed or the guardianship order contains sufficient powers for them to be able to undertake such planning. In the case of *McDowall v IRC*[17] the gifts made by

---

[15] See Table I.
[16] See Table II.
[17] [2004] S.T.C. (S.C.D.) 22.

the attorney were voidable as the attorney did not have specific power to carry out such planning. An attorney should also be aware of any conflict of interest and take advice before carrying out any such planning.

Chapter 16 covers the IHT and CGT tax planning that can be made following an individual's death by granting a deed of variation within two years of the date of death.

Clients may also wish to consider structuring their assets so that they qualify for business property relief (BPR) or agricultural property relief which can provide 50 per cent or even 100 per cent relief from inheritance tax. Structured products are available to reduce the investment risk. Clients involved in family businesses may have even more opportunities for planning, providing the business is not involved in one of the non-qualifying activities of dealing in securities, stocks or shares, land or buildings or making or holding investments.[18] There is also a deferred form of IHT relief known as woodlands relief which offers the opportunity to defer an IHT liability on the value of the timber (but not on the value of the land).[19] BPR of 100 per cent may instead be available if the woodlands are managed on a commercial basis. Each relief has strict conditions but the relief opportunities are extremely valuable.

Many clients, particularly the elderly, have the majority of their wealth tied up in their home and therefore find it difficult to undertake successful lifetime gifting for IHT planning as they do not wish to gift away funds which could leave them in a difficult financial position. As a result equity release is becoming a more popular option enabling the client to extract wealth from their home which they can gift away/use for other purposes, without the upheaval of moving or selling their home.

Venture capital trusts and enterprise investment schemes can be attractive products for clients due to their special tax treatments but proper financial advice should be taken in relation to the client's overall financial situation and objectives before selecting any such investment.

In terms of inheritance tax planning there are several anti-avoidance provisions which place restrictions on the planning that an individual can undertake. The reservation of benefit rules were introduced in 1986[20] and provide that for lifetime gifting, if the transfer falls to be treated as a gift with reservation then the asset transferred is treated, for the purposes of inheritance tax, as still forming part of the estate of the transferor. Although there are some *de mimimis* reliefs[21] the rules state that a transfer will be treated as a gift with reservation where either:

- the donee does not assume bona fide possession and enjoyment of the property at the date of the gift or seven years before the donor's death, if later; or

---

[18] Inheritance Tax Act 1984, s.105(3).
[19] Inheritance Tax Act 1984, ss.125–130.
[20] Finance Act 1986, s.102.
[21] See Revenue Interpretation 55 (November 1993) for good examples.

- at any time in the period ending with the donor's death and beginning seven years before that date or, if later, from the date of gift, the property is not enjoyed to the entire exclusion or virtually to the entire exclusion of the donor.

The Finance Act 2004[22] introduced an income tax charge known as Pre-Owned Assets Tax on benefits received by a former owner of property. If an individual continues to receive benefits from certain types of property they owned after March 17, 1986 but disposed of since, the charge may apply and has effect for the tax year commencing April 6, 2005 and subsequent years. If the individual who has disposed of the property did so by way of gift or, in some circumstances, sale, or contributed towards the purchase of the property in question and they continue to receive some benefit from the property, they are potentially liable to the charge. There are certain exclusions to the charge, and the rules do not apply where the property falls within the gifts with reservation rules or the donor has specifically elected for IHT to apply to the asset that was previously owned.

A common tax planning route for a married couple/civil partners, with estates in excess of the nil rate band for inheritance tax, is to have their wills drafted establishing a discretionary trust on the first death and leaving the residue of their estates to the survivor of them. This is an attractive route for elderly clients in particular as no transfers are undertaken until the time of the first death and a well drafted will can provided flexibility and a number of options for the use of the trust. The trust assets may be loaned to the survivor, normally in return for a debt or a charge over the property, allowing the survivor the benefit of the use of the assets but keeping the value out with their estate for tax purposes. However, the will must contain sufficient powers and the correct paperwork must be put in place for the planning to work. The case of *Phizackerley v CIR*[23] highlighted the need for careful consideration in the drafting of the wills and that the couple's asset ownership and financial contribution background be carefully reviewed if the house is likely to be an asset forming part of the trust assets. Anti-avoidance rules[24] prevent the deduction of a debt where the property originally derived from the deceased. Thus if one party has contributed more to an asset and gifted it to the other during their lifetime specific care will be needed. Nevertheless, with proper advice tax planning through a will, and indeed the use of a discretionary trust which receives assets equivalent to the nil rate band, remains a popular and flexible option where tax savings can be made.

## Capital gains tax

Capital gains are assessed annually each tax year and should be reported **2–12** on the client's tax return. Any CGT due should be paid, along with the income tax for that tax year by the January 31 following the end of the tax year. The capital gains tax annual exemption for the tax year ending April 5, 2008 is £9,200. Gains in excess of this are taxed at the individual's marginal

---

[22] Finance Act 2004, s.84 and Sch.15.
[23] [2007] S.T.C. (S.C.D.) 328.
[24] Finance Act 1986, s.103.

savings rate (10 per cent, 20 per cent or 40 per cent). Any losses incurred in previous tax years that have not been utilised may be carried forward.

The capital gains tax calculation involves deducting from the proceeds of the assets the cost or deemed acquisition value, any enhancement expenditure, indexation relief (only available up to 1998 for individuals), capital gains tax taper relief and any other expenditure incurred in the acquisition or disposal of the assets such as stamp duty land tax or commission. Clients who have held assets from before March 31, 1982 can elect to have the acquisition cost re-based to this date. There are also special rules for shares disposed of which were owned prior to April 6, 1965.

Any transfers between connected persons are deemed to pass at market value regardless of any sum paid and CGT will be due in the normal way. If the market value results in a capital loss this loss may be carried forward but may only ever be offset against gains incurred from transfers to the same connected person. Clients should therefore think carefully about when to gift an item.

There is a free capital gains tax uplift on assets on death. Therefore it may be preferable to retain assets which are laden with gains and to bequeath them under the will. Capital gains tax losses incurred during lifetime in the year of death can be carried back three years, and be offset against taxable capital gains, taking the latest gains first.

Spouses and civil partners should consider their capital gains tax positions together to ensure that both of them are utilising their capital gains tax exemptions. There are numerous planning opportunities available considering that transfers between spouses and civil partners are deemed to pass at no gain/no loss and the transferee inherits the acquisition date of that of the transferor. One option for crystallising gains where one spouse/civil partner is given advance warning of their likely death is to pass the assets into their name for the free uplift on death, only to receive them back IHT free under the other's will on their death. The new deemed acquisition date and value is that of the other's death.

Many assets such as premium bonds and gilts are exempt from capital gains tax and are therefore useful to use as part of overall tax planning if the client feels comfortable to make gifts during lifetime perhaps to utilise their annual IHT exemption or as a PET.

**Income tax**

2–13        Elderly clients in particular are keen to maximise their income where possible. Financial advice is recommended to ensure that the client structures his or her assets as efficiently as possible and tailors their income plans with their overall tax planning. State benefits do not all have the same tax treatment[25] and where there is a choice the decision should be made carefully.

---

[25]  See Table III.

## Table III Tax Treatment of State Benefits

**Taxable**

Incapacity benefit[26] (excluding first 28 weeks)

Jobseeker's allowance

Statutory sick pay

Statutory maternity pay, statutory paternity pay and statutory adoption pay

Carer's allowance

Bereavement allowance and widowed parent's allowance

Income support

State pension

**Exempt from income tax**

Attendance allowance

Bereavement payment

Child tax credit

Winter fuel allowance for pensioners

Christmas bonus for pensioners

Disability Living Allowance

Pension Credit

Working Tax Credit

Housing benefit and Council tax benefit

Income Support

Industrial injuries benefit

Guardian's allowance

Although tax returns and tax affairs often make clients feel nervous HMRC have published a lot of useful information that is accessible to the public. These include guidelines specifically relating to pensioners. The Pension Service's *Pensioners' Guide* can be located at *http://www.thepensionservice. gov.uk/pdf/pensionersguide/pg3oct06.pdf* [accessed August 29, 2007].[27]

Clients should be encouraged to view the annual formality of submitting their self-assessment tax return or repayment claim forms as an opportunity to review their affairs. HMRC have indicated that there are high proportions of pensioners who do not reclaim tax due to them. In the case of repayments individuals can claim refunds of the tax due to them before the end of the tax year on tax deducted from bank and building society interest if the repayment due is £50 or more. Interest on the repayment due will also be awarded. Clients should be aware that the time limit for making a repayment claim is 5 years and 10 months from the end of the tax year.

---

[26] Income Tax (Earnings and Pensions) Act 2003, s.663 provides that no liability to income tax shall arise on long-term incapacity benefit if the period of incapacity for work for the purposes of benefit is treated as having begun before April 13, 1995 and the part of that period which is treated as having fallen before that date includes a day for which that person was entitled to invalidity benefit.

[27] See also the Chartered Institute of Taxation's Low Income Tax Reform Group report *Older people on low incomes—The case for tax reform* at *http://www.litrg.org.uk/uploadedfiles/ document/1_437_pensionersreportA4(1).pdf* [accessed August 29, 2007].

Clients should be encouraged to structure their finances to compliment their circumstances. For example in considering income and potential tax reclaims clients should be aware that the notional dividend tax credits are never repayable, and therefore they may wish to consider transferring funds in a bank account or gilts so that the tax (if deducted at source) may be reclaimed: or looking at tax efficient savings vehicles such as ISAs or tax exempt investments such as premium bonds. Renting out a room in the individual's home can provide tax-free income up to £4,250 per tax year. As with all other taxes, spouses and civil partners should ensure that their finances are structured in the most efficient way and that they both utilise their personal allowances, unless there are other good reasons for holding particular assets in the name of one of them.

The income tax treatment of the elderly client's income is more favorable than that of the younger generation. More generous personal allowances are available.[28]

### Table IV Allowances for the tax year ending April 5, 2008

| | |
|---|---|
| Standard personal allowance (under 65) | £5,225 |
| 65–74 | £7550* |
| 75 and over | £7690* |

* If the individual's income is in excess of £20,900 the allowance will be reduced, although for the personal allowance the minimum is the standard personal allowance.

Married couples allowance acts as a tax reducer and is available where one spouse/civil partner was born before April 6, 1935. The rate of the allowance is £6,285 where the oldest spouse is aged 70–74, and £6,365 where the oldest spouse is aged 75 or over, both of which are restricted to relief at 10 per cent. As with the enhanced personal allowance the married couples allowance is restricted where the individual's income is in excess of £20,900. The minimum allowance is £2,440.

Blind persons allowance of £1,730 for the tax year ended April 5, 2008 is available to those individuals who are registered blind. An unused blind persons allowance may be transferred to a spouse/civil partner.

Individuals who pay maintenance to a person from whom he or she is separated or divorced can claim a deduction for the maintenance paid providing at least one of the individuals was born before April 6, 1935, the person receiving the maintenance has not remarried and the payments are made under a court order or written agreement. The maximum amount of relief is £2,440 restricted to 10 per cent for the tax year ended April 5, 2008.

State pension is paid gross to pensioners but is taxable. Normally any other pension provider will have been provided with the client's tax code (based

---

[28] See Table IV.

on the previous year's income) and will deduct tax at source based on the net allowances available to the individual.

Individuals who are non-taxpayers because their level of income falls within their personal allowance can complete Form R85 to ensure that their bank and building society interest is paid gross. HMRC have a help sheet for calculating whether or not an individual is eligible to claim or not,[29] and there is also an online calculator on their website. Once the form has been completed it should be handed to the bank, building society or local authority. More than one account with each organisation can be recorded on each form but if new accounts are opened or for accounts at different organisations new forms must be completed.

Gift aid relief can reduce an individual's tax liability, and any gifts made under the Gift Aid Scheme (or existing charitable covenants) should be reported on the self assessment/repayment claim form. Gift aid can only be claimed where the individual is liable for at least the equivalent tax (notional dividend tax credits do qualify).

On reaching retirement clients should ensure that they take up their invitation to claim their state pension and send their P45 from their employer to the Revenue so that their tax code can be adjusted. Again, HMRC have published a useful booklet, *Approaching Retirement*, which can be located at *http://www.hmrc.gov.uk/leaflets/ir121.pdf*.[30]

In looking at overall tax planning clients should be wary of the pre-owned assets rules which can result in income tax charges or accepting the IHT reservation of benefit position, which could contradict the purpose of the planning.

Insurance bonds and life policies are also useful products for overall tax planning and should be considered. When structured correctly they can minimise income tax liability (the annual payment can be treated as a return of capital) and when written in trust can be treated as outwith the individual's estate for IHT purposes.

**Council tax**

Council tax is regularly viewed as a burden on elderly clients, particularly **2–14** for those on low incomes. The client's circumstances should be reviewed regularly and advice taken from the local authority. Properties can be treated as exempt if they are unoccupied as a result of the client moving into a nursing home, receiving long-term care in hospital or elsewhere. Where a spouse/civil partner/co-habitee moves out or dies the 25 per cent single occupancy relief should be claimed for the remaining resident.

It is also worth noting that council tax banding can be reduced by one band if a property has been adapted because an individual is disabled. Council tax

---

[29] *http://www.hmrc.gov.uk/taxback/forms.htm* [accessed July 18, 2007].
[30] *http://www.hmrc.gov.uk/leaflets/ir/21.pdf* [accessed August 20, 2007].

benefit is also available for those on low income which can contribute up to 100 per cent of the liability.

### Value added tax

**2–15**    From July 1, 2007 there is a reduced rate of VAT of five per cent for certain home adaptations that support the needs of an elderly person. Furthermore, if a bathroom, washroom or lavatory in a property requires to be adapted or extended as a result of an individual's disability the cost of such work is not liable to VAT.

### National insurance

**2–16**    Elderly clients who are still in employment are provided with relaxed treatment in relation to national insurance contributions. Class 1 contributions are normally due for an individual where he or she is an employed earner[31] (if the individual is self employed Class 2 and 4 contributions may be due), if the threshold of £100 (for the tax year ended April 5, 2008) has been exceeded. Both primary (employee) and secondary (employer) contributions normally require to be paid, however, individuals who have attained pensionable age (currently men over 65 and woman over 60) who fall within the employed earner status are exempt from making primary Class 1 contributions[32] but their employer must still make secondary Class 2 contributions.

It is clear that there is a multitude of issues to be considered when looking at the elderly client's tax affairs. Therefore, their affairs should generally, if possible, be dealt with by individuals who are aware of the planning being done in other areas to ensure that opportunities are identified and any planning is complementary to that being carried out in other areas or included in the client's will.

---

[31]  Social Security Contributions and Benefits Act 1992, s.2(1)(a).
[32]  Social Security Contributions and Benefits Act 1992, s.6(3).

# CHAPTER 3

# TRUSTS

## INTRODUCTION

Trusts can be extremely useful vehicles not only for tax planning but also for **3–01** flexible, efficient and protective planning. They can be established during lifetime (*inter vivos* trusts) or on death (*mortis causa* trusts).

The attraction for the elderly client is often the ability to maintain an element of control (possibly as a trustee) while providing for the future generations and/or charities. There are a number of different trust vehicles allowing the client to select the trust purposes, fixed beneficiaries and/or those who could potentially benefit from the trust. Legal advice should be taken before deciding which option should be taken and the tax position should also be reviewed in relation to the consequences of setting up the trust and the liabilities the trust vehicle may be subject to. Ideally any trust deed should be carefully worded and consideration should be given to the trust powers that are being granted to the trustees.

As well as selecting the trustees, trust purposes and the beneficiaries the settlor may also reserve in the deed an element of control in relation to the assumption or appointment of future trustees, but this should be given careful consideration.

If the settlor (and/or their spouse/civil partner) retains a right to the trust income or assets the settlor will remain liable for income tax on the income generated by the trust assets. Similarly, in such circumstances capital gains will be assessed on the settlor and they may be liable for capital gains tax (CGT), although they may recover any liability from the trustees. Settlor interested trusts also do not qualify for CGT holdover relief for the assets transferred into the trust.

The operation and taxation of trusts have been hot topics recently for the government who have sought to impose stricter tax charges particularly where assets are held in trust for a beneficiary beyond the age of 18. Many clients have expressed disappointment with this as the principal purpose for trust creation is often for the protection of the beneficiary and inheriting at too young an age could defeat this purpose. Nevertheless the rules stand and any planning should be done carefully with an appreciation that the rules could change yet again at any time.

## TRUST CREATION

**3–02** Once the terms of the trust have been established consideration must be given to the sum or value being transferred to the trust and the inheritance tax (IHT) implications. Couples are assessed separately for IHT purposes and it may be sensible to have contributions made jointly instead of from one individual.

### Trusts for the disabled

**3–03** These, including trusts created for the settlor him/herself to provide for future disability, are special trust vehicles given exclusive trust status. The transfer into the trust will be treated as a potentially exempt transfer for lifetime transfers. For *mortis causa* trusts, IHT will be due if the estate exceeds the taxable threshold.

### Charitable trusts

**3–04** These are discussed in detail below but on creation, if charitable status and tax exemption is achieved the transfers into the trust will be exempt transfers for IHT purposes. Additionally, the transferor should be able to claim gift aid relief for income tax and capital gains tax purposes on lifetime transfers. There are also special capital gains tax reliefs if shares or property are gifted to a charity treating the transfer on a no-gain/no-loss basis.

### All other trusts[1]

**3–05** Inheritance tax is due at 20 per cent on the value over the nil rate band (£300,000 for the tax year ending April 5, 2008) on lifetime transfers. The form IHT100 and supplementary pages must be completed at the time of transfer. The transfer value must be grossed up if the settlor pays the tax (to ensure the net amount received by the trust is the intended amount). No grossing up is required if the trustees are to pay the tax from the trust funds received. Form IHT100 need not be submitted if:

- the total value of the individual's transfers in the financial year do not exceed £10,000; and
- the cumulative value of all transfers in the previous 10 years does not exceed £40,000.

Trustees of an interest in possession trust[2] do not have to deliver an account for terminations of a person's beneficial interest where:

- that person's annual exemption[3]; or
- marriage or civil partnership[4] gift exemption,[5]

are made available to the trustees.

---

[1]  Finance Act 2006.
[2]  IHTM16061. HMRC Inheritance Tax Manual can be accessed at *http://www.hmrc.gov. uk/manuals/ihtmanual/index.htm* [accessed August 29, 2007].
[3]  IHTM14141.
[4]  IHTM11032.
[5]  IHTM14191.

For inheritance tax purposes if the settlor dies within seven years of the transfer, the transfer is brought back into account and additional tax may be repayable based on the death rate after deduction of the nil rate band less any prior gifts within seven years before death and deduction of lifetime tax already suffered.

Special capital gains tax holdover rules exist whereby a gain accrued on business assets being transferred into the trust, or where IHT is due on the gift being transferred into the trust, may be able to be held over and the liability deferred.[6]

## ONGOING ADMINISTRATION

Once established, the trust itself (excluding trusts for the disabled, charitable **3–06** trusts and accumulation and maintenance trusts specifically allowing for the beneficiary to inherit at no older than 18[7]) is liable for IHT and the trustees have a duty to ensure that liabilities are met. The IHT charges for trusts (other than disabled and charitable trusts) are:

(1) 10-year anniversary charges; and
(2) exit charges.

On both occasions Form IHT100 must again be completed recording the position. However, trustees of an interest in possession trust do not have to deliver an account for terminations of a person's beneficial interest where that person's annual exemption or marriage or civil partnership gift exemptions are made available to the trustees.

The Finance Act 2006 introduced significant changes from March 22, 2006 to the taxation of trusts and as a result there are fresh rules plus transitional rules and the opportunity for adjustment up until April 6, 2008. The rules are complex and professional advice should be taken.[8]

Accumulation and maintenance trusts which provide for the beneficiary becoming absolutely entitled by the age of 18 (or have been varied to provide for this) are exempt from the 10-year charge and exit charges for the purposes of IHT.

Special rules exist reducing the charges where a beneficiary inherits at an age greater than 18 but less than 25.

## INTEREST IN POSSESSION TRUSTS

Many clients elect to use interest in possession trusts as they allow a prin- **3–07** cipal beneficiary/beneficiaries to be named and can also direct what happens to the trust funds on the termination of the principal's interest. As a result liferent trusts are often incorporated into wills entitling a surviving spouse

---

[6] Taxation of Chargeable Gains Act 1992, ss.152–159, 260.
[7] Finance Act 2006, Sch.20.
[8] See HMRC BN 25–*Aligning The Inheritance Tax Treatment For Trusts*, as found at *http://www.hmrc.gov.uk/budget2006/bn25.htm* [accessed September 13, 2007].

(or another individual) to the use and enjoyment of the residue of an estate but directing where these funds where will go if the survivor remarries/enters in a civil partnership/co-habits or dies.

The tax position for interest in possession trusts is that any income generated is assessable on the liferenter (the person who is entitled to the income and the use of the trust funds), and the value of the trust is aggregated with the value of the liferenter's estate on death for the purposes of inheritance tax (the trustees have responsibility for meeting the trust's share of the IHT liability). Any taxable capital gains generated during the liferent are taxable on the trustees at 40 per cent after deducting the trust annual exemption of half the normal rate (£4,600 for the tax year ending April 5, 2008, although if the settlor has set up more than one trust this half exemption amount is divided further between all the other trusts created).

## DISCRETIONARY TRUSTS

**3–08** These trusts allow for the most flexibility and are often accompanied by a "Letter of Wishes" prepared by the settlor detailing their intentions for the trust. Such letters are not legally binding but commonly provide the trustees with useful guidance on how the trust assets should be distributed and which beneficiaries they should consider benefiting.

As none of the beneficiaries has a right to the trust assets the trustees are subject to income tax and capital gains tax on the income and gains generated from the trust assets. Additionally for inheritance tax the exit and 10 year charges detailed above apply.

## TRUSTS FOR THE DISABLED

**3–09** The changes brought about by the Finance Act 2006 have re-generated the trust vehicle for the disabled (previously the desired result could be achieved by an alternative vehicle). Section 89(5)[9] sets out the strict criteria for meeting the disabled status.

These trusts enjoy special treatment for income tax and capital gains tax purposes. The charges for the trustees are equivalent to those that would be the trigger had the income/gain been received directly by the beneficiary. These trusts also have the added benefit that there are no inheritance tax ten-year charges or exit charges.

## GENERAL

**3–10** As well as the protection and tax benefits a trust vehicle can offer there is additionally the privacy element that attracts many clients. Unlike companies, trusts do not have to disclose information to any organisations such as

---

[9] Finance Act 2006, s.89(5).

Companies House or lodge accounts which are publicly available (charitable trusts however must submit accounts and annual returns to the Office of the Scottish Charity Regulator). Prior to the Finance Act 2006 liferent trusts (and this still applies to liferent trusts in existence at March 22, 2006) were exempt from exit and ten-year charges and were often used by individuals in favour of themselves. This allowed the administration of their assets on their death to be carried out by the trustees without the need for Confirmation to the estate which puts information regarding assets held into the public domain.

## RULES FOR TRUSTEES

The role of a trustee comes with responsibility, and acceptance of office 3–11 should not be taken lightly. The current rules allow for flexibility in terms of investment options but trustees must ensure that at all times they are acting in the interests of the beneficiaries and take professional advice where appropriate. Good practice is to have a regularly reviewed investment strategy tailored to the trust and its assets and the needs of the beneficiaries.

The trust rate for income tax is 40 per cent, with dividends taxed at the lower rate of 32.5 per cent for discretionary and accumulation and maintenance trusts. For the tax year from April 6, 2007 these trusts are also entitled to a basic rate band for the first £1,000 of income.

## CHARITABLE TRUSTS

There is a great attraction for many in having your own charity, for which 3–12 you can select your own name and maintain an element of control in how funds are used. Chapter 16 identifies that establishing a charitable trust is often an attractive option for executing a deed of variation, but many individuals chose to do so during their lifetime or to provide for such in their wills. Many elderly people select to benefit a purpose close to their heart and one which has been relevant to them at some point during their lifetime. Not only does an established charity serve the good of the country but those donating to it and the charity itself are provided with certain tax benefits.

### The Charity Test

For a trust[10] in Scotland to achieve charitable status it must be approved by 3–13 the Office of the Scottish Charity Regulator[11] (OSCR) who seek to ensure that:

(1) its purposes consist only of one or more of the charitable purposes; and
(2) it provides (or, in the case of an applicant, provides or intends to provide) public benefit in Scotland or elsewhere.[12]

---

[10] A trust is not the only vehicle for a charity, companies and scottish charitable incorporated organisations are commonly used vehicles.

[11] OSCR have a very helpful team and their website offers useful guidance, such as *Guidance on Meeting the Charity Test http://www.oscr.org.uk/publicationitem.aspx?id=aec25378-896e-448a-bb07-906b8b715a96* [accessed July 18, 2007].

[12] Charities and Trustee Investment (Scotland) Act 2005, s.7(1).

**Charitable Purposes**

3–14   (1) The prevention or relief of poverty.

(2) The advancement of education.

(3) The advancement of religion.

(4) The advancement of health (including the prevention or relief of sickness, disease or human suffering).

(5) The saving of lives.

(6) The advancement of citizenship or community development (including rural or urban regeneration and the promotion of civic responsibility, volunteering, the voluntary sector or the effectiveness or efficiency of charities).

(7) The advancement of the arts, heritage, culture or science.

(8) The advancement of public participation in sport (and "sport" means sport which involves physical skill and exertion).

(9) The provision of recreational facilities, or the organisation of recreational activities, with the object of improving the conditions of life for the persons for whom the facilities or activities are primarily intended, and only in relation to recreational facilities or activities which are primarily intended for persons who have need of them by reason of their age, ill-health, disability, financial hardship or other disadvantage, or available to members of the public at large or to male or female members of the public at large.

(10) The advancement of human rights, conflict resolution or reconciliation.

(11) The promotion of religious or racial harmony.

(12) The promotion of equality and diversity.

(13) The advancement of environmental protection or improvement.

(14) The relief of those in need by reason of age, ill-health, disability, financial hardship or other disadvantage (including relief given by the provision of accommodation or care).

(15) The advancement of animal welfare.

(16) Any other purpose that may reasonably be regarded as analogous to any of the preceding purposes (and the advancement of any philosophical belief (whether or not involving belief in a god) is analogous to the purpose set out in (3) above).[13]

**Public Benefit**

3–15   The Charities and Trustee Investment (Scotland) Act 2005[14] details what OSCR must have regard to when determining whether a body provides or intends to provide public benefit. This includes any:

(1) benefit gained or likely to be gained by members of the body or any other persons (other than as members of the public); and

(2) disbenefit incurred or likely to be incurred by the public, in consequence of the body exercising its functions compares with the benefit gained or likely to be gained by the public in that consequence,

---

[13] Charities and Trustee Investment (Scotland) Act 2005, s.7(2).

[14] Charities and Trustee Investment (Scotland) Act 2005, s.8.

and where benefit is, or is likely to be, provided to a section of the public only, whether any condition on obtaining that benefit (including any charge or fee) is unduly restrictive.[15]

**Application Process**

The application process to OSCR involves completion of the following:  **3–16**

- application form;
- charity trustee declaration form—to ensure that the prospective charity trustees are aware of their responsibilities and are not disqualified from acting as charity trustees;
- the trust deed;
- a recent statement of accounts (if applicable); and
- document detailing intended activities.

**Tax Position**

Once charitable status has been achieved and a charity number allocated  **3–17** the charitable trust will be exempt from IHT, CGT, and income tax providing HMRC recognise the trust as charitable. Furthermore, as previously mentioned individuals transferring assets to the trust will not be liable for IHT, can avoid triggering a CGT charge and can apply for gift aid relief if they are a UK tax payer.

It is important to be aware of what is expected from acting as a charitable trustee and to ensure that the individual taking on board the appointment is aware of these duties and feels able to adhere to them. OSCR offer a useful leaflet *Guidance for charity trustees.*[16]

Ongoing compliance to ensure that charitable status is maintained includes completion of the annual return and submission of the charity accounts, as well as continuing to illustrate public benefit.

## SUMMARY

Trusts can offer effective solutions for planning matters particularly for the  **3–18** elderly client who may wish to provide for the younger generations or for charitable purposes. Proper advice should be taken at all times and careful planning should be undertaken before the trust deed is executed to ensure that there are sufficient powers to be able to achieve what the settlor intends. Despite the stricter tax rules as a result of the Finance Act 2006 trusts remain a popular option for flexible planning.

---

[15] Charities and Trustee Investment (Scotland) Act 2005, s.8(2).
[16] Available from OSCR at *http://www.oscr.org.uk* [accessed August 21, 2007].

# CHAPTER 4

# ASSETS AND BENEFITS

## THE FAMILY HOME

**4-01** For many people, the family home will be their most valuable and largest asset, and it is important to them that the assets they have worked hard to accumulate can be passed on to their children and grandchildren. This thought is uppermost in their minds when they ask if it is sensible to pass the house on to the children now rather than waiting to pass it under a will.

### Giving away the family home—the key points

**4-02**
- It is important that before clients do so the implications of transferring the home are fully understood so that the advantages can be weighed against the disadvantages and they can make the appropriate decision for them.
- The law says that responsibility lies with the owner of a property although the donor may choose to give away his home and may agree to be responsible for the buildings insurance and general maintenance. The donor might initially be quite happy with the responsibility but what may seem straight forward in the early stages could cause problems later on if his circumstances change and can no longer finance these payments. To prevent any future problems, the issue needs to be openly discussed and agreement reached over who is to pay for all major outgoings of the home.
- Although the property is still the donor's home, the general rule is as the donor no longer owns it, he does not have the right to live in the house. The donor could be asked to pay rent by the owners. The owners may even sell the property and the donor may end up with no home.
- If a person transfers his home to somebody, there is some risk (1) that there will be a falling out amongst the parties; (2) that one of the people who now owns the house will become bankrupt; (3) that one of the people who now owns the house predeceases the donor leaving their share of the house to a spouse or children (or anybody else or a charity); or (4) that one of those persons divorce. In any of these situations the donor may end up with no home. Consider if any of these situations is likely, discuss the issues fully and ask questions to see if there is any real risk. The persons to whom the client transfers his home will need to make provision for the donor's occupancy with their own will or wills.
- Once the person's home has been transferred out of his name it does not belong to him and will not be disposed of in his will. This may save on expenses administering his estate on death. However the value of the property may be added to his estate for inheritance tax purposes to

calculate whether any inheritance tax is payable particularly where no or little rent is paid as the donor has retained a benefit in the asset.

- Inheritance tax may be payable on the donor's death on assets including savings and investments and property over the nil rate band, which is currently £300,000 for tax year ending April 5, 2008. Inheritance tax is payable on the amount over this figure at a rate of 40 per cent. The figure is generally reviewed annually in the Budget. If the deceased has made gifts from capital, of money or assets in his lifetime exceeding £3,000 per annum and within seven years of his death, the value of these gifts may be added to whatever other assets he owns at death to determine the overall tax payable. There are complicated tax implications if a person transfers his home and continues to live in the home if the value of his total assets including the value of the home exceeds the nil rate band.

- If a person owns his home and lives there, no capital gains tax is payable, on transfer, on any gain made on the original purchase or acquisition price under the current law. Usually, the person receiving the gift will be deemed to acquire it at the current market value at date of transfer. There may be tax payable by them when they eventually dispose of the property and they should be advised to obtain independent advice on the implications.

- If the donor is in receipt of means tested state benefits such as income support and gives away an asset such as the home, *and* it appears to the Department for Work and Pensions (DWP) that this was done with the intention of reducing his assets so as to qualify for certain benefits, they may assess him as if he still owns the asset.

- Similar rules apply to financial help which may be available from local authorities, e.g. should the donor subsequently need to move into a care home. If at a future date the donor applies for financial assistance from the DWP or local authority, no matter how much time has passed and whatever the reason for the transfer, the value of the asset may be taken into account when assessing entitlement to financial support if the DWP or local authority in any way deem that one of the reasons was to avoid paying for his own care. The current DWP and local authority view is that all people of a certain age should realise care is a possibility and so such transfers are automatically deemed to be deliberate deprivation of assets in order to avoid paying for their own care.

## MOVING/DOWN-SIZING

For some people, as they age, the family home whilst full of happy **4-03** memories may now be too large, too expensive to heat and repair, and generally have become a burden financially, physically and psychologically. The large garden which was formerly a hobby may now be a chore as it is simply too demanding.

### Retirement flat/house

A retirement housing complex, assuming the person is at least 55, might **4-04** be a logical step. The exact manner of ownership, the service provided and the monthly charge for those services will vary from development to development and the terms of purchase and the titles must be checked carefully to see if the flat or bungalow is suitable for the client in question.

Most clients will ask their lawyer not just for legal advice on this matter but also "Am I doing the right thing?" Rather than giving an outright opinion perhaps the appropriate role is to play "Devil's Advocate". The client's reason for moving should be teased out.

What is the attraction in moving, is it:

- the presence of a warden?
- the comfort of a secure environment?
- the removal of responsibility for repairs?
- no more gardening?
- the appeal of a smaller and therefore more manageable property?
- to be surrounded by people with similar interests and concerns?

It may be that remaining in their own home with some extra security or support might actually be preferable for some people.[1]

Good advice to clients should underline that moving away from friends and family and a mixture of neighbours to mix with people mainly of their own age group only, may not appeal to them in the long term. At first it may seem a relief to have somebody else managing matters but is the client really ready to cede control? How will they feel about being bound by majority decisions? Will the care and attention offered by the warden and perhaps your neighbours be welcome or will it seem like loss of independence? Will the same property be suitable if the client becomes frail, e.g. would it accommodate a wheelchair? Are pets allowed?

Before the client purchases such a property he will have to research the matter carefully, checking location, medical and dental services in the area, transport, car parking, management of the development and its cost, and the different ways of ownership.

In some developments clients will be offered 100 per cent ownership and will simply pay the monthly service charge, council tax, etc. Some housing associations will offer a part purchase and part rental sheltered housing. The client buys a portion of the property at a portion of the market value and pays rent for the remaining portion. The client will need a substantial income to cover the rental and the service charge monthly.

Information can be obtained from Age Concern, the Elderly Accommodation Counsel or the HOMAS Mobility Scheme Helpline 0845 080 1089. Local housing associations will also be able to provide information for the local area.

If the client has insufficient capital to purchase a property or a share of a property then an interest only mortgage could be available. Interest is paid monthly and the capital sum remains the same until the sale of the property

---

[1] See Ch.13 for options.

or the death of the borrower. A family member may purchase the property on behalf of the client but will be bound by age restrictions and of course there are risks to the client in living in a property which belongs to someone else. Additionally, there would be no CGT principal private residence relief on the sale of the property as it would not be the family member's principal home.

The deed of conditions for the housing development should be read carefully and explained in even greater detail than usual to the client as the restrictions are generally far tighter than those in normal properties. The deed of conditions is not the full story however due to the terms of the Title Conditions Act (Scotland) Act 2003 which may apply to such developments.

A useful checklist is contained in Age Concern's factsheet entitled "Buying Retirement Housing".[2]

## RAISING EQUITY FROM THE HOME

The Sunday papers are always full of advertisements for equity release **4–05** schemes which appeal to many clients who may have limited savings and income but own an extremely valuable property. Many are reluctant to sell up and move from the house that has been home for so many years, and consider an equity release scheme may be their only option.

These schemes vary in content and some are definitely better than others.

- The common themes are that there is a minimum age for participating, a maximum percentage of the property they will loan, that the client must be the home owner, that the property must have a minimum value, there is little or no mortgage remaining and with some there may be a minimum amount of borrowing and there will be a limit on the type and construction of the property.
- There will be valuation and legal fees and possibly arrangement fees to be paid. There may be penalties for early repayment of loans.
- The owner remains responsible for repairing and insuring the building and the scheme provider will be entitled to insist that maintenance is to a reasonable standard. This is probably where most clients will be put off these schemes as, if they are already quite tight for money, the house is probably already not in the best of repair.
- The owner may wish or need to move at some time in the future and any restrictions or costs relating to this must be investigated fully before the original scheme is entered into.
- All anticipated changes in circumstances must be considered and the effect of these on the plan and vice versa investigated thoroughly before embarkation.
- The effect of equity release on means-tested benefits such as pension credit, income support or council tax benefits can be quite drastic. This means that the benefits of having additional income emanating from the invested capital are extinguished by the loss of the benefits and the loss

---

[2] *http://www.ageconcernscotland.org.uk/Publications/fact.asp?newsid = 398* [accessed August 8, 2007].

of associated entitlements such as free dental treatment and glasses and the right to grants or loans from the Social Fund would disappear.

## FINANCIAL ASSISTANCE FOR REPAIRS AND ALTERATIONS

**4–06** The law on improvement and repairs grants[3] means that grants may be available from the local authority to assist owners in repairing, improving or adapting the home. Owners can mean owners, agricultural and crofting tenants, disabled tenants and liferenters. It is always worth asking for sight of the local authority's policy on grants and asking for an application form before embarking on works to repair, improve or adapt a house, especially if there is any reason to believe it is currently below the tolerable standard[4] or lacks the standard amenities.[5]

For people with disabilities, advice on adaptations will be available from the Social Work Department and they may also be able to provide funding for the works. This is because the Social Work Department has a duty to provide certain services to disabled people.[6] This can mean that if a grant application fails, the Social Work Department might be obliged to assist instead.

## STATE BENEFITS AND OTHER SOURCES OF FUNDING

**4–07** Many people as they age may find that they are having to live on limited incomes and may find that their savings have dwindled over time either literally or due to inflation.

If a person has a low income he may be entitled to certain state benefits. Convincing clients that they are entitled to these and that it is not shameful to claim them is the lawyer's first task. Once that hurdle is overcome there is a range of options.

### Pension credit for people of 60 and over

**4–08** Pension credit has to be claimed and has two elements; the guarantee credit and the savings credit.

- The guarantee credit is designed to ensure that everyone has a minimum income. The current levels are £119.05 per week for a single person and £181.70 for a couple, at least one of whom must be over 60. These are minimum amounts and the amounts can be higher if a person is severely disabled, or is a carer entitled to carer's allowance or a home owner with housing costs such as mortgage interest to pay.
- The savings credit part can be claimed by people of 65 or over and provides extra cash if they have a "qualifying income" of more than the

---

[3] Housing (Scotland) Act 1987, as amended, and Housing (Scotland) Act 2001.
[4] Housing (Scotland) Act 1987, s.86 (1) as amended by Housing (Scotland) Act 2001, s.102(1).
[5] Housing (Scotland) Act 1987, s.244 and Housing (Scotland) Act 2001, s.102(2).
[6] Chronically Sick and Disabled Persons Act 1970.

savings credit threshold but below a certain level. The amounts vary for disabled people, carers and homeowners as above.

### Working tax credit

This can be claimed by single people or couples whether employed or self- **4–09** employed, and there is no upper age limit. Disabled people may get extra money. Jobcentreplus will be able to explain the intricacies of claiming.

### Housing benefit and council tax benefit

Housing benefit helps towards rent and some service charges but if the **4–10** client lives in a sheltered housing complex the local authority's Social Services Department under a system called "Supporting People" is the appropriate place to claim.

For tax year ending April 5, 2008, having savings of over £6,000 will affect the amount of housing and/or council tax benefit received and there is a £16,000 upper savings limit, however those receiving the guarantee part of pension credit should be entitled to full help with rent and council tax (and there is no upper savings limit).

If neither housing benefit nor main council tax benefit is available due to the client having more than £16,000 of savings, they may be able to get second adult rebate. The second adult rebate scheme can help some people who cannot get benefits based on their own income and savings but who live with one or more persons on a low income.

In summary, whether financial help is available and the amount to which the client might be entitled depends on his income and savings, the people in his family, any disablement and the amount of rent and council tax actually paid.

### The Social Fund

The Social Fund may provide lump sum grant payments to cover **4–11** expenses such as funeral payments, community care grants to help with repairs, redecoration, etc. or may provide budgeting loans and crisis loans. Loans are repaid by deductions from benefits over the following months.

### Help with house repairs

If a person is in receipt of pension credit he may be able to get a com- **4–12** munity care grant or budgeting loan to help with the cost of minor repairs or decoration. Help can mean providing a grant, loan, materials or other form of assistance through a discretionary scheme which should give priority to vulnerable and older people for adaptation or improvement to living conditions. Each local authority will have its own published policy describing the sort of help it offers in this area.

### Disabled facilities grants

These are administered by local authorities and are means tested. **4–13**

**Charities**

**4–14**     There are many charities and charitable trusts which may offer funding to the elderly in need. Local libraries, Age Concern and local solicitors may be able to locate a suitable charity or trust to help.

**Health costs**

**4–15**     Treatment from the NHS is generally free. People over 60 will get free prescriptions and if the client is in receipt of the guarantee part of pension credit he will also be entitled to free dental treatment, free travel costs to visit hospital, free sight tests and help towards paying for spectacles. A person who receives the disability element of working tax credit will also get financial help. A client who does not have any of these benefits but has a low income and savings of below £16,000 (for the tax year ending April 5, 2008) may still get some financial help. Application forms for this are available from dentists, opticians, etc. and should be sought before paying for treatment.

**Fuel bills and heating**

**4–16**     The Social Fund may help towards heating by giving cold weather payments of £8.50 per week available in the weeks when the weather is especially cold to people who are aged over 60 and receive pension credit.

Most people aged over 60 are entitled to winter fuel payments of £200 for an eligible household and £300 if one person in the house is aged 80 or over.

The Scottish Government has a programme of free installation of central heating to households with older residents. The two main grants available, the warm deal and central heating can be investigated by contacting Eaga Partnership Limited.[7]

**Retirement pension**

**4–17** •     The basic state pension is payable to people who have reached pension age (currently 60 for women, and 65 for men, rising to 65 for both genders in 2010 and there is a proposal to raise it to age 68 after 2024) and have paid or been credited with sufficient national insurance contributions; insufficient contributions will mean a reduced pension or no pension at all.
   •     Other peoples' contributions can have an effect in that a married woman can claim a pension on her husband's contributions but may not get this if she has her own pension and her own contributions.
   •     Divorcees and widows/widowers and dissolved civil partners may be able to use their former spouse or civil partner's record to get a pension or an increase.
   •     People can put off drawing their pension for so long as they want in order to receive a lump sum or an increased pension once they do draw it. Reaching 80 entitles the person to an increase in retirement pension

---

[7]  For useful addresses, see Appendix 1: Useful contacts.

and an entitlement to a certain basic pension if not entitled to a normal basic pension.

- If approaching retirement age it is useful to get a pension forecast and to decide whether to make voluntary contributions to increase the pension. Someone who has been receiving jobseeker's allowance or cannot work due to being ill or disabled or has been receiving a carer's allowance will get credits towards their pension. It is important to check whether the person needs to claim or whether it has been done automatically.

**Bereavement benefits**

Many marriages and civil partnerships may have two people with a sig- **4–18** nificant age gap between them. Bereavement benefits are available to both men and women under pension age. The three bereavement benefits are all dependent on the national insurance contributions of the person who has died. The survivor may qualify for the £2,000 lump sum bereavement payment, the bereavement allowance paid for 52 weeks or the widowed parents' allowance for people with dependent children. If the survivor is over pension age he or she can only get the lump sum bereavement payment if his or her spouse or civil partner had not reached pension age or started drawing their state pension at the time of death.

**Incapacity benefit**

This is due to people who are unable to work because they are sick or **4–19** disabled. It is usually based on national insurance contributions, and is not normally means tested but may be reduced if there is a personal or occupational pension being drawn. At pension age incapacity benefit will stop and the state retirement pension should be drawn instead.

**Severe disablement allowance**

This has been abolished for new claimants but will continue for people **4–20** who were receiving it before April 5, 2001 providing they continue to fulfil the conditions. There is a basic rate plus various increments to the payments relating to age and to whether the person has dependents.

**Attendance allowance**

This is for people who are ill or disabled (whether mentally or physically) **4–21** and need help with personal care or require supervision by another person. There is no upper age limit for attendance allowance, it is not means tested and does not depend on national insurance contributions. Under 65s should instead apply for disability living allowance. There are two rates of attendance allowance, the lower rate is appropriate if assistance is required during the day or during the night and the higher rate is appropriate if assistance is required in both day and night time. The entitlement to attendance allowance is not based on whether a person is receiving help but the fact that the person actually needs help.

### Disability living allowance

**4–22**    This is aimed at people who become disabled and make a claim before reaching the age of 65. The claim should be made whether help is being received or not as the entitlement is not based on whether a person is receiving help but the fact that the person actually needs help.

### The Independent Living (1993) Fund

**4–23**    Payments under this cease at age 65.

### Carer's allowance

**4–24**    This is paid to people who are caring for someone who receives the top or middle rate care part of disability living allowance or to someone who receives either rate of attendance allowance. There are strict rules about the amount of care (i.e. number of hours) being given and any other earnings the carer may have. The rules about the interaction of carer's allowance and other benefits being received by the carer, and the interaction of carer's allowance and benefits being received by the invalid, are complex and a claim could reduce the amount of benefit received from other sources by the invalid. This should be researched before a claim is made.

### Industrial Injuries Scheme

**4–25**    This Scheme provides help to people who have been disabled by an accident at work or an industrial disease. The most likely benefit to come from this is disablement benefit which can be paid in addition to other benefits; the level of payment being based on an assessment of the disability.

### War pension

**4–26**    This is payable to:

- people who have been disabled as a result of war;
- people who were servicemen in the Armed Forces in peacetime who have been disabled as a result of that service; and
- war widows and widowers.

Check with the Veterans Agency.[8]

### Council tax reductions

**4–27**    Council Tax is calculated by the value of a property but also to some extent on the people who are resident in the property. Always ensure that a single client is receiving the 25 per cent discount for living alone as this reduction is not means tested.[9]

---

[8] For useful addresses, see Appendix 1: Useful contacts.
[9] For travel concessions, see Ch.14. For exemption to pay TV licences, see Ch.14.

# CHAPTER 5

# ADVANCE DIRECTIVES

## LIVING WILL

When instructing the preparation of wills and powers of attorney many **5–01** clients express a wish to prepare an "end of life" advance directive usually termed a "living will". Many solicitors will provide a *proforma* document with detailed instructions on how to complete it rather than preparing the document for the client.

There follows an example of the living will which will satisfy most end of life situations although it is fair to say that the law in Scotland is far from clear.

TO:    **FIRST:    MY FAMILY**
           **SECOND:    MY DOCTOR and any DOCTORS attending me**

**THIS is a formal ADVANCE DIRECTIVE made by ME to record my wishes in case I become unable to communicate, and cannot take part in decisions about my medical care.**

Name    ...................................................................................

Address    ..............................................................................
...................................................................................................
...................................................................................................

**I have discussed this Living Will with the following Doctor**

Doctor's Name    ........................................................................

Doctor's Address    ....................................................................
...................................................................................................
...................................................................................................
Date of Discussion    ..................................................................

**I DECLARE and DIRECT as follows:-**

1. I am of sound mind, have taken all the advice which I consider necessary, and have given careful consideration to these instructions.
2. If the time comes when I can no longer take adequate part in decisions about my own future, this Directive is to take effect and to be respected as a proper record of my wishes.
3. If in the opinion of my Doctor or of the other Physicians attending me:-

- I have a physical illness or condition from which there is no likelihood of recovery *and* the illness is so serious that my life is nearing its end

Or

- My mental functions have become permanently impaired **and** the impairment is so serious that I do not understand what is happening to me **and** there is no likelihood of improvement **and** my physical condition then becomes so bad that I would need medical treatment to keep me alive

Or

- I become permanently unconscious **and** there is no likelihood that I will regain consciousness

I DO NOT WANT TO BE KEPT ALIVE BY MEDICAL TREATMENT. I WANT MEDICAL TREATMENT TO BE LIMITED TO KEEPING ME COMFORTABLE AND FREE FROM PAIN FULLY ACCEPTING THAT SUCH AN AMOUNT OF DRUGS MAY HASTEN MY DEATH. I REFUSE ALL OTHER MEDICAL TREATMENT AND DECLARE THAT I AM TO BE ALLOWED TO DIE WITH DIGNITY.

**Specific views of particular treatments or tests (if any)**
Please speak to your doctor before you write anything in this section.

........................................................................................................

........................................................................................................

........................................................................................................

**This Living Will is to remain effective until or unless I make it clear that my wishes have changed.**

SIGNED by me at (place) .....................................

Date ................................................................

before this witness

....................................................Witness Signature

....................................................Witness Name

....................................................Witness Address

....................................................

....................................................Witness Occupation

**Dates I have reviewed my decisions since signing this Living Will**.

Date ............................................ Date .......................................

Date ............................................ Date .......................................

Date ............................................ Date .......................................

## COMPLETING YOUR LIVING WILL EXPLANATORY NOTES

These notes explain how to fill in your living will and give an explanation of the meaning and effect of the living will. **5–02**

### What is a living will? **5–03**

A living will only takes effect if you become unable to tell people your wishes about your medical treatment so cannot take part in the decisions to be made.

The living will lets you say in advance of a situation or set of circumstances what your wishes would be about medical treatment. These statements are called advance directives.

A living will cannot deal with funeral instructions or your possessions or property after you die. You need an ordinary will for these matters.

In Scotland the law is *probably* that an advance refusal of treatment is legally binding on doctors and medical staff as long as:

(1) you made your refusal when you were mentally capable of making such a decision;
(2) you meant that refusal to apply to the circumstances, which have now occurred;
(3) you understood what the consequences of the refusal would be in those circumstances; and
(4) you made the decision freely and were not influenced or coerced by someone else.

You cannot insist on receiving a particular treatment.

The British Medical Association supports the use of living wills *but* only where it appears that the conditions for the living will being valid are met.

### How to proceed? **5–04**

Think about your wishes carefully.

You are not obliged to speak to someone else before you complete this form but we suggest that you speak to a doctor (preferably your own GP) to discuss healthcare options and complete the form. His or her details and the date of the discussions should be written into the living will. This helps to show that the four conditions above have been met. You may also want to discuss your plans with family, friends, healthcare workers or religious organisation.

### 5–05  What if I change my mind after it is signed?

The wishes are not necessarily final. They can be changed at any time you are still mentally capable of doing so. The change can be spoken, it need not be in writing, but of course if you change your mind you should have the existing copies of the living will destroyed, just to be sure. Make sure that your doctor and family know that you have changed your mind.

### 5–06  Your wishes and completing the form

Fill in the form using black ballpoint pen or ink.

Fill in your name and address.

Fill in the name and address of any doctor with whom you have discussed your wishes and the date of such discussions.

Score out any part of the wishes that do *not* apply.

Sign and date the form in front of a witness who is age 16 or over. The witness should also sign and complete his or her details.

The witness should NOT be a relative or your partner, or anyone who will gain by your death.

### 5–07  What to do with the completed form?

Make sure the people close to you know about the form and where to find it. Make sure your doctor knows about it and that a copy is added to your notes if you go into hospital.

Make sure you review the form from time to time and sign and date it when you do so to help indicate that the conditions for the living will being valid are met.

### 5–08  Other welfare matters

You may wish to consider instructing a solicitor to prepare a welfare power of attorney for you which will give a chosen person (the Attorney) certain rights to make medical and other welfare decisions for you in the event of you being unable to do so yourself.


### ADVANCE STATEMENTS

5–09  The Mental Health (Care and Treatment) (Scotland) Act 2003 allows individuals to write advance statements[1] which set out how they would wish to be treated (or would rather not be treated) for mental disorders should

---

[1]  Mental Health (Care and Treatment) (Scotland) Act 2003, s.275.

their ability to make treatment decisions become impaired in the future. Those dispensing treatment have a duty to regard such advance statements[2] since past and present wishes must be acknowledged but if the person is at risk and the other grounds for compulsory treatment apply, the doctor may consider overruling the terms of the statement by using compulsory treatment measures which exist under the Act.

The person signing such a statement must have the legal capacity to do so and the test of capacity is akin to the test for taking medical decisions, and in addition the person must understand the consequences of the decision. If preparing statements or witnessing statements for a person, it is wise to consult the Scottish Executive Guidance[3] and the Mental Health Act Code of Practice.[4]

To be valid the person must have capacity, the statement must be in writing and signed by the person making it. It must be witnessed by one of a prescribed group of persons[5] and the witness certifies that in their opinion the person making it has the capacity at the time to do so.[6]

There is no equivalent measure in the Adults with Incapacity (Scotland) Act 2000 but welfare powers of attorney, if suitably worded, can allow the named attorney to make decisions about personal welfare and medical treatment (within set parameters and subject to the safeguards set out in the Act). However, even if the power of attorney specifies a power of refusal of a treatment and the attorney decides a treatment should be refused, the medical profession can overrule this and provide treatment in certain circumstances.[7] It is an offence for anyone exercising personal welfare powers (whether attorney, guardian or intervener) under the Act to ill-treat or wilfully neglect the adult.[8] Moreover the Adults with Incapacity (Scotland) Act 2000 requires as one of the principles that the past and present wishes of adults are considered.

## INTERACTION OF MENTAL HEALTH (CARE AND TREATMENT) (SCOTLAND) ACT 2003 (MHCT) AND ADULTS WITH INCAPACITY (SCOTLAND) ACT 2000 (AWISA)

AWISA provides a new framework for regulating decision making relating **5–10** to the welfare, finances and property of adults who lack capacity to make those decisions for themselves.

The MHCT provides a new legal framework for the treatment and support of people with mental disorders whether in hospital or in the community.

---

[2] Mental Health (Care and Treatment) (Scotland) Act 2003, s.276.
[3] The new Mental Health Act: A guide to advance statements, Scottish Executive (2004).
[4] Mental Health (Care and Treatment) (Scotland) Act 2003, s.274.
[5] Mental Health (Advance Statements) (Prescribed Class of Persons) (Scotland) (No.2) Regulations 2004 (SSI 2004/429), reg.2.
[6] Mental Health (Care and Treatment) (Scotland) Act 2003, s.276(2).
[7] Adults with Incapacity (Scotland) Act 2000, s.47 and s.50.
[8] Adults with Incapacity (Scotland) Act 2000, s.83.

MHCT relates to all adults with a mental disorder whether they have capacity or not and includes provisions relating to voluntary and compulsory treatment and outlines the service provision required for people with mental disorders.

The definition of capacity varies between the two Acts which means that health professionals will have to be very clear about their definitions before deciding which measures to adopt under which Act in each situation.

The two Acts have a different focus but will both apply in some cases to the one individual. An example of this is a 17-year old who has a mental disorder and lacks capacity in respect of some decisions about his or her daily life.

Medical practitioners may begin to learn about which legislation to use to treat certain adults and the appropriate use of compulsory treatment and welfare guardianship orders. The sheriff court and the Mental Health Tribunal are two entirely different bodies which may at times be making separate decisions about the same people.

Different sets of guidelines exist and there may be confusion rather than clarity about which set of principles to apply.

CHAPTER 6

# POWERS OF ATTORNEY

Many clients will consult lawyers after a significant event has occurred **6–01**
which has triggered concern for the future. The event could be a change in
family or financial circumstances, a medical diagnosis or reading an article
about inheritance tax in a Sunday broadsheet. Most practitioners will be
accustomed to the article in the Sunday papers leading to the telephone
ringing merrily on Monday morning. Many solicitors operate a holistic
approach to clients and will regularly contact clients to hold review meetings
and at any of these occasions, whatever the reason for the client's visit, it
would be appropriate to suggest that the client should plan for the future in
case at any time in that future he or she is unable to make or communicate
sensible decisions about financial matters, property or indeed personal
wellbeing.

## PRE-1991

Up until January 1, 1991 a document could be executed appointing an **6–02**
attorney as factor and commissioner. The document conferred on a person
or persons certain powers to act on behalf of the granter, largely for convenience, e.g. during a period of absence, etc. In law, such a document, no
matter of the terms of it, was to cease to have effect in the event of the
mental incapacity of the granter; mental incapacity being defined at the time
as a mental disorder meaning "mental illness (including personality disorder) or mental handicap however caused or manifested".[1]

In practice where these powers of attorney would be in use for ageing and
ailing clients who had simply lost interest in his or her financial affairs they
would continue to be used if the person slipped into mental incapacity.

Note that the temporary insanity of the granter would not cause the power
of attorney or factor and commission to fall.[2] The correct procedure on
mental incapacity was to have a *curator bonis* appointed, which was cumbersome, expensive and in reality only suitable for large estates.

---

[1] Mental Health (Scotland) Act 1984, s.1.
[2] *Wink v Mortimer* (1849) 11 D. 995.

## JANUARY 1, 1991–APRIL 1, 2001

**6–03** The common law was changed on January 1, 1991 to "Any rule of law by which a factor and commission or power of attorney ceases to have effect in the event of the mental incapacity of the granter shall not apply to a factor and commission or power of attorney granted on or after the date on which the Section comes into force".[3] So a power of attorney, or factor and commission signed after that date continues on the subsequent mental incapacity of the granter, unless the document states otherwise.

## APRIL 2, 2001 ONWARDS: THE ADULTS WITH INCAPACITY (SCOTLAND) ACT 2000

**6–04** The Adults with Incapacity (Scotland) Act 2000 ("the Act") made sweeping changes and introduced a whole new regime for managing the affairs of an adult who has become mentally incapacitated.

## ADULTS WITH INCAPACITY (SCOTLAND) ACT 2000

**6–05** It is worth outlining the main thrust of the legislation as follows.

- Under Pt 1 of the Act it is provided that certain principles must be applied to any intervention in the affairs of an adult under the Act.[4] This is both in deciding what measure of intervention to seek and then in each and every operation of that, or another, intervention thereafter.
- These are easily abbreviated and remembered thus:
  (1) Principle 1—Benefit.
  (2) Principle 2—Minimum intervention.
  (3) Principle 3—Take account of wishes of adult.
  (4) Principle 4—Consultation with relevant others.
  (5) Principle 5—Encourage adult to exercise his skills.

- Under Pt 2 of the Act there is a new regime for people who foresee the possibility of their incapacity. It allows them to grant a power of attorney in relation not just to property and financial affairs as they could under the previous law, but also now in relation to personal welfare. There is a new framework for creating and exercising these powers of attorney.
- Under Pt 3 of the Act a person may apply to the Public Guardian for authority to access funds in an account in the sole name of an adult to provide for the adult's day-to-day care. A joint account held with the adult may continue to be operated by the another account holder providing it is an either/or signature.
- Under Pt 4 authorised establishments (care homes and hospitals) may manage the funds of a resident up to a prescribed limit.
- Under Pt 5 medical practitioners are given a general authority to treat adults if there is a certificate of incapacity. There are of course

---

[3] Law Reform (Miscellaneous Provisions) (Scotland) Act 1990, s.71.
[4] Adults with Incapacity (Scotland) Act 2000, s.1,

safeguards and exceptions to this general rule. Certain medical research
is also permitted where an adult cannot consent.

- Under Pt 6 of the Act a person may apply to the sheriff for an intervention order to deal with financial, property and/or personal welfare
matters in relation to an adult. This is appropriate to generally one-off
situations rather than ongoing management situations. Also under Pt 6
guardianship orders can be applied for to deal with similar matters but
on an ongoing basis.

- Codes of practice[5] providing guidance for exercise of functions under
the Act are published for local authorities, chief social workers and
mental health officers, continuing and welfare attorneys, those authorised under intervention orders, guardians, withdrawers, managers of
care homes and hospitals and those authorised to carry out medical
treatment or research.

However in this chapter we shall concern ourselves only with the client being
able to take control of a situation and make choices ahead of the event,
namely the preparation of a continuing and/or welfare power of attorney.

## CONTINUING AND WELFARE POWERS OF ATTORNEY

Continuing attorneys are attorneys with powers of property and financial **6–06**
affairs and the document containing the powers is a continuing power of
attorney.[6] Welfare attorneys are attorneys with powers over personal welfare and such a document containing such powers is called a welfare power
of attorney.[7]

The Act and the code of practice for continuing and welfare attorneys are
essential reading materials.

## PRE-ACT POWERS OF ATTORNEY

From April 1, 2001, any person already appointed as an attorney under a **6–07**
contract of mandate or agency with powers relating solely to the property or
financial affairs of an adult shall become a continuing attorney under the
Act, an attorney under contract of mandate or agency with powers relating
solely to the personal welfare of an adult shall become a welfare attorney
under the Act and an attorney under a contract of mandate or agency with
powers relating both to the property and financial affairs and to the personal welfare of an adult shall become a continuing and welfare attorney
under the Act[8] (this removes any doubt over whether it was competent to
appoint a welfare attorney pre-2001).

This does not mean that the registration process applies but does mean that
the attorney will have to follow the general principals contained in s.1 of the

---

5  Adults with Incapacity (Scotland) Act 2000, s.13
6  Adults with Incapacity (Scotland) Act 2000, s.15.
7  Adults with Incapacity (Scotland) Act 2000, s.16.
8  Adults with Incapacity (Scotland) Act 2000, Sch.4.

Act and indeed the courts could order that a pre-Act financial attorney should be placed under the supervision of the Public Guardian or a pre-Act welfare attorney should be supervised by the local authority or indeed that the attorney could have to report to the court.


## REGULATION OF ATTORNEYS

**6–08** The relationship between granter and attorney is one of absolute trust. However in order to protect vulnerable adults there are regulatory bodies in relation to attorneys, i.e. the Public Guardian,[9] the courts,[10] local authority[11] and the Mental Welfare Commission for Scotland.[12]


## THE PUBLIC GUARDIAN

**6–09** The Public Guardian's first function is to establish, maintain and make available to the public on payment of the prescribed fee registers of all documents relating to continuing powers of attorney and all documents relating to welfare powers of attorney governed by the Law of Scotland.

The Public Guardian also offers guidance for attorneys.

Additional functions of the Public Guardian relate to the investigation of any complaints regarding the attorney, investigating circumstances where property or financial affairs seem to be at risk, providing a continuing attorney with information and advice if so requested, supervising a continuing attorney and receiving accounts to audit if so ordered by a sheriff, consulting with the Mental Welfare Commission and any local authority where there is a common interest.


## THE COURTS

**6–10** All court applications are to the sheriff who has a wide discretion conferred upon him.

> "In any application or any other proceedings under this Act, the Sheriff may make such consequential or ancillary order, provision or direction as he considers appropriate."[13]

---

9   Adults with Incapacity (Scotland) Act 2000, ss.6 and 7.
10   Adults with Incapacity (Scotland) Act 2000, s.3.
11   Adults with Incapacity (Scotland) Act 2000, s.10.
12   Adults with Incapacity (Scotland) Act 2000, s.9.
13   Adults with Incapacity (Scotland) Act 2000, s.3.

# LOCAL AUTHORITIES

Local authorities will supervise welfare attorneys where ordered to do this **6–11** by the sheriff. They will consult with the Public Guardian and Mental Welfare Commission where there is common interest, investigate complaints and suspicious circumstances about welfare powers and investigate potential risks to the personal welfare of an adult where they are aware of such risk.

# MENTAL WELFARE COMMISSION FOR SCOTLAND

The Commission has a role solely where incapacity is the result of mental **6–12** disorder (and not where failure to communicate is because of a physical disability). The Commission has powers to visit adults, investigate complaints about welfare powers where the Commission feels the local authority action is inappropriate or indeed where the local authority fail to act. They can look into any circumstances in which an adult seems to be at risk even if there is not actually a complaint.

# CREATING A CONTINUING PERSONAL AND WELFARE POWER OF ATTORNEY

A continuing power of attorney is a written document which must be signed **6–13** by the granter and must incorporate a statement that it is intended to continue in spite of incapacity and must incorporate a certificate in the prescribed form signed by a solicitor (and this means a Scottish solicitor) a practising member of the Faculty of Advocates or a registered medical practitioner.[14] There must be separate certificates for continuing and welfare powers of attorney whether the powers are contained all within one document or in separate documents.

*Forms of Certificate*                                                           **6–14**

Continuing Power of Attorney

This Certificate is incorporated in the document subscribed by ............ ("the granter") on ........................................................ that confers a Continuing Power of Attorney on .........and/whom failing ................

I certify that:

A. I interviewed the granter on ............................................. immediately before he/she subscribed this Continuing Power of Attorney and
B. I am satisfied that, at the time this Continuing Power of Attorney was granted, the granter understood its nature and extent:

I have satisfied myself of this:

1. because of my own knowledge of the granter and

---

[14] Adults with Incapacity (Scotland) Act 2000, s.15(3).

   2.  because I have consulted the following persons, who have knowledge of the granter on the matter :
     >

AND

C.  I have no reason to believe that the granter was acting under undue influence or that any other factor vitiates the granting of this Continuing Power of Attorney.

| | |
|---|---|
| Signature | .................................................................... |
| Date: | .................................................................... |
| Full Name: | > |
| Profession: | > |
| Address: | > |

Welfare Power of Attorney

This Certificate is incorporated in the document subscribed by ........ ("the granter") on ............................................................. that confers a Welfare Power of Attorney on .............and/whom failing ............

I certify that:

A.  I interviewed the granter on ........................................... immediately before he/she subscribed this Welfare Power of Attorney and
B.  I am satisfied that, at the time this Welfare Power of Attorney was granted, the granter understood its nature and extent:

I have satisfied myself of this:

   1.  because of my own knowledge of the granter and
   2.  because I have consulted the following persons, who have knowledge of the granter on the matter :
     >

AND

C.  I have no reason to believe that the granter was acting under undue influence or that any other factor vitiates the granting of this Welfare Power of Attorney.

| | |
|---|---|
| Signature | .................................................................... |
| Date: | .................................................................... |
| Full Name: | > |
| Profession: | > |
| Address: | > |

**Signatory on certificate**

If X is a person appointed whether as attorney, joint or substitute **6–15** attorney, in a power of attorney, then X cannot be the signatory to the certificate, even if appropriately qualified.

If the person appointed is a solicitor in a firm, another solicitor (including another partner of the firm) in the same firm may sign but where the firm itself is being appointed as a continuing attorney it is good practice for the certificate to be signed by someone independent of the firm.

Those who certify are advised to keep a clear note of the pre-signing interview and to make sure the opinion of others is sought should there be any hint of a doubt about any of the three requirements of being satisfied. In Ch.1 we set out the meaning of incapable in relation to the Adults with Incapacity (Scotland) Act 2000 and this governs the preparation of powers of attorney.

**Who can be an attorney**

A continuing attorney can be an individual or can be a corporate body. A **6–16** welfare attorney can only be an individual. Any solicitors would be well advised not to accept the position as a welfare attorney for two reasons. First, it is unlikely that the solicitor will know his or her clients sufficiently well to make good quality welfare decisions; and secondly the solicitor should not be paid for exercising the power of attorney containing welfare powers although expenses can be charged if the power specifies this.

**Advising the client on choosing an attorney**

Pre-Act, it was common to appoint a person and "whom failing for any **6–17** reason" another person. This made the first appointed a sort of senior figure who was the chosen or preferred attorney but the second named party could step in and out at any time (say when the first was simply unavailable).

Under the Act the position differs in that it is a substitution when the first ceases to be able to operate the power of attorney. A popular choice for married clients is to appoint a spouse whom failing all children jointly and severally, with perhaps a declaration that should the children not be able to agree, a particular named child has the "casting vote".

True joint appointments are less popular for reasons of convenience with families being so geographically spread.

It is possible to create one document which gives attorney A a certain set of powers and attorney B a separate set. An example of this would be appointing a solicitor for the financial aspects of life and family or friend for welfare, but the split need not be in that manner.

### Registration

**6–18** Once the power of attorney is signed, there is a registration form to be completed and then signed by the appointed (but not the whom failing) attorney/s. The power of attorney, certificate/s and form are all sent together to the Office of the Public Guardian with the relevant fee (currently £60 per power of attorney) and once the document is registered a copy of the power of attorney with the registration certificate is posted out to the submitting agent with a copy being sent to the granter.

### Powers

**6–19** In relation to inheritance tax planning as set out in para.2–11 the case of *McDowall* is essential reading.[15] It is likely that the vast majority of powers of attorney prepared between 1991 and 2001 will lack the necessary power to make gifts and so it is prudent to review existing powers of attorney and encourage clients to refresh the powers and indeed consider granting a welfare power of attorney.

The following is a fairly typical set of powers suitable for a continuing attorney and for a welfare attorney to address most situations.

**6–20** SCHEDULE OF CONTINUING POWERS referred to in the foregoing Power of Attorney by JOHN SMITH

1. To open, operate, overdraw and close any account in my name at any Bank and to borrow or lend, with or without security, and to grant security for any sum.
2. To claim and receive any pensions, benefits, allowances, services, financial contributions, repayments, rebates and the like to which I may be entitled.
3. To take possession of, and complete my title to, and to buy, lease, sell and otherwise deal with any interest in property heritable or moveable.
4. To execute and deliver deeds and documents including granting or executing any Affidavit, Declaration, Consent or Renunciation required under the Matrimonial Homes (Scotland) Act 1981 as amended or similar statute.
5. To maintain, repair, renew improve or extend and erect additional buildings and structures and to pay any expenses in connection with my property heritable or moveable.
6. To deposit for safe custody in any bank or other depository any property or document and to withdraw any property or document deposited by me or on my account.
7. To effect, pay the premiums on, alter or surrender any insurance policy.
8. To make, settle, compromise, discharge and refer to arbitration, and raise, defend, compromise and settle any court action and enforce any decree in respect of, any claim.
9. To make tax returns and settle, adjust and compromise any claim for tax and in accordance with such professional advice as my Attorney may consider it appropriate to seek, to review my tax affairs and potential

---

[15] *Executors of William C McDowall v The Commissioners of Inland Revenue* SC 3135/2001.

liabilities, plan to mitigate tax costs and implement such tax-planning arrangements.

10. To attend and vote in person or by proxy, at any meeting of any company or corporation in respect of any investment and to exercise any right arising from it.

11. To appoint a solicitor, accountant and other professional advisers and pay their usual charges and where any of my Attorneys is one of the foregoing to pay his or her usual charges.

12. To make, vary and dispose of investments and deposits.

13. To make any payments for which I may be contractually or legally liable and to continue all payments I have customarily made including gifts and charitable contributions.

14. To set up a Trust or Trusts to benefit me and/or any beneficiary or beneficiaries. To make gifts whether from income or capital on my behalf for any reason, (to my exclusion) including for tax planning purposes, to or to benefit any beneficiary or beneficiaries (including my Attorney, but not to benefit my Attorney more than any other members of my family who have the same relationship to me).

15. To have access to confidential information relative to my property and financial matters only to which I am entitled to have access, including the contents of my Will.

16. To run, sell or wind up any business which I may own whether alone or in conjunction with others; to appoint or employ any person (including my Attorney) in any capacity in relation to that business and pay suitable remuneration and to delegate any part of the running of such business.

17. To receive, renounce or vary in whole or in part any testamentary or other entitlements due to me and to exercise or consent to the exercise of powers to restrict or terminate any trust interest to which I am entitled or prospectively entitled including those where such action will directly benefit my Attorney and to pay any tax referable to such action.

18. To purchase in the name of another (including my Attorney) a motor vehicle or use for my benefit and to pay the insurance and running costs whether my Attorney benefits from the vehicle or not.

SCHEDULE OF WELFARE POWERS referred to in the foregoing Power **6–21** of Attorney by JOHN SMITH

1. To take decisions as to where I should live and what level of care may be appropriate for me.

2. To consult with board authorities regarding home care, community care and residential/nursing care.

3. To authorise my placement in any establishment or facility.

4. To decide if I should remain at a particular address.

5. To return me to that particular address or to authorise others so to return me to that particular address.

6. To decide on my dress, diet and personal appearance.

7. To have access to confidential information relating to myself where I would have access to such documents or information on a personal basis, such as access to medical records or personal files held by the social work services.

8. To have access to all personal information concerning myself, held by any organisation.
9. To consent or withhold consent to any medical, dental or nursing treatment, procedure or therapy for myself, where not specifically disallowed by the Act.
10. To pursue, defend or compromise any legal action or complaints procedure involving my personal welfare.
11. To make decisions on the social, cultural and religious activities that I may pursue.
12. To decide with whom I should or should not consort.
13. To take me on holiday or authorise someone else to do so.
14. To indicate my wishes regarding donating my organs after death.
15. To be reimbursed for any reasonable outlays or out of pocket expenses incurred while acting as my Welfare Attorney.

**Powers which cannot be used even if given**

**6–22**    A trustee cannot delegate his functions to an attorney.[16] An executor cannot delegate his function under a power of attorney. An executor who lives abroad can grant a power of attorney in favour of someone in Scotland, in a particular format, authorising him to give up an inventory, make oath thereto and expede confirmation in his, her or their names, but it is the executor who is confirmed, not the attorney. In intestacy, an additional power to present the petition can be included. Powers to realise the estate can also be included if wished.[17] The same provisions do not apply for an executor who is merely in ill health.[18] An attorney cannot vote in an election as there is a specific proxy procedure in law for this purpose which must be followed.[19] An attorney cannot on behalf of the granter, consent to marry,[20] give evidence, sign an affidavit nor make or revoke a will. In relation to the Matrimonial Homes (Scotland) Act 1981, as amended, affidavits are no longer required and have been replaced by declarations and attorneys are specifically empowered to execute declarations in relation to dealings of property[21] and granting of standard securities.[22]

Some practitioners take the view that every client of whatever age or circumstance needs a power of attorney: it is risk management for the future.

The creation of continuing and welfare powers of attorney are largely similar processes. The main differences are in who can be appointed, when the power of attorney can be used and the termination provisions.

A continuing power of attorney relating to financial or matters of property can be used with the blessing of the granter as soon as it has been registered. This means that the power of attorney can be used like a traditional power

---

[16]    *Freen v Beveridge* (1832) 10 S. 727.
[17]    *Currie on Confirmation of Executors* (8th edn), para.8.14.
[18]    *Leishman,* unreported, December 17, 1980.
[19]    Representation of the People Act 2000, s.12.
[20]    Marriage (Scotland) Act 1977, ss.13 and 19.
[21]    Family Law (Scotland) Act 2006, s.6.
[22]    Family Law (Scotland) Act (Consequential Amendments) Order 2006, s.3.

of attorney for periods of absence or indeed for convenience whereas a welfare power of attorney can only be used if the granter is incapable of making those welfare decisions by him or herself.

Once registered, whether or not being used, the Public Guardian must be informed of any change in the granter's address, any change in the attorney's address, death of granter or any event which results in the termination of the power of attorney.

For guidance on exercising continuing powers of attorney, see Ch.7.

### Interviewing the client

When discussing continuing or welfare powers of attorney with a client it **6–23** is sensible to use a client questionnaire to catch information and record the client's thoughts on powers, who could be appointed and, of course, your notes on your assessment of capacity.

It makes sense in your terms and conditions of business to have the client sign a copy and indicate to you that the power of attorney is a precaution for the future that the client does not yet know rather than a knee jerk reaction to imminent incapacity. The reason for this relates to subsequent applications for financial assistance with care home costs more fully discussed in Ch.13.

Many councils will have a policy of viewing the creation of a power of attorney as indicative of impending incapacity therefore being indicative of anticipating a need for care. If the creation of the power of attorney coincides with the divesting oneself of many assets, this will be seen as bolstering the local authority's case that the gift was deliberate deprivation. A good file note indicating that the power of attorney is simply a precaution for the future and that there is a firm policy of advising all clients at all times to consider creating a power of attorney should help rebut this presumption.

### Layout of power of attorney

A style using schedules to separate the powers into financial and property **6–24** and welfare makes the concept clear to both granter and attorney so that the attorney once operating the powers will know which "hat to wear" depending on the decision in front of the attorney. The difficulty with this is the need for additional signatures on the extra pages, perhaps by somebody who is older or becoming infirm. Notarial executions do assist where signatures are becoming impossible due to e.g. stroke, arthritis or poor eye sight (see Ch.1).

## TERMINATION

### Revocation by the granter

**6–25**    Revocation is possible by the granter before or after registration providing the granter still has capacity. It is debatable what capacity or lack thereof means in relation to this.

### Resignation by attorney

**6–26**    If the power of attorney has been registered, the attorney must write to the granter and the Public Guardian[23] (and depending on the situation perhaps the guardian, primary carer or local authority) giving notice of intention to resign. The resignation will not take affect for 28 days after the Public Guardian receives written notification.[24] If the resigning party is a joint attorney the notice should be accompanied by evidence that the other joint attorney is willing to continue to act. If there is a substitute attorney appointed in the power of attorney then evidence that that person is willing to act should accompany the notice. This would probably take the form of a registration form signed and completed by the substitute. In such a situation the substitute attorney would take over immediately and there would be no 28-day period.[25]

### Splitting up

**6–27**    If the granter and attorney are married to each other unless the power of attorney says otherwise it will come to an end on a decree of separation, a decree of divorce or a declarative nullity of the marriage.[26] The same provisions apply to civil partners.[27]

### Guardianship

**6–28**    If a guardian is appointed the authority of an attorney will end in relation to any matter over which the guardian is given powers.[28]

### Bankruptcy

**6–29**    A continuing power of attorney will end if the continuing attorney becomes bankrupt or the granter becomes bankrupt. Bankruptcy does not affect a welfare power of attorney. This is not spelt out in the Act.

### Recovery of faculties

**6–30**    If the adult recovers sufficient capacity so as to be able to revoke the power of attorney, and does so, the power of attorney will come to an end.

---

[23]    Adults with Incapacity (Scotland) Act 2000, s.23(1).
[24]    Adults with Incapacity (Scotland) Act 2000, s.23(2).
[25]    Adults with Incapacity (Scotland) Act 2000, s.23(4).
[26]    Adults with Incapacity (Scotland) Act 2000, s.24(1).
[27]    Family Law (Scotland) Act 2006, s.36.
[28]    Adults with Incapacity (Scotland) Act 2000, s.24(2).

## Death

Death of the granter, which should be intimated by the attorney to the **6–31**
Public Guardian,[29] or death of the attorney, which should be intimated by
the personal representatives of the attorney to the Public Guardian,[30] will
end the power of attorney.

## Court order

The order of the sheriff may revoke a power of attorney, continuing or **6–32**
welfare.[31]

Any attorney who is unaware that the powers have been terminated will not
be liable for any act undertaken in good faith.[32]

## WHO IS THE CLIENT

Beware of the situation where an elderly person is brought into the office by **6–33**
a younger friend or relative who may initiate the conversation by saying "I
need a power of attorney for my Uncle".

The client is the person granting the power of attorney. The client should be
interviewed alone to ensure that he or she wishes to prepare a power of
attorney, actually wishes to appoint the party in question, understands the
implications of the power of attorney and is not being pressured in any way.
See Ch.1 regarding office policy and best practice.

For many practitioners, older clients will come in confirming that the GP or
hospital has given a diagnosis of some form of dementia and indicating that
a power of attorney should be prepared as a matter of urgency before there
is a decline in capacity. This is quite a comforting position in that any
doubts the solicitor may have about capacity are largely ironed out by the
GP's letter.

## CASE STUDY

Whilst aging but competent, A granted a continuing power of attorney in **6–34**
favour of a relative, X. After the passage of time, A's capacity began to fade
and the power of attorney was brought into operation, capacity became
patchy with some lucid moments.

X had access to the will and was aware A had bequeathed the credit balance
in a particular account to B. X rearranged A's finances including moving
funds out of the said bank account, effectively disinheriting B. Coincidently
X's family's potential under the will improves.

---

[29] Adults with Incapacity (Scotland) Act 2000, s.22(1).
[30] Adults with Incapacity (Scotland) Act 2000, s.22(2).
[31] Adults with Incapacity (Scotland) Act 2000, s.3.
[32] Adults with Incapacity (Scotland) Act 2000, s.24(4).

A seemed sufficiently aware of the situation and gave instructions to his/her lawyer to amend legacy to outright cash instead of funds in account

Two doctors gave opinions that the client no longer has capacity to revoke the power of attorney nor to amend the will.

The suspicion has to be that X has acted improperly but how would that be proved if the decision can be shown to fall in with the principles in the Act?

Lessons for lawyers:

- capacity in practice is a frustratingly grey area;
- advise the client bluntly to choose attorneys wisely; and
- draft wills flexibly to acknowledge changing circumstances and the fact that the client may not always be able to do a new will as life changes.

# CHAPTER 7

# OPERATING A POWER OF ATTORNEY

## OPERATING A CONTINUING AND/OR WELFARE POWER OF ATTORNEY

### Duty of care

An attorney has at common law a fiduciary duty to the granter and a duty **7–01** of care but there is no specific statutory duty to act (although failure to act is probably a breach of the common law duties). In fact, even if the attorney is empowered to do certain actions, he or she is not obliged to carry them out if doing so would in relation to its value or utility be unduly burdensome or expensive.[1] A continuing or welfare attorney has no power to act until the document is registered with the Office of the Public Guardian.[2] In exercising the powers the general principles of the Adults with Incapacity (Scotland) Act 2000 must be observed and the attorney must be pro-active[3]. The code of practice[4] sensibly sets out exactly how to operate a continuing power of attorney in a proper manner.

The salient point is that the attorney must check he has the power to do what it is that is required to benefit the adult. If the power is lacking then an alternative measure under the Act may be required.

A continuing or welfare attorney must keep records of the exercise of the powers.[5]

If in doubt as to what is the best course of action, the advice of the Public Guardian in a welfare or financial matter[6] or Mental Welfare Commission and/or local authority in a welfare matter[7] can be sought. If the attorney feels in a conflict of interest situation regarding the adult then independent advice can be taken from a solicitor, the Public Guardian (and local authority, Mental Welfare Commission) can be consulted or ultimately the attorney can make an application to the sheriff court for directions.[8]

---

[1] Adults with Incapacity (Scotland) Act 2000, s.17.
[2] Adults with Incapacity (Scotland) Act 2000, s.19 (1).
[3] Adults with Incapacity (Scotland) Act 2000, s.1.
[4] Adults with Incapacity (Scotland) Act 2000, s.13.
[5] Adults with Incapacity (Scotland) Act 2000, s.5.
[6] Adults with Incapacity (Scotland) Act 2000, s.6.
[7] Adults with Incapacity (Scotland) Act 2000, ss. 9 &10.
[8] Adults with Incapacity (Scotland) Act 2000, s.3.

### Solicitors as attorneys

**7–02**     Where a solicitor is an attorney with financial powers, in addition to the foregoing, there are specific rules contained in Solicitors' (Scotland) Accounts Etc. Rules 2001 on how the solicitor should operate the power of attorney.[9] Because of these additional matters to be observed, most solicitors would be well advised not to take on joint appointments with persons outside his or her own firm, as it is hard to keep track of another person's intromissions and record them fully and timeously on the client ledger.

The guarantee fund and indemnity insurance offer additional safeguards and comfort to the adult and his family.

*"Rule 8 Solicitors' (Scotland) Accounts Etc. Rules 2001*

#### Accounts required to be kept in books of solicitor
**8.**—(1) A solicitor shall at all times keep properly written up such books and accounts as are necessary—

(a) to show all his dealing with—
  (i) clients' money held or received or paid or in any way intromitted with by him;
  (ii) any other money dealt with by him through a client account;
  (iii) any bank overdrafts or loans procured by him in his own name for behoof of a client or clients; and
  (iv) any other money held by the solicitor in a separate account in the title of which the client's name is specified; and
(b) (i)   to show separately in respect of each client all money of the categories specified in sub-paragraph (a) of this paragraph which is received, held or paid by him on account of that client; and
  (ii) to distinguish all money of the said categories received, held or paid by him from any other money received, held or paid by him.

(2) Without prejudice to paragraph (1) above, this Rule shall apply to money received or payments made by a solicitor by virtue of any power of attorney in his favour.

*Rule 23 Solicitors' (Scotland) Accounts Etc. Rules 2001*

#### Powers of Attorney
**23.**—(1) This Rule shall, subject to paragraph (2) below, apply to monies received or payments made by a solicitor by virtue of any power of attorney in his favour.

(2) In the event of any power of attorney granted in favour of a solicitor continuing to have effect by virtue of sections 15 or 88 of the Adults with Incapacity (Scotland) Act 2000 any money of the granter held or received by the solicitor shall be clients' money.

---

[9]   Solicitors' (Scotland) Accounts Etc. Rules 2001.

(3) Every solicitor shall deliver to the Council a list of any powers of attorney in the solicitor's favour held or granted during an accounting period, the list to be as set out in the Certificate".

### Fee structure

Terms and conditions of business should be issued annually by the firm  **7–03** acting to the solicitor attorney. Include in this the fact that the file will be sent to an independent auditor or law accountant to fix the fee and that the auditor's/accountant's fee will be paid for by the estate of the adult.

### Fees

Whether terms and conditions are issued or not, a solicitor who acts as an  **7–04** administrator of a client's funds under a power of attorney should have his fees assessed independently by an auditor of court to afford protection and reassurance to those interested in the estate and to the solicitor in relation to a challenge on the amount of the fee. In these circumstances it will be sufficient to forward the file to an auditor for assessment of the fee without the need for a formal taxation.

A solicitor who is a co-attorney with an unqualified person should not make a unilateral reference to an auditor for taxation of the account. Such a reference will need the concurrence of the other attorney(s), and the auditor may require intimation of the taxation to any other party with an interest in the residue of the estate.

Where the granter of a power of attorney is still capable of giving instructions the fee note should be copied to the grantor when it is prepared following assessment by the auditor.

Apart from the risk of a complaint to The Law Society of Scotland any person can complain against the attorney to the Public Guardian. This can be either because they have bypassed the attorney and gone straight there, or it can be because they are not satisfied with the attorney's response to the issues raised with the attorney. The Public Guardian's duty is to receive and investigate all such complaints. The matter may not stop there as a person who is dissatisfied also has recourse to the sheriff.

### Getting started

In order to look after the affairs of the adult, the attorney must either  **7–05** have the express permission of the adult to act or must be sure that the adult lacks capacity in relation to the matter he or she is about to delve into.

In relation to financial matters, most institutions will require sight of the registered power of attorney or a certified true copy of the registered power of attorney and will also ask for two forms of identification for the attorney for copying and return. Some may ask for sample signatures for the attorney.

This process can be carried out in person by visiting banks, etc. or by letter.

# Chapter 8

# COURT ORDERS: GUARDIANSHIPS AND INTERVENTION ORDERS

## Background

**8–01**     Where it is clear that an adult has incapacity as defined in the Adults with Incapacity (Scotland) Act 2000[1] ("the Act") (see Ch.1) all available measures will have to be considered and adopted or rejected as appropriate.

However, the Act does not contain all the relevant law relating to someone who has some form of incapacity. For example, consent to marriage or the making of a will are not, in Scotland, matters where another party can obtain authority to carry out the deed for someone who is deemed incapable in that area of his or her life. Moreover, the Act does not contain all the possible measures to help a person who has a degree of incapacity so, e.g. it remains open to a relative or other benevolent third party to set up a trust with assets of their own to benefit an adult who is incapable.

## Brief overview of the Adults with Incapacity Act

**8–02**     Part 1 of the Act sets out the definitions of "adult", "incapacity" and the "general principles" which determine whether to intervene and, if so, in what way and at what level. It also sets out the general provisions regarding proceedings, appeals, powers of the sheriff and of the Court of Session, general provisions about the roles of the Public Guardian, Mental Welfare Commission and local authorities. This part of the Act also contains the provisions about investigations, codes of practice, and appeals against decisions of incapacity.

## The general principles

**8–03**     Section 1(1) of the Act provides that the following principles must be applied to any intervention in the affairs of an adult under the Act. This is both in deciding what measure of intervention to seek and then in each and every operation of that intervention thereafter. They are the bedrock of the legislation.

"(2) there shall be no intervention in the affairs of an adult unless the person responsible for authorising or effecting the intervention is

[1]   Adults with Incapacity Act 2000, s.1(6).

satisfied that the intervention will benefit the adult and such benefit cannot reasonably be achieved without the intervention

(3) Where it is determined that an intervention as mentioned in subsection (1) is to be made, such intervention shall be the least restrictive option in relation to the freedom of the adult, consistent with the purpose of the intervention

(4) In determining if an intervention is to be made and, if so, what intervention is to be made, account shall be taken of—

(a) the past and present wishes of the adult so far as they can be ascertained by any means of communication, whether human or mechanical aid (whether of an interpretative nature or not) appropriate to the adult;

(b) the views of the nearest relative, named person and primary carer of the adult, insofar as it is reasonable to do so;

(c) the views of

  (i) any guardian, continuing attorney or welfare attorney of the adult who has powers relating to the proposed intervention: and

  (ii) any person whom the sheriff has directed to be consulted, in so far as it is reasonable to do so; and

the views of any other person appearing to the person responsible for authorizing or effecting the intervention to have an interest in the welfare of the adult or in the proposed intervention where these views have been made known to the person responsible, in so far as it is reasonable and practicable to do so.

(5) Any guardian, continuing attorney, welfare attorney or manager of an establishment exercising functions under this Act or under any order of the sheriff in relation to an adult shall, in so far as it is reasonable to do so, encourage the adult to exercise whatever skills he has concerning his property, financial affairs or personal welfare, as the case may be, and to develop new such skills."

The principles can be summarised under five key principles:

- Principle 1—Benefit.
- Principle 2—Minimum intervention.
- Principle 3—Wishes of adult past and present.
- Principle 4—Consultation with relevant others.
- Principle 5—Encourage adult to exercise his skills.

If the nearest relative appears unsuitable it is possible for the adult[2] (either because they are able to enunciate the wish or because evidence is presented in the application to the court), although not ahead of an incapacity,[3] (which means a person cannot simply decide he dislikes his nearest relative and think to himself, well if I am ever incapable, I certainly don't want you involved so I think I'll get an order right now just in case!) to apply to the

---

[2] Adults with Incapacity (Scotland) Act 2000, s.4(1).
[3] Adults with Incapacity (Scotland) Act 2000, s.4(4).

court to have the nearest relative displaced or to have information withheld from that nearest relative. Any person appointed under an intervention order or appointed as a guardian would need to be aware of this.

Under Pt 2 of the Act a person can appoint a continuing and/or welfare attorney. This part of the Act contains the provisions about creation, registration and operation.[4]

Under Pt 3 of the Act a person may apply to the Public Guardian for authority to access funds in an account in the sole name of an adult to provide for the adult's day-to-day care. There is a code of practice which relates to this. A joint account held with the adult may continue to be operated by the other account holder providing it is an either/or signature.[5]

Under Pt 4, authorised establishments (care homes and hospitals) may manage the funds of a resident up to a prescribed limit. There are similar codes of practice for managers and supervisory bodies.

Under Pt 5 medical practitioners are given a general authority to treat adults if there is a certificate of incapacity. There are of course safeguards and exceptions to this general rule. Certain medical research is also permitted where an adult cannot consent. There is a code of practice for persons authorised to carry out medical treatment and research.

Under Pt 6 of the Act a person may apply to the sheriff for an intervention order or guardianship order to deal with financial, property and/or personal welfare matters in relation to an adult. Intervention orders are appropriate generally to one-off situations rather than ongoing management situations. Guardianship orders are generally more suited to deal with the same sort of matters on an ongoing basis.

### Court orders

**8–04**     The greatest level of intervention in an adult's life is through a court order of some form. If there is no other lesser measure appropriate to assist the person then this will have to be considered. Intervention is used in the Act in two senses. Intervention means to intervene and so any "interference" or "assistance" is an intervention in the adult's life. An intervention order is a specific court order empowering a person to do specific tasks for the adult. For the sake of clarity, in this chapter we shall call such a person so authorised an "intervener" although this term is not used in the legislation.

The application is to the sheriff court to seek power to carry out certain specified actions on behalf of an adult for whom the applicant can produce the appropriate statutory evidence of incapacity in relation to those actions. The matter in hand may relate to finance, property and/or personal welfare or a mixture of issues.

---

⁴  See Chs 6 and 7.
⁵  Adults with Incapacity (Scotland) Act 2000, s.32.

One-off decisions or actions will usually call for an intervention order and ongoing situations will generally call for a guardianship order. However this is not a hard and fast rule. A situation may be ongoing but still an intervention order is the appropriate measure when taking into account the five principles of the Act. If there is an existing power of attorney which is operational but simply lacks a specific power to carry out a one-off task, then an intervention order would be sought to carry out the task say to sell a house, and to pass the funds to the attorney to be managed by the attorney using the relevant powers in the power of attorney.

## PROTECTION FOR THE ADULT AND REGULATION OF THOSE AUTHORISED

If a person grants a power of attorney, he or she is making a conscious **8–05** decision to appoint a chosen person to act on his or her behalf in the event of incapacity. The appointment and relationship is therefore one of absolute trust.

Being given the power to intervene or being appointed as a guardian is quite different in flavour. These are court appointments by a sheriff who has considered all the relevant evidence and then issued an interlocutor. The sheriff does require to take the adult's wishes into account but it may not be possible to find out what the past wishes are if the adult had never discussed the issue with anyone, and the present wishes may be impossible to find out (e.g. the person is in a coma). Notice will be given (except in exceptional circumstances) to the adult that there is an application and he or she is told of the hearing date but the sheriff's decision does not require the consent/ agreement of the adult. Therefore, logically a greater level of protection must be built in to the procedure as the element of choice by the adult is absent.

### Public Guardian

The functions of the Public Guardian are set out in s.6 of the Act. In **8–06** relation to intervention orders and guardianship orders, in general the Public Guardian has a function of keeping public registers of all documents relating to guardianship orders and intervention orders granted under the Act.[6]

If an intervention order or guardianship order is granted in relation to property or financial affairs, then the Public Guardian automatically has a supervisory role of the authorised person and his exercise of the function.[7]

The Public Guardian has a duty to receive and investigate any complaints about the intervener or guardian regarding the exercise of the functions in

---

[6]   Adults with Incapacity (Scotland) Act 2000, s.6(2)(b).
[7]   Adults with Incapacity (Scotland) Act 2000, s.6(2)(a).

relation to property or financial affairs,[8] or where it has been made known that the property or financial affairs of an adult seem to be at risk.[9]

The Public Guardian has a duty to advise the intervener or guardian if so requested[10] and to consult with Mental Welfare Commission or local authorities where there appears to be a common interest.[11]

### The courts

**8–07**    Applications for orders are made to the sheriff court and so it is the sheriff who makes specific orders under the Act.[12]

The application to the sheriff may be made by any person (including the adult himself) claiming an interest in the property, financial affairs and/or personal welfare of an adult, if the sheriff is satisfied that the adult is incapable of taking the action, or is incapable in relation to the decision about his property, financial affairs and/or personal welfare to which the application relates, make an order (in the Act referred to as an "Intervention Order").[13]

An application may be made under this section by any person (including the adult himself) claiming an interest in the property, financial affairs and/or personal welfare of an adult to the sheriff for an order appointing an individual or office holder as guardian in relation to the adult's property, financial affairs or personal welfare.[14]

The sheriff has a large amount of discretion and flexibility to make such consequential or ancillary order, provision or direction, as he considers appropriate.[15] This includes making the order subject to conditions,[16] insisting on reports,[17] insisting on further enquiry or information,[18] making interim orders,[19] or indeed appointing a safeguarder to represent the adult's interests[20] or convey his views.[21]

### Local authorities

**8–08**    The local authority has a duty to apply for an intervention order[22] if it appears to the local authority that (a) the adult is incapable and no application has been made or is likely to be made for an intervention order in

---

  [8]  Adults with Incapacity (Scotland) Act 2000, s.6(2)(c).
  [9]  Adults with Incapacity (Scotland) Act 2000, s.6(2)(d).
 [10]  Adults with Incapacity (Scotland) Act 2000, s.6(2)(e).
 [11]  Adults with Incapacity (Scotland) Act 2000, s.6(2)(f).
 [12]  Adults with Incapacity (Scotland) Act 2000, s.2(1).
 [13]  Adults with Incapacity (Scotland) Act 2000, s.53(1).
 [14]  Adults with Incapacity (Scotland) Act 2000, s.57(1).
 [15]  Adults with Incapacity (Scotland) Act 2000, s.3(1).
 [16]  Adults with Incapacity (Scotland) Act 2000, s.3(2)(a).
 [17]  Adults with Incapacity (Scotland) Act 2000, s.3(2)(b).
 [18]  Adults with Incapacity (Scotland) Act 2000, s.3(2)(c).
 [19]  Adults with Incapacity (Scotland) Act 2000, s.3(2)(d).
 [20]  Adults with Incapacity (Scotland) Act 2000, s.3(4).
 [21]  Adults with Incapacity (Scotland) Act 2000, s.3(5).
 [22]  Adults with Incapacity (Scotland) Act 2000, s.53(3).

relation to the decision in question and (b) the intervention order is necessary for protection of the property, financial affairs and/or personal welfare of the adult.

A similar duty to apply for a guardianship order exists[23] where it appears to the local authority that (1) the adult is incapable as mentioned in s.58(1)(a) and (2) no application is made or is likely to be made for guardianship and (3) guardianship is necessary for the protection of the property, financial affairs or personal welfare of the adult. The sheriff may direct that the person authorised under an intervention order is subject to local authority supervision[24] and the local authority has a duty to supervise a welfare guardian in exercise of the functions in relation to the adult.[25] The local authority has a duty to receive and investigate any complaints relating to the exercise of the functions relating to the personal welfare of an adult by a guardian or intervener.[26]

## Mental Welfare Commission for Scotland

The Mental Welfare Commission has a role if a court order concerns the **8–09** welfare of an adult whose incapacity is as a result of mental disorder. The duties and powers are set out partly in the Adults with Incapacity (Scotland) Act 2000 (AWISA)[27] and partly in the Mental Health (Care and Treatment) (Scotland) Act 2003 (MHCTA).[28] The Commission will offer information and advice to interveners and guardians.

## Protection of intervener/guardian and limitation of liability

There is no liability for any breach of care or fiduciary duty owed to the **8–10** adult if the authorised person has acted reasonably and in good faith and in accordance with the general principles *or* has failed to act and the failure was reasonable and in good faith and in accordance with the principles.[29] This heavily underlines the importance of the principles and the application of them by those who act.

An intervener or guardian or attorney is held at common law to have a duty of care to the adult whose affairs are being managed and so must act with skill and care in exercising the powers. Neglect or abuse can be an offence.[30] There is naturally a higher duty of care demanded of a professional who must show the skill and care expected of a reasonably competent member of that profession. As a fiduciary duty is owed to the adult the possibility of a conflict of interest must be borne in mind.

For example if the intervener or guardian is related to the adult there may be a conflict of interest between their personal interests and the fiduciary duty

---

[23] Adults with Incapacity (Scotland) Act 2000, s.57(2).
[24] Adults with Incapacity (Scotland) Act 2000, s.10(3).
[25] Adults with Incapacity (Scotland) Act 2000, s.10(1)(a).
[26] Adults with Incapacity (Scotland) Act 2000, s.10(1)(c).
[27] Adults with Incapacity (Scotland) Act 2000, s.9.
[28] Mental Health (Care and Treatment) (Scotland) Act 2003, Pt 2.
[29] Adults with Incapacity (Scotland) Act 2000, s.82(1).
[30] Adults with Incapacity (Scotland) Act 2000, s.83.

to the adult. What a dilemma if the guardian is a niece or nephew who has been bequeathed the house in the will but the proper course of action to look after the adult would involve the sale of the property and conversion of it to cash to spend on the needs of the adult. The subject of the special legacy would therefore cease to form part of the estate as at the date of death, the legacy is adeemed and so nothing is due to the beneficiary.[31]

It is not a conflict of interest if the guardian or intervener happens to benefit from correct and properly thought out action taken on behalf of the adult.

### Resolving conflicts of interest

**8–11**    The guardian/intervener could:

- engage an independent solicitor to represent the adult;
- engage an independent advocate who could be obtained from an advocacy service to ensure the adult's wishes are properly represented;
- consult the Public Guardian;
- if the matter involves a welfare issue, consult the local authority or Mental Welfare Commission; and
- apply to the sheriff to seek direction under s.3 of the Act.

## WHICH ORDER: INTERVENTION OR GUARDIANSHIP

**8–12**  An intervention order is ideal for single decisions or actions, or actions which have a long time scale, provided the benefit can be clearly stated and there is a definite outcome. For example buying or selling property is, although a complicated and often long drawn out affair, really a one-off action consisting of a beginning, a middle and an end so an intervention order would be suitable. Intervention orders are less suited to dealing with issues where flexibility is required, an outcome of the decision or action is not known within clearly set parameters. For example the ongoing management of a share portfolio is more suited to a guardianship order.

It is not possible to be categorical as to which actions fall within intervention and which within guardianship. The appropriate way forward will present itself once the general principles are applied to the circumstances and of course there is always an element of judgement to be applied to the situation. Helpfully, if one aims too high, the sheriff may treat a guardianship order application as being one for an intervention order if the sheriff decides that would be a more appropriate order to grant.[32]

### Termination

*Death*

**8–13**    An intervention order or guardianship will end on the adult's death[33], and similarly on the death of the guardian or intervener.

---

[31]   *McArthur' Exrs.v Guild*, 1908 S.C. 743.
[32]   Adults with Incapacity (Scotland) Act 2000, s.58(3).
[33]   Adults with Incapacity (Scotland) Act 2000, s.77.

*Variation/recall/cancellation by sheriff*

The intervener, the adult or anyone else with an interest in the finances or **8–14** property or welfare may apply to the sheriff for an order varying or cancelling the intervention order.[34] The sheriff can replace or remove a guardian or recall or vary a guardianship on application to him by the guardian, the adult or any other person claiming an interest.[35] There will be no removal of a guardian unless the sheriff is satisfied there is a suitable substitute or that the remaining joint guardian is prepared to act or that the guardianship is no longer necessary. A substitute guardian can be appointed for a temporary period. [36]

*Variation/recall/cancellation by Public Guardian*

The Public Guardian can at his own instance or application by any per- **8–15** son, including the adult, claiming an interest, recall the powers of the guardian. The Mental Welfare Commission or local authority can recall the powers of a welfare guardian at their own instance or as a result of an application by any person claiming an interest in the personal welfare of the adult.[37]

A joint guardian or a guardian who has been substituted may resign by giving notice in writing of his intention to do so to the Public Guardian and the local authority and the Mental Welfare Commission.[38]

## EFFECT OF AN ORDER

### Terms of the order

Once the sheriff makes an order the adult cannot enter into any trans- **8–16** action relating to a matter within the authority of the intervener or guardian. The intervener or guardian supersedes the authority of anyone with a power of attorney covering the same matters.[39] The terms of the order may allow the guardian or intervener to allow the guardian to enter into certain transactions or types of transactions, e.g. many people with guardianship orders will go food shopping although do not have the capacity to run all their finances. The adult retains capacity in relation to any matter not specified on the order.

### Order relating to heritable property forming home of adult

If the heritable property is deemed by the sheriff to be the *home* of the **8–17** adult then the Public Guardian must be approached to consent to the sale of the house or any purchase of a house to form the home of the adult.[40] The Public Guardian's procedure requires the submission of a specific form with

---

[34] Adults with Incapacity (Scotland) Act 2000, s.53.
[35] Adults with Incapacity (Scotland) Act 2000, s.71(1).
[36] Adults with Incapacity (Scotland) Act 2000, s.63.
[37] Adults with Incapacity (Scotland) Act 2000, s.73(3).
[38] Adults with Incapacity (Scotland) Act 2000, s.75(1).
[39] Adults with Incapacity (Scotland) Act 2000, s.67(1).
[40] Adults with Incapacity (Scotland) Act 2000, Sch.2, para.6.

a 21-day waiting period and the adult, nearest relative and primary carer are informed. The Public Guardian can decide to notify other people. Anyone with an interest can object and if there is an objection the Public Guardian will remit the matter to the sheriff whose decision is final.

If the Public Guardian refuses an application the guardian must be offered a chance to respond and either the guardian or the Public Guardian can refer the matter to the sheriff.

Whilst any decision of the Public Guardian can be appealed to the sheriff whose decision is final, it is not possible to appeal against the approval of the purchase or sale price.

The Register of Scotland's practice is to accept that a transfer by a guardian is not a dealing to which s.106 of the Civil Partnership (Scotland) Act 2004 applies and so the Keeper will enter the usual unqualified statement without seeing evidence. However the Family Law (Scotland) Act 2006 provides for the guardian to grant appropriate evidence. The practice is for the Keeper to archive any such evidence submitted without comment.

### Powers of interveners or guardians

**8–18**      Court orders can authorise the raising, or defence, of an action of divorce, separation or nullity of marriage on behalf of the adult. [41] A guardian exercising welfare powers can be reimbursed for expenses[42] but would not expect to receive a fee for acting unless there is a particular reason for this. The local authority cannot receive payment for acting as a guardian nor be reimbursed for providing items which it would normally provide without cost.[43] The guardian is not limited to exercising welfare powers to periods of time when the adult is in Scotland.[44]

A guardian acting in financial and property matters can claim reimbursement for any expenses[45] and a financial guardian can charge a professional fee for acting unless the order prohibits this.[46] The fee levels are commissions fixed by the Public Guardian but the guardian can appeal to the sheriff against the Public Guardian's decision on the fee levels, on the matter of payment of fees to account or on the expenses which he or she wishes to recover.[47] Where the guardian is in breach of any duty of care, fiduciary duty or obligation imposed by the Act, anyone claiming an interest in the adult's property, financial affairs or personal welfare can apply to the sheriff who can order the forfeiture (in whole or in part) of any remuneration due to the guardian.[48]

---

[41]   Adults with Incapacity (Scotland) Act 2000, s.64(1)(c).
[42]   Adults with Incapacity (Scotland) Act 2000, s.68.
[43]   Adults with Incapacity (Scotland) Act 2000, s.68(4)(b).
[44]   Adults with Incapacity (Scotland) Act 2000, s.67(3).
[45]   Adults with Incapacity (Scotland) Act 2000, s.68.
[46]   Adults with Incapacity (Scotland) Act 2000, s.68(4)(b).
[47]   Adults with Incapacity (Scotland) Act 2000, s.68(8).
[48]   Adults with Incapacity (Scotland) Act 2000, s.69.

## Powers which cannot be granted

A guardian cannot place an adult in a hospital for the treatment of a **8–19** mental disorder against his or her will.[49] Instead provisions under the MHCTA 2003 would have to be used. A guardian cannot make a will and cannot marry off the adult, nor can a guardian consent to organ donation.[50]

## Gifts

A financial guardian wishing to make a gift out of an adult's estate will **8–20** require authority from the Public Guardian.[51] There is a standard form for such applications. The authority given will either be a general authority or will be for a specific gift or event.

As with the procedure for dealing with the purchase or sale of a dwelling house, notice is given to all relevant parties to give them an opportunity to object. There is a right of appeal to the sheriff and under s.66(4) the need to give notice can be dispensed with if the value of the proposed gift does not warrant notice being given.

## Discharge procedure

Following the termination of a financial guardianship for whatever rea- **8–21** son, the guardian may apply to the Public Guardian for discharge of his duties in respect of the adult's estate.[52] If the reason is the death of the guardian, his or her personal representatives may apply for the discharge.

The Public Guardian gives notice to all relevant parties and will hear any objections. If the application for discharge is to be rejected, the Public Guardian must give the person applying for the discharge the opportunity to make representations. Any decision in relation to the discharge may be appealed to the sheriff whose decision is final. The Public Guardian also has the opportunity to remit the matter to the sheriff for a decision.

## Complaints

Any complaint about an intervener or guardian who has financial and/or **8–22** property powers should be made to the Public Guardian.

Complaints about interveners or guardians with welfare powers can be made to the local authority and if dissatisfied with the result there to the Mental Welfare Commission.

## Duties of interveners or guardians

Interveners and guardians, whether with financial, property or welfare **8–23** powers, must bear in mind the principles of the Act. Failure to consider the principles may result in the loss of benefit of the indemnity provisions and forfeiture of any remuneration due (it would be highly unusual for a welfare

---

[49] Adults with Incapacity (Scotland) Act 2000, s.64(2)(a).
[50] Adults with Incapacity (Scotland) Act 2000, s.64(2)(e).
[51] Adults with Incapacity (Scotland) Act 2000, s.66.
[52] Adults with Incapacity (Scotland) Act 2000, s.72.

guardian or welfare intervener to be remunerated in any event) or be required to repay the adult's funds, with interest.

Guardians and interveners owe a duty of care to the adult and can be liable for not protecting the adult's interests or are negligent in considering what those interests might be. Ill treatment or wilful neglect of the adult is a criminal offence carrying fines or imprisonment, or both.[53] Interveners and guardians must keep records of the exercise of powers.[54]

Interveners and guardians can delegate duties or parts thereof but cannot abdicate, i.e. surrender or transfer those duties.[55] For many lay interveners or guardians this means that they can allow someone else such as a solicitor to carry out the day-to-day duties for the adult but will remain ultimately responsible.

Interveners and guardians must keep the Public Guardian advised of any change of his or her address or the adult's address.

Joint guardians may act individually and must take reasonable steps to ensure that the other guardian does not breach his or her duty of care to the adult.[56] Sensible joint guardians will always consult the other guardian before acting and if they disagree on how to act either or both can apply to the sheriff for directions.[57]

### Management of estate of adult

8–24     Unlike curatories where the duty of the *curator bonis* was to preserve the value of the person's estate, the principles make it clear that the guardian should use the assets/money to benefit the adult. Income and capital can be used to buy items, services or accommodation to enhance the adult's quality of life, as long as the guardian acts within the parameters of the terms of the guardianship order.

Schedule 2 to the Act sets out the procedure for management of the adult's estate by a guardian.

The guardian must prepare an inventory of the estate within three months of registration of the guardianship order. The prescribed form of the inventory can be obtained from the Public Guardian.

A financial and management plan must be drawn up and approved by the Public Guardian. This must be done within one month of submitting the inventory. The guardian must review the plan periodically and it would be sensible to ask the Public Guardian to approve the variation. In the case of disagreement between the guardian and the Office of the Public Guardian, the sheriff can be applied to for a determination, which will be final.

---

[53]  Adults with Incapacity (Scotland) Act 2000, s.83.
[54]  Adults with Incapacity (Scotland) Act 2000, s.65(1).
[55]  Adults with Incapacity (Scotland) Act 2000, s.64(6).
[56]  Adults with Incapacity (Scotland) Act 2000, s.62(7).
[57]  Adults with Incapacity (Scotland) Act 2000, s.62(8).

The guardian must open a separate (from the guardian's own funds) bank account for the adult's money and this must be an interest bearing account if the balance is over £500.

Existing investments may be retained but the guardian must seek advice from an independent financial adviser (and in the case of a solicitor who is appointed guardian this specifically excludes one's own firm or a subsidiary) if the investments are in excess of currently £25,000. Any alterations to investments will form part of the management plan and will be approved or otherwise by the Public Guardian.

The Public Guardian requires the guardian to submit regular financial statements and will write to remind the guardian when they are due. In the early days full accounts with supporting vouchers were required in every instance but now more often than not, a statement for review can be submitted on the basis that a full account with supporting vouchers can be required at a later date. The accounts may be approved if there are minor errors or inconsistencies if it appears that the guardian has acted reasonably and in good faith but the Public Guardian can require the guardian to make up any shortfall.

## APPLICATION PROCEDURE

After considering the adult's current position regarding personal welfare, **8–25** property and financial matters it will be possible to determine which needs of the adult are not being met and consequently what measures or actions should be taken to plug the gap. Applying the five principles should lead to a suitable course of action.

After verifying that the adult does not have sufficient capacity to take decisions in these particular matters and is unable to appoint an attorney to take the decision and no other form of assistance seems likely to be sufficient, then some form of court order will be required.

### Legal aid

In an application for intervention or guardianship, if there is a welfare **8–26** element then non-means tested civil legal aid will be available for the application. If the application is for financial and property matters only then civil legal aid, based on the adult's (and not the applicant's) financial situation may be available if the adult qualifies (in either case, civil advice and assistance may be available for the preliminary advice if the adult's means qualify).

**Reports**

8–27     The applicant must obtain two medical reports both carried out not more than 30 days before the submission of the application to the court. At least one of the reports must be from an approved medical practitioner (psychiatrist).[58]

If the application has a welfare element, a mental health officer must also supply a report. If the applicant is not the local authority the applicant must notify the chief social work officer by recorded delivery letter of the proposed application and the mental health officer must report within 21 days of the date of the notice.[59] The mental health officer must interview and assess the adult not more than 30 days before the lodging of the application confirming whether the order would be appropriate and that the person nominated is suitable. If the adult's incapacity is because of communication needs rather than mental disorder, the chief social work officer will report instead of a mental health officer.[60]

There are prescribed forms for the doctors and mental health officer's reports under the Adults with Incapacity (Reports in Relation to Guardianship and Intervention Orders) (Scotland) Regulations 2002 (SSI 2002/96).

Where there is no welfare element, instead of a mental health officer's report, the applicant must obtain a report from someone who can confirm that the intervention order or guardianship order is appropriate and that the nominated intervener or guardian is suitable.[61] As would be expected this person must interview and assess the applicant no earlier than 30 days prior to the lodgement of the application. As before there is a prescribed form for the report. There is no need to notify the chief social work officer of an application where there is no welfare element. Preparing such reports contains an element of being a referee for the applicant and solicitors should apply caution to the situation to ensure they are not endorsing a person they have barely met.

**Role of sheriff**

*Application*

8–28     Once the writ (Form 23) and the three reports (and copy notice with recorded delivery slip) and any other productions have been submitted with the court dues of £57, the sheriff will issue an order for intimation of the application on any interested parties including the adult unless he or she is the applicant or unless the medical reports have specified that intimation would cause undue distress.

---

[58]   Adults with Incapacity (Scotland) Act 2000, s.57(3) as amended by Mental Health (Care and Treatment) (Scotland) Act 2003.
[59]   Adults with Incapacity (Scotland) Act 2000, s.57(4).
[60]   Adults with Incapacity (Scotland) Act 2000, s.57(3)(b).
[61]   Adults with Incapacity (Scotland) Act 2000, ss.53(4) and (57(3).

*Intimation*

Intimation is by recorded delivery with a prescribed form (Form 20) and **8–29** copies of the application and the accompanying reports. Interested parties will be the nearest relative,[62] the adult's primary carer, named person, any existing guardian, intervener or attorney, the Public Guardian, local authority if welfare powers are being sought, the Mental Welfare Commission where welfare powers are being sought and the incapacity is by reason of mental disorder and any other person directed by the sheriff.

Where the adult lives in a care home or hospital, service on the adult is by Form 21 and the manager completes Form 22 and returns it to the sheriff court.

*Certificates of delivery*

Recorded delivery slips are attached to certificates of delivery and **8–30** returned to the sheriff court prior to the hearing.

At the same time as making an order for intimation the sheriff fixes a hearing date at which the application may or may not be opposed.

**Representation at the hearing**

The applicant will need to attend the court or be legally represented to **8–31** answer any questions about the application. The adult can be separately legally represented. Anyone with an interest in the application can also be heard personally or through a solicitor.

After the hearing the application may be granted, the sheriff can request further reports, can make an interim order or can grant the order subject to conditions or restrictions.

**Bond of caution**

Where there is an application in relation to finance and/or property the **8–32** sheriff will require a bond of caution (insurance policy) from the applicant whether for intervention or guardianship. The sheriff may waive this requirement if caution cannot be obtained by the applicant but the sheriff still considers he or she is a suitable person to act.[63] The Adult Support and Protection (Scotland) Act 2007 now allows the sheriff discretion in every case but previous practice in many sheriff courts was to exercise the discretion "on cause shown".[64]

**Duration**

For a guardianship the maximum period for an initial appointment is **8–33** three years unless cause can be shown for a longer duration.[65] The renewal process is procedurally largely the same except that the application is by

---

[62] Mental Health (Care and Treatment) (Scotland) Act 2003, s.1.
[63] Adults with Incapacity (Scotland) Act 2000, ss.53 and 58.
[64] The Adult Support and Protection (Scotland) Act 2007, s.61(3)(a)(ii).
[65] Adults with Incapacity (Scotland) Act 2000, s.58(4).

minute rather than by Form 23. The maximum period for renewals is five years.[66] Providing the renewal is applied for before expiry of the original grant, the original order continues to have effect until the renewal application is determined, so that there is no gap where the adult is bereft.[67]

### Protection of third parties

**8–34**     Where an intervention order or guardianship authorises dealings with a house or land, the order must be registered at the General Register of Sasines or the Land Register and a copy of the registration certificate sent to the Public Guardian.[68]

Anyone who deals in good faith with an intervener or guardian will be protected. The transaction for a value between a third party and the intervener/guardian is valid even if the intervener/guardian has exceeded his or her authority or indeed is in breach of the order.[69]

That being said, the intervener or guardian is liable for any transaction carried out outwith the scope of the order and any transaction entered into without disclosure that he or she is acting under the intervention or guardianship order will render them personally liable. The intervener or guardian can seek re-imbursement from the adult's estate if he or she has not breached any other provision of the Act relating to the order.[70]

## LESSENING NEED FOR WELFARE GUARDIANSHIP ORDERS

**8–35** Section 64 of the Adult Support and Protection (Scotland) Act 2007 came into force in March 2007. It inserts extra provisions into the Social Work (Scotland) Act 1968 (s.13ZA) and clarifies the power of local authorities to take steps to provide care services to an adult with incapacity. If a local authority assesses an adult as needing community care services and that adult is not capable of making decisions about those services, the local authority can take any steps it considers necessary to help the adult benefit from such services; and this includes the right to move the adult into a care home. This cannot be operated where there is a welfare guardian or attorney with appropriate powers or where a court action to have a guardian has commenced.

As such moves into care were one of the main reasons, although not the only reasons, for requiring welfare guardianship orders, it can be expected that there will be fewer applications.

---

[66]   Adults with Incapacity (Scotland) Act 2000, s.60(4)(b).
[67]   Adults with Incapacity (Scotland) Act 2000, s.60(1).
[68]   Adults with Incapacity (Scotland) Act 2000, ss.56 and 61.
[69]   Adults with Incapacity (Scotland) Act 2000, ss.53(11) and (13) and s.67.
[70]   Adults with Incapacity (Scotland) Act 2000, ss.53(14) and 67(4).

# CHAPTER 9

# ALTERNATIVE MEASURES TO A POWER OF ATTORNEY

## INTRODUCTION

There are several scenarios when other measures may be required; whether **9–01** the person in question has lost capacity incrementally and slowly, or suddenly and dramatically.

- He or she may never have appreciated that life can change suddenly and may have missed the opportunity to make a power of attorney.
- He or she may have outlived his/her appointed attorneys.
- The attorneys may have become incapacitated.
- The document may simply not have a broad enough range of powers to deal with the current situation.

In such situations, if it is certain that a fresh power of attorney cannot be granted, then another route must be found to assist the person to function.

## ADULTS WITH INCAPACITY (SCOTLAND) ACT 2000 MEASURES

### Access to funds

There is a process under the Adults with Incapacity (Scotland) Act 2000[1] **9–02** which allows access to the funds of a person with incapacity. This process is much less complicated and much less onerous and less costly than a guardianship or intervention order. On application[2] to the Public Guardian, signed by the applicant and countersigned by a "prescribed person",[3] accompanied by fairly short medical reports, a single person (not a statutory body) is given a certificate which allows access to the adult's funds in bank, building society or post office accounts (but not a joint account) for certain specific purposes as laid down in the statute[4] and certain others over which the Public Guardian has discretion. If access is refused by the Public Guardian, an appeal can be made via the sheriff court.[5] If a financial guardian is appointed or an intervention order is granted which relates to the account, or a continuing attorney acquires authority in relation to the

---

[1] Adults with Incapacity (Scotland) Act 2000, s.25.
[2] Adults with Incapacity (Scotland) Act 2000, s.26.
[3] Adults with Incapacity (Countersignatories of Applications for Authority to Intromit) (Scotland) Regulations 2001 and Adults with Incapacity (Countersignatories of Applications for Authority to Intromit) (Scotland) Amendment Regulations 2005.
[4] Adults with Incapacity (Scotland) Act 2000, s.28.
[5] Adults with Incapacity (Scotland) Act 2000, s.26(8).

account in question, the authority to *intromit* ceases.[6] There is a code of practice which gives full guidance.

### Hospitals/care homes

**9–03**    For those in hospital, the Health Board can take on responsibility for managing financial affairs and for those in care, some care homes may similarly be willing to take on such a role although not all are prepared to do so.[7] The matters[8] which they can manage are fairly restricted and relate to:

- dealing with all aspects of state benefits;
- claiming, receiving and holding and spending any money the resident/patient is entitled to; and
- holding and disposing of other moveable property.

There are safeguards for the patient/resident[9] and the general principles of the Act must be adhered to in the management of the affairs.

### Liability

**9–04**    Guardians, continuing attorneys, welfare attorneys, interveners, withdrawers and the managers of residential establishments shall not be liable for any breach of any duty of care or fiduciary duty owed to the adult if they have acted reasonably and in good faith and in accordance with the five principles[10] or have failed to act and the failure is reasonable and in good faith in accordance with the general principles.[11]

The warning is stark. It is essential for anyone appointed to familiarise themselves with the general principles and apply them properly to each and every decision and to every step of each and every decision.

## OTHER MEASURES

### Negotiorum gestio

**9–05**    This is the legal principle under which a person with no legal authority intervenes in the management of the affairs of another who, whether temporarily or permanently, is unable to manage them himself, and in the circumstances where it is reasonable to assume that such legal authority *would* have been conferred had the circumstances made it possible to apply for it.[12] This applies in many cases including where a person has become insane.[13] The gestor is entitled to reimbursement for expenses if acting properly even if the action is not actually beneficial[14] and to be relieved of all liabilities. The gestor must account for his intromissions with the estate of

---

6    Adults with Incapacity (Scotland) Act 2000, s.31(7).
7    Adults with Incapacity (Scotland) Act 2000, s.35.
8    Adults with Incapacity (Scotland) Act 2000, s.39(1).
9    Adults with Incapacity (Scotland) Act 2000, ss.40–41.
10   See para.8–03.
11   Adults with Incapacity (Scotland) Act 2000, s.82.
12   Erskine, *Institute* III, 3, 52; Bell, *Principles*, s.540.
13   *Dunbar v Wilson & Dunlop's Tr* (1887) 15 R. 210.
14   Stair, *Institutions* I, 8, 3.

the person and is only liable for losses caused by a failure to exercise the care and diligence which a prudent man would have shown in relation to his own property.[15] Since this principle exists, why would anyone need the formal measures available under the Act?

There are two clear reasons why *negotiorum gestio* should be seen as an emergency fallback only.

- The other or third party need not co-operate, e.g. a nursing home might not take on a new client unless the client can make the decision to move into the home and sign the form, or there is someone formally appointed to make the decision and carry out the signing on their behalf. In other words not all organisations will be happy to act on the word of another who has no written authority. Red tape gone mad or proper and just protection of the vulnerable? Is it fair that someone can do what they perceive as "the right thing" at the cost of the person's human rights for example?
- Even if the organisation in question is willing to act on such instructions, is there really sufficient protection of the gestor, in today's litigious and complaints-orientated society to make acting informally a good option? Each situation would have to be summed up and judged on its own merits as to whether it matched the "care and diligence of a prudent man in relation to his own property".

### State benefits and state pension

Those on benefits may have very modest assets and may feel either they **9–06** lack the funds to pay for the preparation of a power of attorney document, or that there would be no need for a formal arrangement in relation to their finances.

- Many elderly people will appoint a friend, relative or carer etc. to collect benefits on their behalf. This can be a temporary or intermittent arrangement by signing the payment slip as and when required to allow that person to collect the benefit. Of course if a person has lost capacity, this arrangement should not be used, whether they can still form their signature or not!
- Instead, if someone applies in writing (there are application forms available) to the benefit supervisor in the local office, they may be appointed to receive and spend the benefits on behalf of the incapacitated person. The accepted practice is to appoint a relative who lives with or cares for or visits often as the appointee. If there is no one suitable, someone from the care home where the person lives can be appointed.

### Bank accounts

- Whilst still having legal capacity, a person can sign a third party man- **9–07** date allowing someone who is not the account holder to operate the account. The exact procedure will vary from bank to bank (or building society to building society), e.g. for some institutions it is a one-off

---

[15] *Kolbin & Son v United Shipping Co*, 1931 S.C. (H.L.) 128.

instruction which persists until recalled whilst for others, an instruction or mandate is required for each separate operation of the account by the third party.

- Joint accounts seem a better prospect as most will be "either/or survivor" accounts and so the joint account holder who still has capacity can continue to operate the account: unless there is a court order saying otherwise or the terms of the account prevent this.[16]

**Trusts**

9–08    If an adult has fluctuating capacity or has been given a diagnosis which indicates a future decline in capacity is likely, he or she, whilst lucid could easily transfer their assets to a trust so that there are trustees in place with valid authority and proper legal control over assets when incapacity strikes (although consideration must be given to the tax implications).[17]

---

[16]  Adults with Incapacity (Scotland) Act 2000, s.32.
[17]  See Ch.3.

CHAPTER 10

# ADVISING ON INCAPACITY

## CASE STUDY

In the real world, most solicitors will come across guardianships in one of **10–01** two ways; the minor brush and the real involvement. The minor brush may be when offering to purchase a house and finding that the seller is a financial guardian or has powers to sell under an intervention order.[1]

Real involvement often follows a call coming in from a client saying a power of attorney is needed for a relative, whether spouse or parent, who is ser-iously ill. On further probing it seems unlikely a power of attorney can be granted as capacity seems to be lacking for that.

In such situations it is sensible to have a full checklist to hand at the meeting which will make sure the five principles of the Act are applied to every step of the decision-making process in choosing how to assist the person whose capacity is lacking. If a power of attorney cannot be granted for capacity reasons, a guardianship may still not be appropriate as it may not satisfy all five of the principles as it may not be the least amount of intervention in relation to the assets of the individual.

The matter may be clearer cut as in the following example, but it is still sensible to use a checklist to capture the correct information and show the principles were properly applied at all stages before the advice was given.

**The details**

Your clients, Mr and Mrs A have been married for 58 years. Mr A **10–02** comes to see you and tells you that Mrs A was diagnosed with Vascular Dementia around three or four years ago and Mr A has looked after her in the family home until becoming physically unable to do so himself due to a heart condition. Neither has ever granted a power of attorney and now that Mr A is unable to support his wife as he was before, it has become clear to all around them that Mrs A's illness is actually far worse than anyone outside the home had realised. Mrs A is then admitted to the Dementia Unit of a local NHS Hospital under a short term detention order[2] and is assessed. The psychiatrist and Social Work Department conclude after assessment that Mrs A can only be

---

[1] See para.8–17 for details of the procedures and the likely effect on the purchasing process.

[2] Mental Health (Care and Treatment) (Scotland) Act 2003, s.44.

discharged from hospital into a suitable dementia unit at a care home. In order to arrange a home, a welfare guardianship is required as the family wish to make the decisions on care rather than having them made by the local authority. In order to be able to sort out the finances to do this, either an intervention order or financial guardianship order is required.

**Thought process to arrive at correct advice**

10–03 
- Who is the client? It is the person seeking the lawyer's advice on the best way to help the adult.
- Does the client have capacity to be a guardian/intervener? As they are an elderly couple, the client may also have capacity issues.
- Seek up-to-date identification required for client and adult for money laundering purposes.
- Where is the adult living just now? This will determine jurisdiction, i.e. the correct sheriff court.
- Adult's date of birth: Is the person an adult, i.e. over 16 years of age?[3]
- What should the letter of engagement to client say? What is actually to be done?
- Collate details of children and family tree. Some of this detail is necessary information to apply for a guardianship and is useful for the future especially if adult does not have a will and there is a likelihood of an intestacy in the future.
- Collate details of nature of the adult's difficulties and what is it he or she needs to do but cannot.
- Consider all other lesser options.[4]
- Consider all of the above in relation to the five principles.
- What guardianship or intervention orders have previously been granted, and subsequently varied?
- Are any other "interventions", under the Act or otherwise, in force; how will the application affect them (e.g. guardian superseding attorney); and if they will continue, how will they inter-relate?
- Can a guardianship be shown to be necessary and the least restrictive option?
- Details of assets and general financial information required to make sure appropriate powers are sought. Can the powers sought all be shown to be necessary and to represent the least restrictive option. Are the powers sought adequate to meet existing and reasonably foreseeable needs?
- If instructions have been given to seek management powers, are any welfare powers needed, and vice versa?
- Does incapacity arise solely from physical inability to communicate?
- Where the applicant claims an interest in the adult's personal welfare, is notice needed to the chief social work officer?
- Having regard to powers sought and the cause of incapacity, determine what reports are required? Will two doctors certify incapacity in relation to the matters in hand?

---

[3] Adults with Incapacity (Scotland) Act 2000, s.1(6).
[4] See Ch.9 for more detail.

- When received, do the reports comply with the forms in the regulations and do they confirm incapacity in terms of s.1(6) in relation to all of the powers sought?
- Who might know the present and past wishes and feelings of the adult?
- Who are the nearest relative and primary carer; is there a named person?
- Should any other views be ascertained?
- Can it be shown that the proposed guardian (or each proposed guardian) is suitable and has consented to be appointed? Any skeletons?
- Should any interim order be sought?
- Should interim appointment be sought?
- Should a direction be sought that intimation should not be given to the adult?
- If financial or property powers are sought, is caution available, and, if not, should the sheriff be asked to dispense with caution?
- If property and/or financial powers are sought, should the sheriff be asked to dispense with a management plan?
- If any heritable property is to be covered by the order sought, has a proper conveyancing description for each property been obtained for inclusion in the application?
- Should the sheriff be asked to confer powers which may be exercised prior to approval of the management plan?
- Should the sheriff be asked to specify anyone whom the guardian should consult when exercising his functions?
- Should powers be sought to enable the guardian to authorise transactions or categories of transactions by the adult?
- Should the appointment be for some period other than three years?

Obtaining full information will allow the best decision to be reached. For example, a guardianship is seen by many as a last resort as it is quite cumbersome, onerous and costly on an annual basis. If there is a trust already in existence for the benefit of the adult, it may make sense rather than obtaining a guardianship order, instead to apply for an intervention order permitting the transfer all the adult's assets to the trust, thereby ensuring the protection of the adult and his assets as part of the normal administration of the trust rather than under the auspices of the Office of the Public Guardian.

### Style letter explaining the process to the client

"We discussed your wife's current state of health and concluded that a **10–04** court action seeking a guardianship order is required to give you authority over her finances, property and personal welfare initially to allow respite care to be arranged and funded and thereafter to allow you to make decisions about her future.

I recommend that a court application is made on your behalf, seeking powers to make decisions about her welfare, for example deciding where she will live etc.

As part of this, as you already have full access to the joint finances and are able to manage them as they are, I do not see the need for ongoing financial guardianship as the costs of this would outweigh any benefit. I recommend that we incorporate an intervention order into the application asking for permission to sign paperwork such as social work applications for financial assistance and contracts with the nursing home, etc.

You may wish to consider asking for someone else to be appointed alongside you as a joint guardian as this is good risk management for the future.

The application is called a writ and explains to the sheriff what your wife's current situation is, what you would like to do to assist and the powers you need to be able to do this. As part of this, we order reports from GP, psychiatrist, and the chief social worker who will have a Mental Health Officer prepare a suitability report. The purpose of these reports is to ensure that all relevant parties are consulted (including your wife) and offered the opportunity to put forward his/her view so the Sheriff has all the facts before making a decision.

The GP and psychiatrist will charge for their reports (usually around £150 each). There are court costs of £57 and there will be legal fees of up to but not exceeding £..... plus VAT.

Once the reports have arrived, the writ is submitted to the court and a hearing date is set. The sheriff, at that stage tells us who is to be intimated about the hearing and copies of all the documents are sent by recorded delivery to all the people he decides are to receive an intimation. The sheriff may appoint a Safeguarder, who is a professional person whose job is to ensure the adult's position is protected. The Safeguarder will visit you and your wife and will charge a fee (around £500) which is one of the costs of the application.

During this time, we will have to approach an insurance company to obtain a bond of caution, which is a form of insurance to protect the assets of your wife against the guardian's misdeeds. This costs around £ ... based on the value of her assets you disclosed to me.

The intimation gives all relevant parties the chance to object or to appear at the hearing.

After the hearing the sheriff will then give his decision and tell us if the application is granted and on what terms.

Civil Legal Aid can be applied for and the Legal Aid application will take around 8 weeks to be processed. Any work carried out prior to that decision will not be covered by Legal Aid. If you do not wish to wait that long, you will have to accept that you would have to meet the costs yourself (although in that case we would seek approval from the Sheriff that your wife's assets will meet the costs of the application in full).

After the decision is given, the guardian registers the decision with the Office of the Public Guardian (OPG). Where there is a house involved, the decision is also recorded in the Sasine Register or Land Register for which there is a fee of £30.

After the decision is given, the guardian must then prepare an inventory of the assets and a management plan of how the assets are to be managed for the following year. This is submitted to the OPG who will oversee the guardian's actions forevermore. The Public Guardian will charge a fee for the submission of the plan, the inventory and at some point the application to sell the house. They will require annual accounts to be submitted and will charge for auditing them every year.

The bond of caution will be renewed every year at an annual cost of say £300. All in all being a guardian is quite onerous and a guardianship is expensive on an ongoing basis.

I would like to be sure that you appreciate this fully before deciding to become guardian. There is a very helpful Code of Practice which I have enclosed for you to read. I have marked the relevant parts for you

Once you and the family have all discussed the matter, I will be very pleased to speak to you again, to issue my firm's Letter of Engagement and then to initiate proceedings."

## Style checklist with two appendices

**10–05**

| Incapacity Instruction Checklist | | |
|---|---|---|
| **Applicant**<br>**Client's Name:**_____ Client Code_____ Matter Code_____ | | |
| **Adult**<br>**Name:**_____ Client Code_____ Matter Code_____ | | |
| *Note: Where □ Please √ as appropriate* | *Fee earner please complete, initial and date as appropriate* | |
| **Does Client have Legal Capacity? Yes □ No □** | | |
| **Client Proof Of ID:** | | |
| **Adult Proof Of ID:** | **Domicile:**<br><br>**Residence:**<br><br>**Jurisdiction:**<br><br>**N I number:** | |
| **Letter of engagement sent?**          □ | | |
| **Client :**<br>**Address:**<br><br><br>**Postcode:**<br>**Tel:**<br>**Mobile:**<br>**Email:** | **Adult:**<br>**Former Address:**<br><br><br>**Postcode:**<br>**Tel:**<br>**Mobile:**<br>**Email:** | **Current address:** |
| **Date of Birth:**<br>**Relationship to Adult:** | **Date of Birth:**<br>**Age > 16?** | |
| **Does Adult have children: Yes □      No □** | | |

| Name of Child 1:<br>Address:<br><br>Postcode:<br>Tel:<br>Mobile:<br>Email:<br>Date of Birth: | Name of Child 2:<br>Address:<br><br>Postcode:<br>Tel:<br>Mobile:<br>Email:<br>Date of Birth: | Name of Child 3:<br>Address:<br><br>Postcode:<br>Tel:<br>Mobile:<br>Email:<br>Date of Birth: |
|---|---|---|

**Details of any predeceasing children**

**Name:**

**Date of Death:**

**Age:**

**SKETCH OF FAMILY TREE.**

**Nature of Adult's Difficulties:**

**Five Principles:**

Principle 1 – Benefit
Principle 2 – Minimum intervention
Principle 3 – Take account of wishes of Adult
Principle 4 – Consultation with relevant others
Principle 5 – Encourage adult to exercise his skills and develop new ones

**INITIAL ADVICE**

| Is there an existing<br>Continuing P of A?<br>Where is it?<br>Mandate to obtain it?<br>Is it registered?<br>Is the Attorney willing to act?<br>Are the powers sufficient? | ☐ | Is Adult able to grant a<br>Continuing P of A?<br><br>If unsure, Consult GP?<br><br>Visit Adult and take instructions. | Any existing<br>Interventions?<br><br>Access to Intromit<br>intervention order<br>Welfare Guardian<br>financial guardian<br>Negotiorum Gestio<br>DSS Appointee<br>Named person | |
|---|---|---|---|---|

**ASSETS: Is there a Will?**

| Heritable Assets: Power for <u>each one</u><br><br><br><br>**WHERE ARE TITLES?** | Equivalent Abroad: |
|---|---|

**Moveable Assets:**

| Investments: | |
|---|---|
| Estate Abroad: | |
| **Has a foreign Will been prepared?** | |
| Interest in Another Trust: | |
| Spouses Assets:<br><br>Separation of assets recommended for couples where one may be about to go in to care. | |
| **INCOME and Benefits** | |
| Income sources: | Notes: |
| Benefits claimed: | Notes: |
| Tax return: | Notes: |
| **OUTGOINGS** | |
| 1.<br><br>2.<br><br>3.<br><br>4.<br><br>5.<br><br>6.<br><br>7.<br><br>8. | Notes: |

| | |
|---|---|
| 9.<br><br>10. | |
| **Debts:**<br>1.<br><br>2.<br><br>3.<br><br>4.<br><br>5. | **Notes:**<br>1.<br><br>2.<br><br>3.<br><br>4.<br><br>5. |
| **ADVISE CLIENT ABOUT:** | |
| **Five Principles:**<br><br>**Principle 1—Benefit**<br>**Principle 2—Minimum intervention**<br>**Principle 3—Take account of wishes of Adult**<br>**Principle 4—Consultation with relevant others**<br>**Principle 5—Encourage adult to exercise his skills and develop new ones** | **Notes:** |
| **Options:**<br>**No action**<br>**Continuing Power of Attorney**<br>**Access to funds and joint accounts**<br>**Management of Resident's finances**<br>**Intervention order**<br>    **Welfare**<br>    **Financial**<br>    **Both**<br>**Guardianship order**<br>    **Welfare**<br>    **Financial**<br>    **Both** | **Notes:** |
| **Summary of recommendations:** | |
| 1.      **Benefit:** | |
| 2.      **Minimum Intervention:** | |
| 3.      **Adult's previous and present wishes:** | |
| 4.      **Consult with Others:**<br><br>**Nearest relative (See MHCTSA 2003)**<br>**Adult**<br>**Named person**<br>**Applicant**<br>**Carer**<br>**Attorney**<br>**Intervener**<br>**Guardian**<br>**Anyone else** | **Is there a Section 4?** |

| | | | |
|---|---|---|---|
| **Reports:**<br>**Psychiatrist**<br>**GP**<br>**Chief Social Work Office (if Welfare) Should take 21 days to reply**<br>**AWI Suitability report on Guardian/Intervener** | | | |

| | | | |
|---|---|---|---|
| **All 3 reports to be < 30 days old. Dated** | **Date ordered** | | **Added to**<br>**Diary** |

| | |
|---|---|
| **Draft Initial Writ Form 23**<br>**Consider Principles**<br>**Consider Assets**<br>**Consider Powers**<br>**Heritage? Powers for each property and**<br>**contents powers.**<br>**Welfare – Powers**<br>**Approve with Applicant**<br>**Order reports**<br>**Redraft Initial Writ**<br>**Send signed copies to Sheriff Court**<br>**£57 fee**<br>**Copy Notice and Recorded Delivery slip** | |
| **Interlocutor**<br><br>**Serve Notices as directed**<br><br>**Form 20 – Notice**<br>**Form 21 – Nursing Home Notice**<br>**Form 22 – Nursing Home Certificate** | **Nearest Relative.**<br>**Primary Carer.**<br>**Guardian/Attorney.**<br>**OPG.**<br>**Local Authority**<br>**MWC**<br>**Anyone else Sheriff directs.**<br>**Named person** |
| **Property to sell**      Yes ☐ No ☐ | **Notes:** |
| **Property to let**      Yes ☐ No ☐ | **Notes:** |
| **Stockbroker**      Yes ☐ No ☐ | **Notes:** |
| **IFA**      Yes ☐ No ☐ | **Notes:** |
| **Send Letter of Engagement**<br><br>**Fee quote** | |

| HEARING | | |
|---|---|---|
| **Date.** | ☐ | **NOTES:** |
| **Tell Client.** | ☐ | |
| **Pre Hearing Meeting** | ☐ | |
| **Property : Register Interlocutor at Sasine/Land Register** | ☐ | |
| **Send endorsed Interlocutor/ Land Certificate to OPG for registration.** | ☐ | |
| | ☐ | |
| **Inventory Lodge** | | |
| **Management Report Lodge** | ☐ | |
| | ☐ | |
| **MISC NOTES** | | |
| | | |

*Appendix 1 to checklist*

**10–06**     Meaning of "nearest relative"[5]

(1) In this Act, "nearest relative", in relation of a person (the "relevant person"), means—

(a) subject to subsection (3) below, in a case where only one person falls within the list set out in subsection (2) below, that person;

(b) subject to subsections (3) and (4) below, in a case where two or more persons fall within that list, the person falling within the paragraph first appearing in the list set out in subsection (2) below.

(2) The list mentioned in subsection (1) above is—

(a) the relevant person's spouse;
(b) a person such as is mentioned in subsection (7) below;
(c) the relevant person's child;
(d) the relevant person's parent;
(e) the relevant person's brother or sister;
(f) the relevant person's grandparent;
(g) the relevant person's grandchild;
(h) the relevant person's uncle or aunt;
(i) the relevant person's niece or nephew;
(j) the person mentioned in subsection (8) below.

---

[5]  Mental Health (Care and Treatment) (Scotland) Act 2003, s.254.

(3) If the relevant person's spouse—

(a) is permanently separated (either by agreement or under an order of a court) from the relevant person; or
(b) has deserted, or has been deserted by, the relevant person and the desertion continues,

subsection (2) (a) above shall be disregarded for the purposes of subsection (1) above.

(4) Where two or more persons fall within the paragraph first appearing on the list set out in subsection (2) above, the nearest relative shall be—

(a) if those persons agree that one of them should be the nearest relative, that person; or
(b) if those persons do not so agree, the person determined in accordance with the following rules—
    (i) brothers and sisters of the whole blood shall be preferred over brothers and sisters of the half blood; and
    (ii) the elder or eldest, as the case may be, shall be preferred.

(5) A relevant person's nearest relative may decline to be the named person of the relevant person by giving notice to—

(a) the relevant person; and
(b) the local authority for the area in which the relevant person resides,

to that effect.

(6) For the purposes of subsection (2) above—

(a) a relationship of the half-blood shall, subject to subsection (4) (b) (i) above, be treated as a relationship of the whole blood;
(b) the stepchild of a person shall be treated as the child of that person;
(c) if the relevant person is ordinarily resident in the United Kingdom, the Channel Islands or the Isle of Man, any person who is not so resident shall be disregarded; and
(d) any person who is under 16 years of age shall be disregarded.

(7) The person referred to in subsection (2) (b) above is a person who—

(a) is living with the relevant person—
    (i) as husband and wife; or
    (ii) in a relationship which has the characteristics of the relationship between husband and wife except that the person and the relevant person are of the same sex; and
(b) has been living with the relevant person for a period of at least 6 months or, if the relevant person is for the time being in hospital, had been living with the relevant person for such period when the relevant person was admitted to hospital.

(8) The person referred to in subsection (2) (j) above is a person who—

(a) is living with the relevant person and has been living with the relevant person for a period of at least 5 years; or

(b) if the relevant person is in hospital, had been living with the relevant person for such period when the relevant person was admitted to hospital.

*Appendix 2 to checklist: Suitable standard powers*

**10–07** (a) collect, sue for, receive, discharge and settle all sums, property or rights due or which may become due to the adult;

(b) draw cheques on and sign forms of withdrawal to uplift money from, or credit money to, or open or close, any account in the adult's name including accounts held in common with other persons;

(c) authorise expenditure for any service or for the purchase of any items which are required for the adult's benefit, and pay any accounts incurred by the adult or for his benefit;

(d) invest any sum or sums which may be available for investment in such way as the guardian may think best; vary the terms of any investment; and purchase any property heritable or moveable wherever situated including property held in common with other persons;

(e) exchange, sell or lease by any method any part of the means and estate, heritable or moveable wherever situated from time to time belonging to the adult;

(f) have access to any information regarding the adult's financial affairs;

(g) give up and sign on behalf of the adult all returns, claims and forms which may be required in connection with the adult's liability to taxation;

(h) administer and manage any heritable property wherever situated in which the adult may be interested; repair, maintain, renew and improve the same and erect additional buildings and structures; grant, accept, vary and terminate leases and rights of tenancy or occupancy; plan, thin and cut down timber; work or let minerals; grant or accept feus; excamb land; all as the guardian may think proper and as if he were owner of the property;

(i) commence, run, sell or wind up, whether along or in conjunction with other persons, any business; appoint or employ any person including him/herself in any capacity in relation to such a business and pay suitable remuneration; and delegate the running of such a business to any extent he or she may think proper;

(j) raise or defend or compromise any action or judicial or other proceedings in which the adult is or may be interested so far as s/he may consider necessary or expedient; refer to arbitration any question or disputes in which the adult is or may become involved; appeal against, enforce or implement any judgement, order or award; and appear or instruct appearance on the adult's behalf before any tribunal, commission or other official inquiry;

(k) attend, act or vote for the adult at all meetings of any company or partnership in which the adult may be interested;

(l) have access to confidential information about the adult's will and other testamentary provisions;

(m) employ solicitors, factors, stockbrokers, investment managers, bankers or other agents, and delegate to them such power as s/he thinks fit; act her/himself in any of these ways if qualified, and may pay her/himself, if so acting, and for acting as guardian, the usual professional remuneration;

(n) decide what care and accommodation may be appropriate for the adult;

(o) consent to any medical treatment or procedure or therapy of whatever nature which s/he decides is for the benefit of the adult and may provide access for that, or refuse such consent;

(p) consent to any medical research involving the adult but subject to the restrictions in the Adults with Incapacity (Scotland) Act 2000;

(q) make decisions concerning the adult's involvement in education, training, work, holidays, and cultural or social activities;

(r) make decisions concerning the adult's dress, diet and personal appearance;

(s) exercise any rights of access which the adult has in relation to personal data and records;

(t) take any legal action on behalf of the adult involving his personal welfare;

(u) sign any deed or other document necessary to enable the guardian to implement the powers granted by this deed;

(v) be remunerated out of the adult's estate in respect of the exercise of his/her functions as a guardian relating to the property or financial affairs of the adult;

(w) be reimbursed for any reasonable outlays or out of pocket expenses incurred while acting on behalf of the adult as his/her guardian;

(x) without prejudice to the generality of the foregoing powers, power in terms of section 64(1)(a) of the said Act to deal with the following particular matters on behalf of the said adult namely to sell ALL and WHOLE [insert full conveyancing description] together with fixtures and fittings therein and thereon (hereinafter called the dwellinghouse) including but not limited to power to do everything reasonably required for the purposes of marketing the dwellinghouse and negotiating, concluding and implementing a sale of the dwellinghouse including (i) to employ, instruct and appropriately remunerate estate agents, solicitors, surveyors and any tradesman specialist or experts whom surveyors might recommend be instructed (ii) to employ instruct and appropriately remunerate removal contractors (iii) to arrange for termination of responsibility for services at the dwellinghouse (iv) to execute on behalf of the adult a disposition in favour of the purchaser of the dwellinghouse (v) to execute on behalf of the adult any other deed or documents which solicitors employed as aforesaid might advise should be properly or so executed (vi) to repay the existing borrowing secured over the dwellinghouse with [enter lenders details] and any other creditor who may have an interest in the dwellinghouse (vii) to purchase a Title Indemnity Policy (if required) in respect of the adult's inability to sign a Matrimonial Homes Affidavit in connection with the sale of the dwellinghouse.

(y) As regards each item of corporeal moveable property belonging to the adult at the discretion of the guardian (i) to sell same to the purchasers of the dwellinghouse (ii) to sell same to any other party (iii) to retain same in accordance with such arrangements as such guardian may determine (iv) to seek authority under section 66 of the said Act to make a gift thereof.

[repeat x and y for each property]

(z) to pay and apply the price received for the dwellinghouse as follows (i) in meeting the expenses of this application (ii) in meeting the whole costs of sale and removal including all costs properly incurred and in consequence of the exercise of the powers conferred to the pursuer (iii) in investing any remainder thereof for the benefit of the adult in such manner and on such terms as the Public Guardian may approve and to do anything ancillary to or consequential upon the powers above specified which may reasonably be necessary or appropriate for the full and proper exercise thereof.

*Welfare Powers*

(aa) decide what care and accommodation may be appropriate for the adult;
(bb) decide where the adult may live;
(cc) require the adult to remain at a specified address;
(dd) return the adult to a specified address or to authorise other named persons to do so;
(ee) consent to any medical treatment or procedure or therapy of whatever nature which s/he decides is for the benefit of the adult and may provide access for that, or refuse such consent;
(ff) consent to any medical research involving the adult but subject to the restrictions in the Adults with Incapacity (Scotland) Act 2000;
(gg) make decisions concerning the adult's involvement in education, training, work, holidays, and cultural or social activities;
(hh) make decisions concerning the adult's dress, diet and personal appearance;
(ii) exercise any rights of access which the adult has in relation to personal data and records;
(jj) take any legal action on behalf of the adult involving his personal welfare;
(kk) sign any deed or other document necessary to enable the guardian to implement the powers granted by this deed;
(ll) be reimbursed for any reasonable outlays or out of pocket expenses incurred while acting on behalf of the adult as his/her guardian.


THE ADVICE

**General**

10–08    In this instance the advice given was to apply for Mr A to be appointed as welfare guardian and in the same court application seek an intervention order to allow him to arrange his wife's finances to pay for the nursing home. An interim order was granted on a limited basis as a place came up unexpectedly in a suitable nursing home to allow a quick move of the adult and then at the hearing the order was granted in full without any objections or conditions.

**Documentation**

10–09    The following supporting documentation was sent to the court:

1. Four Forms AWI (1).
   a. Dr X—Intervention Order.
   b. Dr X—Welfare Guardianship.
   c. Dr Y—Intervention Order.
   d. Dr Y—Welfare Guardianship.
2. Forms AWI (2) and AWI (10).
   a. Mental Health Officer—Intervention Order.
   b. Mental Health Officer—Welfare Guardianship.
3. Form 23.
4. Copy letter to Chief Social Worker with Recorded Delivery Slip.
5. Cheque for Court dues of £57.

**Terms of the order**

**GUARDIANSHIP ORDER**        10–10

**FORM 23**

**Rule 3. 16.7(1)**

SUMMARY APPLICATION UNDER THE ADULTS WITH
INCAPACITY (SCOTLAND) ACT 2000

SHERIFFDOM OF TAYSIDE CENTRAL AND FIFE AT PERTH

Mr A residing at Main Street Perth - Pursuer

The applicant craves the Court:-

1. To make a guardianship order under Section 58(4) of the Adults with Incapacity (Scotland) Act 2000 appointing Mr A residing at Main Street Perth to be guardian of Mrs A sometime of Main Street aforesaid and now residing at Murray Royal Hospital, Perth ("the Adult"), conferring on him powers in relation to the Adult's personal welfare and in particular conferring on him power to:
   (a) decide what care and accommodation may be appropriate for the Adult;
   (b) decide where the Adult may live;
   (c) require the Adult to remain at a specified address;
   (d) return the Adult to a specified address or to authorise other named persons to do so;
   (e) consent to any medical treatment or procedure or therapy of whatever nature which he decides is for the benefit of the Adult and may provide access for that, or refuse such consent;
   (f) consent to any medical research involving the Adult but subject to the restrictions in the Adults with Incapacity (Scotland) Act 2000;
   (g) make decisions concerning the Adult's involvement in education, training, work, holidays, and cultural or social activities;
   (h) make decisions concerning the Adult's dress, diet and personal appearance;
   (i) exercise any rights of access which the Adult has in relation to personal data and records;

(j)  take any legal action on behalf of the Adult involving her personal welfare;

(k)  sign any deed or other document necessary to enable the guardian to implement the powers granted by this deed;

(l)  be reimbursed for any reasonable outlays or out of pocket expenses incurred while acting on behalf of the Adult as her guardian;

And to grant an Intervention Order under Section 53(1) of the Adults with Incapacity (Scotland) Act 2000 ("the Act") authorising the applicant to

1.  Obtain details of the Adult's financial situation and to disclose them to appropriate authorities in order to obtain financial assistance with the costs of a suitable Nursing Home. To sign and agree all necessary contracts in relation to entry and residence in a Nursing Home and to sign all appropriate application forms in relation to financial assistance therewith.

2.  To find any party opposing this application liable in the expenses thereof and otherwise to award the expenses incurred by the applicant in making this application out of the Adult's estate.

3.  To grant an interim order conferring on the applicant all Powers sought to allow an immediate move of the Adult to a specialist Nursing Home where a place has become available at short notice.

4.  To Dispense with the need for Caution.

5.  And that for an indefinite period from date of appointment or for such other period as the Sheriff may consider appropriate.

## STATEMENT OF FACTS

1.  The applicant is Mr A residing at Main Street, Perth. The present application is made under Section 57 of the Adults with Incapacity (Scotland) Act 2000 in respect of an adult, Mrs A, sometime of Main Street aforesaid and now residing at Murray Royal Hospital, Perth ("the Adult"). The applicant is the Adult's husband and has an interest in her personal welfare. The Adult is habitually resident within the sheriffdom. This Court accordingly has jurisdiction. There is no agreement between the parties prorogating jurisdiction over the subject matter of the present cause to any other Court. There are no proceedings involving the present cause of action and between the parties hereto subsisting in any other Court.

2.  The Adult's date of birth is 15 March 1920. She is 87 years old. She resides at Murray Royal Hospital, Perth. The Adult was diagnosed suffering from vascular dementia in 2003. As a result of this illness she has found it increasingly difficult to act on her own behalf and to make decisions about her personal welfare. She is now disorientated in place and time and cannot engage in any meaningful discussions about her welfare. Her condition is permanent.

3.  It has been determined that the Adult should leave Murray Royal Hospital and the appropriate environment for discharge is a Nursing Home with a specialised care unit for Adults with the particular difficulties suffered by the Adult. As the Adult has been deemed incapable of making any decisions regarding her care the Welfare Guardianship is necessary to choose a Home and thereafter move the Adult there and make ongoing decisions regarding her welfare hereafter. The chosen

Nursing Home will require a contract to be signed on behalf of the Adult and applications will have to be made for financial assistance for her care costs. The Intervention Order is required to allow the financial aspect of going in to care to be addressed.

4.   The applicant therefore seeks a Guardianship Order under Section 58(4) of the Adults with Incapacity (Scotland) Act 2000 ("the Act") appointing the applicant to be Welfare Guardian of the Adult and conferring on him the welfare powers sought and seeks an Intervention Order under Section 53(1) of the Adults with Incapacity (Scotland) Act 2000 ("the Act") authorising the applicant to carry out the intervention sought.

5.   The making of the order sought will benefit the Adult. The appointment of the applicant as guardian will enable him to ensure that all relevant aspects of the Adult's personal welfare are safeguarded and promoted. Such benefit cannot reasonably be achieved without the making of an order. The Adult's health is likely to continue to deteriorate and the extent of her incapacity in relation to her own personal welfare is likely to increase. She requires ongoing care and in the absence of a guardianship order the applicant is likely to require to make regular applications to the court for authority to intervene in relation to the Adult's personal welfare. The intervention sought will allow the applicant to arrange the financial aspects of going into care, once and for all, without the need for a continuing set of powers. The assets of the Adult are such that a Financial Guardianship is inappropriate. No other means provided by or under the Adult's with Incapacity (Scotland) Act 2000 would be sufficient to enable the Adult's personal welfare to be safeguarded and promoted to the appropriate degree. The applicant believes that in the circumstances it would be appropriate to appoint a guardian with continuing powers of the type sought and to authorise the intervention sought. The applicant believes the making of the order sought is the least restrictive option available to the Court in relation to the freedom of the Adult consistent with the aim of safeguarding and promoting the personal welfare of the Adult and arranging the financial aspects of her going into a Nursing Home.

6.   The Adult has been examined and assessed by Dr [...........]of [..........] and by Dr [..............] of [..............]. Dr [..............] is a medical practitioner approved for the purposes of Section 22 of the Mental Health (Care and Treatment) (Scotland) Act 2003]. Reports, in Form AWI[1], which have been prepared by Dr [..........] and Dr [.............] are produced.

7.   The Adult had been interviewed and assessed by [...........................] mental health officer. A report in Form AWI(2) date [...............] prepared by [..............] is produced.

8.   It has been difficult to assess whether the Adult would wish this application to be granted. She feels that this application made no difference to her and she was not sure who Mr A was. She said she did not understand the business of the application and thought that she did not need anyone to make decisions for her either financially or in terms of her welfare. She noted she was happy where she was at the moment although did not think she was in hospital nor did she think she needed to go anywhere in reference to nursing care. She has never offered an

opinion about what she would like to happen should she no longer be in a position to make decisions, even after watching her mother deteriorating with the same condition. The applicant believes the Adult's wishes would be that, if he was not himself capable of caring for her, she would wish him to make arrangements for her care.

9. The nearest relative is the Applicant who supports the application as he wishes to see his wife safely settled in a suitable environment. The Primary Carer is Miss X Staff Nurse of Murray Royal Hospital, Perth who supports the application. Ms A, daughter, of High Road, Perth supports the application.

10. No other intervention order or guardianship order has been previously made in relation to the Adult.

11. By Recorded delivery Letter of [date.....................] the Applicant gave notice of his intention to make this application to [......................] Chief Social Work Officer of [......................] Council, [Address.....................]. A copy of said letter with the recorded delivery slip relative thereto is produced.

### [PLEA-IN-LAW]

The Adult being incapable in relation to making decisions about and acting to safeguard or promote her interests in her personal welfare and the financial and contractual aspects of going into a Nursing Home and being likely to continue to be so incapable, and no other means provided by or under the Adults with Incapacity (Scotland) Act 2000 being sufficient to enable the Adult's interests in her personal welfare to be safeguarded or promoted, the order should be made as craved.

IN RESPECT WHEREOF

SOLICITOR
Address

Agents of Pursuer

CHAPTER 11

# ELDER ABUSE

## INTRODUCTION

The media frequently reports harrowing stories of our elderly and most **11–01** vulnerable members of society being bullied, abused or mistreated. Most of this book so far has dealt with assets, i.e. money and property which does not mean that the authors lack a sense of social responsibility but reflects the overall outlook of Scots law in relation to its older citizens.

Adults with incapacity and those with mental disorders have some comfort as the AWISA and MHCTSA have started to address the issue of protection from bodily harm, protection of general welfare and well being, but there is not a direct body of law aimed at protecting the frail and vulnerable in the way there is for other special groups in society, e.g. children.

For the elderly, protection, and remedies where the protection has failed, will be found scattered across many statutes.

## THE LAW

There is no definition in law of "elder abuse" although the term is starting to **11–02** be widely used. Analysing the duties and powers of local authorities and health services as they relate to the elderly, and then examining areas where problems can arise, sheds light on possible remedies for the abused elderly person.

### National Assistance Act 1948

Whilst in general local authorities will look for co-operation from an **11–03** elderly person who is no longer coping at home, or will ask the family to seek a welfare guardianship order or apply themselves for one, before making a decision about an adult, serious situations sometimes warrant serious measures. The local authority has power to seek a court order to remove a person from his or her home to be placed in a place of safety such as a hospital or care home. The procedure[1] applies to persons who are:

- suffering from grave chronic disease or being aged, infirm or physically incapacitated, are living in unsanitary conditions; *and*
- unable to devote to themselves and are not receiving from anyone else, proper care and attention.

---

[1]   National Assistance Act 1948, s.47, as amended.

Application is made to the sheriff court and to protect the person from "interference" there is a need to submit a certificate by a designated medical officer of health to certify, that after thorough enquiry, he is satisfied that the order is necessary to the interests of the person, or to prevent injury to health or serious nuisance to others. The sheriff can authorise removal of the person to hospital or other suitable premises to obtain necessary care and attention, and also their detention for a period (renewable) of up to three months. There is further protection from over zealous interference in that there is a seven-day notice period except in the emergency procedure.[2]

If a person is admitted to hospital or care and cannot make arrangements to deal with their possessions, the local authority has a duty to take reasonable steps to protect moveable property and this includes personal possessions and pets. They have the power to enter the home, remove possessions and place them in store.[3] There is no duty to ensure the house is secure.

It is an offence to obstruct a person carrying out such duties.

### Social Work (Scotland) Act 1968

**11–04**    Local authorities have a general duty towards persons in need. Included in the definition[4] of "persons in need" are:

- persons who are in need of care and attention arising out of infirmity, youth or age; or
- suffer from illness or mental disorder or are substantially handicapped by a deformity or disability.

Local authorities also have a general duty to promote social welfare by making available advice, guidance and assistance and making arrangements and providing facilities, as the local authority considers suitable and adequate.[5]

The duty to assess those in need and the assessment procedure are covered below.[6] However, what protection is there for the carer who may themselves be elderly and vulnerable? Carers are entitled to ask the local authority to assess the needs of the carer as well as those of the individual towards whom they have the duty of care and further providing the right to carers to request an assessment of their ability to provide care and this right is available even if the one being cared for is not being themselves assessed.[7]

---

[2]  Introduced by the National Assistance (Amendment) Act 1951.
[3]  National Assistance Act 1948, s.48 (as amended).
[4]  Social Work (Scotland) Act 1968, s.94(1).
[5]  Social Work (Scotland) Act 1968, s.12.
[6]  See Ch.12.
[7]  Social Work (Scotland) Act 1968, s.12 as amended by the Carers (Recognition and Services) Act 1995 and Community Care and Health (Scotland) Act 2003.

## Mental Health (Care and Treatment) (Scotland) Act 2003

The Act contains a new definition of mental disorder. "Mental disorder" **11–05**
means mental illness, personality disorder or learning disability.[8] There is no
statutory definition of the three terms and we are left to look at case law.
These terms mean what a reasonable person would understand them to be.[9]

The local authority has responsibility for care and support services, promotion of well being and social development and assistance with travel for
persons with a mental disorder. There are several specific responsibilities
laid out in the Act and these are additional to the duties in the Social Work
(Scotland) Act 1968 and its frameworks and protections.[10]

The Act sets out specific offences in respect to non-consensual sexual acts[11]
in relation to sexual conduct relating to carers (which relates not just to the
hands-on carer but also to those involved in providing the care such as a
hospital manager, volunteer, etc.).[12]

There are certain defences for amongst others, spouse carers.[13] Not knowing, and providing it is reasonable not to be expected to know, that the
person has a mental disorder is also a defence.[14]

There is a six-month time limit from the date when the prosecution service
obtains sufficient evidence to initiate proceedings for proceedings to
commence.[15]

A conviction can result in the offender being included in the Sex Offenders
Register.[16]

It is an offence for a member of the staff or management of a hospital or any
carer in a residential or other setting to ill-treat or wilfully neglect any
person in their care. This also relates to volunteers and volunteer organisations and unpaid carers and friends and relatives.[17]

## National Health Service and Community Care Act 1990

Part II of this Act places a general duty on local authorities to carry out **11–06**
an assessment where a person appears in need of community care services.

---

[8] Mental Health (Care and Treatment) (Scotland) Act 2003, s.328.
[9] *WvL* [1974] Q.B. 711.
[10] Mental Health (Care and Treatment) (Scotland) Act 2003, ss.25–35.
[11] Mental Health (Care and Treatment) (Scotland) Act 2003, s.311.
[12] Mental Health (Care and Treatment) (Scotland) Act 2003, s.313.
[13] Mental Health (Care and Treatment) (Scotland) Act 2003, s.313(3).
[14] Mental Health (Care and Treatment) (Scotland) Act 2003, s.313(3).
[15] Mental Health (Care and Treatment) (Scotland) Act 2003, s.319, and Criminal Law
(Consolidation) (Scotland) Act 1995, s.4.
[16] Mental Health (Care and Treatment) (Scotland) Act 2003, s.313.
[17] Mental Health (Care and Treatment) (Scotland) Act 2003, s.315.

### Criminal Law (Consolidation) (Scotland) Act 1995

**11–07**    A homosexual act is an offence if, even if both consenting males are over the age of 18, one of them has a "mental deficiency" of such a nature or degree that he is incapable of living an independent life or guarding himself against serious exploitation, as he is unable to give consent.[18] There are defences for the party who has thought there was consent if he can show he did not know and had no reason to suspect "mental deficiency" or knew of it but did not know and had no reason to suspect it was of such a nature and degree to mean the consent was not true consent.[19]

### Adult Support and Protection (Scotland) Act 2007

**11–08**    This offers a number of solutions including protection and banning orders (see Ch.12).

### Adults with Incapacity (Scotland) Act 2000 protections and specific offences

**11–09**    Welfare powers of attorney, if suitably worded, can allow the named attorney to make decisions about personal welfare and medical treatment (within set parameters and subject to the safeguards set out in the Act). However, even if the power of attorney allows it and the attorney decides a treatment should be refused, the medical profession can overrule this and provide treatment in certain circumstances.[20] It is an offence for anyone exercising personal welfare powers (whether attorney, guardian or intervener) under the Act to ill-treat or wilfully neglect the adult.[21] Acting in good faith and in accordance with the principles should mean an adult is properly cared for, but where it does not, a person is not liable for breach of duties in such circumstances.[22]

### Civil law

**11–10**    A person who is wronged can raise an appropriate court action to resolve the matter. A bad transaction can be voided, an interdict can keep an abuser away from the person or there can be a damages action.

### Matrimonial Homes (Family Protection) (Scotland) Act 1981

**11–11**    An abusive spouse or civil partner can be excluded from the home no matter what age he or she may be. On application to the sheriff he or she can be ejected from the home.[23] The spouse may also be prohibited from entering the home without consent,[24] and may be prohibited from removing any furnishing and plenishings from the home.[25] The exclusion order may simply apply to the house or an interdict can be sought to extend the exclusion zone.[26]

---

[18]   Criminal Law (Consolidation) (Scotland) Act 1995, s.3.
[19]   Criminal Law (Consolidation) (Scotland) Act 1995, s.3(3).
[20]   Adults with Incapacity (Scotland) Act 2000, s.47 and s.50.
[21]   Adults with Incapacity (Scotland) Act 2000, s.83.
[22]   Adults with Incapacity (Scotland) Act 2000, s.82.
[23]   Matrimonial Homes (Family Protection) (Scotland) Act 1981, s.4(4) (as amended).
[24]   Matrimonial Homes (Family Protection) (Scotland) Act 1981, s.4(4)(b) (as amended).
[25]   Matrimonial Homes (Family Protection) (Scotland) Act 1981, s.4(4)(c) (as amended).
[26]   Matrimonial Homes (Family Protection) (Scotland) Act 1981, 2.4(5) (as amended).

### Race Relations Act 1976

Is the abuse racial, in which case is there a remedy under this Act?    **11–12**

### Sex Discrimination Act 1975

Has there been sex discrimination, in which case is there a remedy under **11–13** this Act?

### Disability Discrimination Act 1995

Has there been discrimination of a disabled person and could the Dis- **11–14** ability Rights Commission help?

### Human Rights Act 1998

Has there been a breach of the person's human rights?    **11–15**

### The Employment Equality (Age) Regulations 2006[27]

Age discrimination is when an employee is discriminated against by an **11–16** employer on the grounds of age. Discrimination takes different forms:

- overt discrimination, e.g. someone being made redundant because they are considered too old for the job;
- indirect discrimination, such as making ageist comments.

Has there been age discrimination?

### Protection from Harassment Act 1997

A person who has been harassed, and many people with physical and **11–17** mental disabilities and simply the very old, who have been harassed, can go to court for an interdict to stop the harassment. The harassment does not have to be physical violence and can include behaviour causing alarm and distress. The court instead may choose to make a non-harassment order instead, breach of which carries a prison sentence of up to five years.

However what if the elderly client simply *feels* harassed? Many older citizens feel rather vulnerable and many do not like change. Unfortunately new neighbours bring change and can bring nuisances with them. If a neighbour is being annoying with noise it is worth having a friendly conversation to find out if they are aware that they are causing problems. It might simply be a different lifestyle or keeping different hours which is causing the real problem and it may be resolved amicably.

Other neighbours may be suffering similarly and perhaps one of them could deal with the matter.

If there is a serious problem mediation may be of help.

There are many legendary ongoing disputes over coniferous hedges. If a neighbour's tree hangs over the adjacent property and the owner has been

---

[27] SI 2006/1031.

asked and failed to trim it back the person encroached upon can trim it back to the boundary line but must offer back the lopped branches.

It is prudent to advise the client to check if there is a tree preservation order before starting to avoid being fined. If an awkward tree is in a dangerous condition it can be reported to the local authority who will have power to deal with it.

Modern life means most families having two or more cars and inadequate offstreet parking. Those who live on a public road do not have any ownership of the road or pavement outside the property and unless there is a parking permit scheme in place, parking is a free for all. However blocking somebody else's driveway is unacceptable and the local authority and police can prevent this particularly if it is an ongoing situation.

### Noise and Statutory Nuisance Act 1993 and Environment Act 1995

**11–18**    The council has a duty to deal with any noise they consider to be a statutory nuisance.[28] The Environmental Health Department is the usual port of call and generally they are best dealing with ongoing noise from factories or the like as opposed to the police who are better dealing with rowdy behaviour, live parties and youngsters tearing about the streets in noisy cars.

### Crime and Disorder Act 1998

**11–19**    A victim of harassment could ask their local authority to seek an anti-social behaviour order or ASBO.[29] The advantage of this over other remedies is that it is the local authority conducting the case not the individual.

### Criminal law

**11–20**    It should be remembered that physical abuse could constitute an assault and existing criminal legislation if not providing a full remedy could at least remove the abuser from his or her position. The victim should report the matter to the police. There is protection for vulnerable and intimidated witnesses.

Many older people do not like to go out at night for fear of mugging. If the person is a victim of a serious violent crime, then criminal injuries compensation will be available in relation to a personal injury or trauma. The compensation does not cover stolen or damaged possessions that are not covered by insurance.

### The Police Act 1997 (Enhanced Criminal Record Certificates) (Protection of Vulnerable Adults) (Scotland) Regulations 2002

**11–21**    Prevention is always better than cure and ideally abusers would never manage to get near our elderly population. A system is in place to ensure that convicted persons are kept from working with those felt to be at risk of abuse.

---

[28]   See the Noise and Statutory Nuisance Act 1993; Environment Act 1995.
[29]   Crime and Disorder Act 1998, s.19.

Organisations providing services to vulnerable adults will seek police checks on all managers, employees and volunteers.[30]

The services are:

- accommodation and nursing or personal care in a care home;
- personal care or nursing or support to live independently in his own home;
- any services provided by an independent hospital, independent clinic, independent medical agency or National Health Service body;
- social services care; or
- any services provided in an establishment catering for a person with learning difficulties.

There are two types of disclosure.

- Standard disclosure, which is for people who will have regular contact with children or vulnerable adults.
- Enhanced disclosure, which is appropriate for people whose work regularly involves care, training, supervision or being in charge of children or vulnerable adults in certain settings.

Vulnerable adults includes not just those who have physical and mental disabilities or illnesses but also those who are simply frail.[31]

Disclosure Scotland provides the service for the police and once they have provided the disclosure certificate it is for the employer to decide whether to employ an applicant or not. However, if the certificate discloses a conviction for an offence punishable by three months imprisonment or more and sentenced to imprisonment (even if deferred or suspended) the person cannot act as a manager or provider of a care service. [32]

## CAVEAT

However, how many frail elderly clients would have the stomach for a court **11–22** action and with memory and eyesight problems, how good a witness might he or she be?

---

[30] Police Act 1997.

[31] Police Act 1997 (Enhanced Criminal Record Certificates) (Protection of Vulnerable Adults) (Scotland) Regulations 2002 (SSI 2002/217).

[32] Regulation of Care (Requirements as to Care Services) (Scotland) Regulations 2002 (SSI 2002/114).

# ADULT SUPPORT AND PROTECTION (SCOTLAND) ACT 2007

## INTRODUCTION

**12–01** The Adult Support & Protection (Scotland) Act received Royal Assent on March 21, 2007 but the only "legal part" of the Act in force is s.64 which inserts a new s.13 (z)(a) into the Social Work (Scotland) Act 1968 clarifying the power of local authorities to take steps to provide community care services to an adult with incapacity.[1] The commencement of the rest of the Act will be as and when the Scottish ministers appoint by order the days on which the other provisions are to commence.

## OVERVIEW OF THE ACT

**12–02** The Act is separated into five parts as follows:

(1) Protection of adults at risk from harm (scheduled to commence Autumn 2008);
(2) Adults with incapacity (scheduled to commence Spring 2008);
(3) Adult support, etc: miscellaneous amendments and appeals (various dates);
(4) Mental health: miscellaneous amendments and appeals (various dates); and
(5) Final provisions.

## PROTECTION OF ADULTS AT RISK OF HARM

**12–03** Part 1 of the Act seeks to address the issue of elderly abuse by defining what is meant by harm, and adult at risk, and introducing a series of measures to first of all identify those individuals, place an onus on local authorities to make enquiries and then take action and gives the local authorities (and others) the necessary tools to stop or prevent that harm.

### Adults at risk

**12–04** Adults at risk are defined as being those aged 16 or over who are unable to safeguard their own wellbeing, property, rights or their interests, are at risk of harm *and*, because they are affected by disability, mental disorder,

---

[1] See para.11–04.

illness or physical or mental infirmity, more vulnerable to being harmed than adults who are not so affected.[2]

### Harm

"Harm" is defined as being all harmful conduct and, in particular, con-  **12–05** duct which causes physical or psychological harm, unlawful conduct which appropriates or adversely affects property, rights or interest or conduct which causes self harm; and conduct includes action or neglect and other failures to act.[3]

### General principle

Following the ethos of the Adults with Incapacity (Scotland) Act 2000, a  **12–06** person may intervene or authorise an intervention in an adult's affairs only where the person is satisfied that the intervention will provide benefit to the adult and that it is the least restrictive option available to meet the objective of the intervention.[4] The feelings of the adult at risk (so far as they can be ascertained) as well as the views of significant individuals who are known to the public body or office holder are given consideration.[5] Consideration has to be given to the importance of the adult participating as fully as possible and that adult should not be treated any less favourably than any other adult in a comparable situation giving due regard to the adult's abilities, background and characteristics.

### Onus on local authority

Local authorities have a duty imposed on them to make enquiries about  **12–07** an adult's wellbeing, property or financial affairs and where a person meets the statutory definition of an adult at risk and the local authority knows or believes it may have to intervene in order to protect the adults wellbeing, property or financial affairs.[6] To try and improve co-ordination of efforts and better protect all vulnerable adults there is a requirement for co-operation amongst various public bodies to co-operate with each other when harm is known or suspected.[7]

It is recognised that often an adult with incapacity will have difficulties communicating and so the local authority is required (once it has determined, following enquiries, that it has to intervene) to have regard to the importance of the provision of appropriate services including in particular independent advocacy services to assist the adult concerned.[8]

---

[2]  Adult Support and Protection (Scotland) Act 2007, s.3.
[3]  Adult Support and Protection (Scotland) Act 2007, s.5(3).
[4]  Adult Support and Protection (Scotland) Act 2007, s.1.
[5]  Adult Support and Protection (Scotland) Act 2007, s.2.
[6]  Adult Support and Protection (Scotland) Act 2007, s.4.
[7]  Adult Support and Protection (Scotland) Act 2007, s.5.
[8]  Adult Support and Protection (Scotland) Act 2007, s.6.

### Power to make investigations

12–08     Local authorities will be entitled to have their relevant officers (defined in s.53) enter premises to make investigations[9] and to interview an adult in private in that place.[10] Health professionals will be entitled to conduct private medical examinations either at the place being visited or (if they have obtained an assessment order under s.11) the person can be taken elsewhere for the medical examination;[11] the adult must be informed of his or her right to refuse to be examined prior to the examination. A health professional is a doctor, nurse, midwife or any other suitably qualified individual in any subsequent order made by Scottish ministers.[12] Council officers are entitled to require those holding health, financial or other records relating to the adults to produce them for inspection but health records can only be inspected by a health professional as defined above.[13]

### Assessment orders

12–09     There is provision under ss.11–13 for the council to make application to a sheriff for an assessment order to allow a council officer to conduct a private interview or a health professional conduct a private medical examination of the adult at risk. This would be necessary and can only be granted if such interview or examination could not take place under a normal visit to the place being visited. Orders remain valid for up to seven days and the sheriff will only grant an order if satisfied that the council has reasonable cause for thinking the subject of the order is an adult at risk who is being or is likely to be seriously harmed and that an order is necessary to establish this fact.

### Assessment orders and warrants for entry

12–10     If a sheriff grants an assessment order he will also grant a Warrant for entry in relation to any visit taking place. If no assessment order is requested or made, the sheriff may only grant a warrant for entry in relation to a visit if satisfied the council officer reasonably expects to be refused entry, largely requires them to be able to carry out the visit.[14] Warrants are only valid for the 72 hours after they are granted.[15] The sheriff must also be satisfied as to the availability and suitability of the place for interview and examination and an assessment order will only be used where it is not possible for the adult at risk to be interviewed or medically examined during the course of a visit. The visits cannot just be at any time and must be carried out at reasonable times and the purposes of the visit must be stated.[16] The council officer can bring with them any person or equipment that they require to complete the visit but cannot use force. If force is required they would need a police officer with a suitable warrant for entry.[17]

---

[9]  Adult Support and Protection (Scotland) Act 2007, s.7.
[10] Adult Support and Protection (Scotland) Act 2007, s.8.
[11] Adult Support and Protection (Scotland) Act 2007, s.9.
[12] Adult Support and Protection (Scotland) Act 2007, s.5(2).
[13] Adult Support and Protection (Scotland) Act 2007, s.10.
[14] Adult Support and Protection (Scotland) Act 2007, s.38.
[15] Adult Support and Protection (Scotland) Act 2007, s.37.
[16] Adult Support and Protection (Scotland) Act 2007, s.36.
[17] Adult Support and Protection (Scotland) Act 2007, s.36 and 37.

## Removal orders

Council officers can apply to the sheriff for removal orders to remove an **12–11** adult at risk to a specified place. These orders are effective for a maximum of seven days. During that period the council can take such steps as the council think reasonable in order to prevent the adult from suffering harm. The removal must happen within 72 hours of the order being granted.[18]

The criteria for granting a removal order are set out in s.15 and the sheriff has an amount of discretion on the matter.[19] An order, once made, can be varied or recalled by an application by the subject of the removal order or anyone claiming an interest in his or her wellbeing or property or by the council themselves. Before granting the variation or recall, the sheriff must be satisfied that the circumstances have changed.[20]

If the council has obtained a removal order in respect of an adult at risk they must take reasonable steps to prevent any property owned or controlled by that person being lost or damaged for the duration of the removal order. No other arrangements have or are being made. This gives the council officer a right of entry and any removed property must be returned to the adult concerned after the removal order ceases to have effect. The council is not entitled to expenses and property does include pets.[21]

A sheriff who grants a removal order will also grant a warrant for entry in relation to any visit taking place.[22]

## Banning orders

The Act introduces a flexible way to effectively keep a person away from **12–12** an adult at risk by banning that person from a place for a length of time to protect the adult at risk.[23]

Only the adult at risk, any other person entitled to occupy the property or the council can apply for a banning order.[24] Banning orders can be temporary.[25]

Councils can only apply for an order if the adult at risk is being or is likely to be seriously harmed by another person and that the adult would be better safeguarded by banning the subject than removing the adult. Councils must also be satisfied that no other person is likely to apply for an order and that there are no other proceedings before a court. If so satisfied the council is under a duty to apply for an order.[26]

---

[18]  Adult Support and Protection (Scotland) Act 2007, s.14.
[19]  Adult Support and Protection (Scotland) Act 2007, s.41(2).
[20]  Adult Support and Protection (Scotland) Act 2007, s.17.
[21]  Adult Support and Protection (Scotland) Act 2007, s.18.
[22]  Adult Support and Protection (Scotland) Act 2007, s.39.
[23]  Adult Support and Protection (Scotland) Act 2007, s.19.
[24]  Adult Support and Protection (Scotland) Act 2007, s.22.
[25]  Adult Support and Protection (Scotland) Act 2007, s.21.
[26]  Adult Support and Protection (Scotland) Act 2007, s.22.

The order can cover more than simply keeping parties apart and the sheriff can apply other conditions and requirements on the subject, the adult and other individuals to allow proper enforcement of the order. The sheriff must have regard to the views of the applicant, the adult at risk, the subject of the order and any other person with an interest in the adult at risk's wellbeing or property. A power of arrest can be attached[27] but the period of the order may not exceed six months.[28]

Section 20 sets out the strict criteria for the granting of an order and the sheriff must be satisfied that the adult at risk is likely to be seriously harmed and that the banning of the other person from the place occupied by the adult will better safeguard the adult's wellbeing and property than removing the adult at risk. The sheriff must be satisfied that the adult at risk is entitled or permitted to occupy the place but neither the adult nor the subject of the order is so entitled or permitted. This means that an adult at risk with no entitlement cannot ban a person who is entitled to occupy somewhere.[29]

If an adult at risk has a right as a non-entitled spouse under the Matrimonial Homes (Family Protection) (Scotland) Act 1981, as amended, having the spouse excluded does not damage the adults at risk's rights.[30]

Banning orders or temporary banning orders can be varied or recalled in an application to the sheriff and will only be granted if the sheriff is satisfied there has been a change in the facts or circumstances.[31]

Those who can make an application for variation or recall are the banned person, the original applicant, the adult who is being protected by the order or any other person claiming an interest in the wellbeing or property of the adult at risk or any other person entitled to occupy the property from which the subject is banned, or the council.[32]

The powers of arrest which can be attached to the banning order or temporary banning order become effective only when served on the subject of the order and will expire at the same time as the order.[33]

The police, via the chief constable, must be notified as soon as possible after any power of arrest attached to a banning order or temporary banning order becomes effective. The police must also be notified in the event of a variation or recall of the banning order.[34] Where the applicant for a banning order or temporary banning order or variation or recall thereof is not the adult at risk the applicant must notify the adult at risk and any other person with an

---

[27]  Adult Support and Protection (Scotland) Act 2007, s.25.
[28]  Adult Support and Protection (Scotland) Act 2007, s.19(5).
[29]  Adult Support and Protection (Scotland) Act 2007, s.20.
[30]  Adult Support and Protection (Scotland) Act 2007, s.23.
[31]  Adult Support and Protection (Scotland) Act 2007, s.24.
[32]  Adult Support and Protection (Scotland) Act 2007, s.24.
[33]  Adult Support and Protection (Scotland) Act 2007, s.25.
[34]  Adult Support and Protection (Scotland) Act 2007, s.27.

interest in the adult's wellbeing or property. Failure to deliver the order does not invalidate it.[35]

Breach of a banning order or temporary banning order can lead to an arrest without warrant if the police officer reasonably suspects the subject to be in breach of the order *and* is likely to breach the order again if not arrested. The arrested person must be told immediately the reason for the arrest and then taken into a police station as soon as reasonably possible.[36] The arrested person will be detained in custody until being brought before the sheriff or accused on petition or charged on complaint of the criminal offence arising from the incident.[37] Sections 30 to 34 set out the procedure.

**Protection orders and visits**

The adult at risk may of course refuse to co-operate with the authorities in   **12–13** their attempts to investigate and prevent or stop harm. In recognition of this, and of the adult's rights as an individual, s.35 addresses the situation by requiring the adult to consent to the granting of a protection order and/or to the proposed action to be taken under it. For these purposes a protection order includes all or any of an assessment order, removal order, banning order or temporary banning order.[38] If the adult at risk refuses the sheriff may not make a protection order. No action can be taken by a person carrying out the protection or if there is a known refusal of consent. The one exception to this is that the refusal can be ignored where the sheriff or person acting reasonably believes the adult at risk to be under the undue pressure to refuse to consent *and* that there are no other steps which could reasonably be taken with the adult's consent which should protect the adult from the harm which the order or action is intended to prevent. Undue pressure is defined in the Act.[39]

Nothing in the Act allows a council officer to carry out an interview or health professional to carry out a medical examination if the adult at risk has refused to consent to this.[40]

**Urgent cases**

Section 40 allows the council to apply to a justice of the peace instead of a   **12–14** sheriff for a removal order or a warrant for entry in respect of visits under s.7. This is *only* possible if it is considered that it is not practical to apply to the sheriff and an adult at risk is likely to be harmed if there is any delay in granting the order or warrant.[41] The criteria for granting and the requirement to grant a warrant for entry is the same as for an application to the sheriff. A removal order is granted by a justice of the peace and will only have a duration of 12 hours starting no longer than 24 hours after the

---

[35]   Adult Support and Protection (Scotland) Act 2007, s.26.
[36]   Adult Support and Protection (Scotland) Act 2007, s.28.
[37]   Adult Support and Protection (Scotland) Act 2007, s.29.
[38]   Adult Support and Protection (Scotland) Act 2007, s.35.
[39]   Adult Support and Protection (Scotland) Act 2007, s.35(4).
[40]   Adult Support and Protection (Scotland) Act 2007, s.35(6).
[41]   Adult Support and Protection (Scotland) Act 2007, s.40.

application. A warrant for entry granted by a Justice of the Peace expires 12 hours after granting.

### Procedure

**12–15**    Section 41 sets out the procedures for making applications for assessment orders, removal orders, banning orders, temporary banning orders or the variation or recall of same. Notice must be given to both the subject of the application and the affected adult at risk. The subject of the application (and the affected adult at risk if the adult is neither the applicant nor the subject) must appear or be represented before the sheriff. The adult can be accompanied by a friend, relative or representative at any such hearing and a safe-guarder may be appointed for the interests of the adult at risk. The sheriff has an amount of discretion and may attach conditions and disapply certain criteria if so doing will protect the adult or will not prejudice any person affected by the decision.

### Adult protection committees

**12–16**    Local authorities are obliged to establish an adult protection committee whose function will be to review the procedures and practices of specified public bodies in relation to the safe-guarding of adults at risk. This is to improve the statutory duty of co-operation and the public bodies involved are the council, Care Commission, health board, chief constable and any other public body as may be specified at a later date by Scottish ministers.[42] Sections 43 to 47 set out the membership, procedures, role, duties and powers of the committee.

Following the model of the Adults with Incapacity (Scotland) Act 2000, the Scottish ministers will prepare and publish a code of practice containing guidance on the operation of the adult protection measures contained in Pt 1.[43]

### Offence under the Act

**12–17**    It is an offence to prevent or obstruct any person from doing anything which he or she is authorised or entitled to do under an assessment order, removal order, banning order, temporary banning order, warrant for entry or any other provision contained in Pt 1 of the Act and it is also an offence to refuse, without a reasonable excuse, to comply with the request to provide information under s.10. Being found guilty of these offences can lead on summary conviction to a fine, imprisonment or both *but* nothing done by the adult at risk will constitute an offence under this section.[44] If an offence is carried out by a corporate body both the individuals who have control within the organisation as well as the organisation itself can be proceeded against and punished.[45]

---

[42]    Adult Support and Protection (Scotland) Act 2007, s.42.
[43]    Adult Support and Protection (Scotland) Act 2007, s.48.
[44]    Adult Support and Protection (Scotland) Act 2007, s.49.
[45]    Adult Support and Protection (Scotland) Act 2007, s.50.

## Appeals

There is no appeal procedure against the granting of an assessment order, **12–18** removal order or a warrant for entry.

The grant or refusal of a grant of a banning order or temporary banning order can be appealed to the Sheriff Principal only with the leave of the sheriff. The Sheriff Principal's decision on appeal can be appealed to the Court of Session but an appeal in relation to a temporary banning order is competent only with the leave of the Sheriff Principal. If a Sheriff Principal decides to quash a banning order or temporary banning order, the order will have effect until the end of the period for appeal if no appeal is made, or if an appeal is made on the abandonment of the appeal or when the decision is confirmed.[46]

## ADULTS WITH INCAPACITY

The Adults with Incapacity (Scotland) Act 2000 is amended by the Adult **12–19** Support and Protection Act 2007 with a view to improving how it operates in practice following a two-year monitoring project on the implementation of the 2000 Act resulting in a consultation paper entitled "Improving with Experience" issued by the Scottish Executive on August 24, 2005.[47] The most substantive part of the reform is the creation of a whole new procedure for intromission with the funds of an adult with incapacity. There are also amendments in relation to powers of attorney, intervention orders, and guardianship orders.

### Independent advocacy services

It is recognised that incapable adults may have difficulty expressing their **12–20** views and so s.3 of the 2000 Act is amended stating that the sheriff must take into account the views expressed on behalf of the incapable adult by a person providing independent advocacy services under all the applications and proceedings of the 2000 Act.[48] Independent advocacy services has the same meaning as in s.259(4) and (5) of the Mental Health (Care and Treatment) (Scotland) Act 2003.

### Nearest relative

Under s.4 of the 2000 Act the adult is entitled to apply to the sheriff to **12–21** have the person who would otherwise be treated as his nearest relative displaced for the purposes of the Act. This is amended so that any person claiming an interest in the adult's property, financial affairs or personal welfare can apply to have the nearest relative displaced and also allows the court to make an order quite different to the one applied for, e.g. appoint a different person from the person specified in the application.[49]

---

[46] Adult Support and Protection (Scotland) Act 2007, s.51.
[47] Available on *http://www.scotland.gov.uk* [accessed July 18, 2007].
[48] Adult Support and Protection (Scotland) Act 2007, s.55.
[49] Adult Support and Protection (Scotland) Act 2007, s.56.

### Powers of attorney

*Certificates*

**12–22**    Chapter 6 sets out the style of certificate to be contained within a welfare and/or continuing power of attorney. This is altered for both the creation of a continuing power of attorney and the creation and exercise of a welfare power of attorney. Where the person signs the certificate does not have sufficient knowledge of the granter it is now to be sufficient that the person consults one person who does have knowledge of the granter to satisfy themselves that the granter understood the nature and extent of the power of attorney. All welfare powers of attorney and continuing powers of attorney which will start on incapacity will have to contain a statement to the effect that the granter has considered how incapacity should be determined. The great media about the definition of solicitor has now clarified and it must be a practising solicitor which is defined as a solicitor holding a practising certificate issued in accordance with Pt 2 of the Solicitors (Scotland) Act 1980 (c.46).[50] A power of attorney which contains welfare and financial powers requires only one joint certificate.[51]

*Revocation*

**12–23**    As mentioned in Ch.6 there was debate as to how a person could revoke a continuing or welfare power of attorney if there was any question of incapacity. The position is now clarified and the revocation must be by the granter of the power of attorney by giving notice in writing to the Public Guardian and incorporate a certificate by a practising solicitor or a member of a prescribed class stating that he or she interviewed the granter immediately before the document was signed, that the granter understands the effect of the revocation and was not under any undue influence. The Public Guardian will then notify the attorney (and if a welfare power of attorney), the Mental Welfare Commission and the local authority.[52]

## NEW REGIME FOR INTROMISSIONS, ACCOUNTS AND FUNDS

**12–24**  Part 3 of the Adults with Incapacity (Scotland) Act will read as follows once the new regime is brought into force (currently scheduled for Spring 2008):

**12–25**                              **"PART 3**[53]
### ACCOUNTS AND FUNDS
*Purposes and application of Part*

**Intromissions with funds**
**24A.**—(1) This Part makes provision for the authorization of persons by the Public Guardian to intromit with the funds of an adult for the purposes mentioned in subsection (2).
(2) Those purposes are—

---

[50]  Adult Support and Protection (Scotland) Act 2007, s.57(1),(2),(9).
[51]  Adult Support and Protection (Scotland) Act 2007, s.57(3).
[52]  Adult Support and Protection (Scotland) Act 2007, s.57(7).
[53]  Adult Support and Protection (Scotland) Act 2007, s.24A.

(a) the payment of central and local government taxes for which the adult is responsible;

(b) the provisions of sustenance, accommodation, fuel, clothing and related goods and services for the adult;

(c) the provision of other services provided for the purposes of looking after or caring for the adult;

(d) the settlement of debts owed by or incurred in respect of the adult, including any prescribed fees charged by the Public Guardian in connection with an application under this Part;

(e) the payment for the provision of items other than those mentioned in paragraphs (a) to (d) such as the Public Guardian may, in any case, authorise.

**Adults in respect of whom applications may be made**

**24B.**—(1) An application to the Public Guardian under this Part may be made only in relation to an adult who is incapable in relation to decisions about, or of safeguarding the adult's interests in, the funds to which the application relates.

(2) But an application may not be made in the case of an adult in relation to whom—

(a) there is a guardian of the type mentioned in section 33(1)(a) with powers relating to the funds in question;

(b) there is a continuing attorney with powers relating to the funds in question; or

(c) an intervention order relating to the funds in question has been granted.

*Authority to take preliminary steps*

**Authority to provide information about funds**

**24C.**—(1) This section applies where a person—

(a) believes that an adult holds funds in an account in the adult's sole name; but

(b) cannot make an application under section 25 or section 26G because the person does not know—

(i) where the account is held;

(ii) the account details;

(iii) how much is held in the account; or

(iv) any other information needed to complete the application.

(2) Where this section applies, the person may apply to the Public Guardian for a certificate authorising any fundholder to provide the person with such information as the person may reasonably require in order to make an application under section 25 or 26G.

(3) Where the Public Guardian grants an application under subsection (2), the Public Guardian must issue the certificate to the applicant.

(4) A fundholder presented with a certificate issued under subsection (3) is not prevented by—

(a) any obligation as to secrecy; or

(b) any other restriction on disclosure of information,

from providing the person who presents the certificate to it with such information as the person may reasonably require in order to make an application under section 25 or 26G about funds held by it on behalf of the adult.

### Authority to open account in adult's name

**24D.**—(1) This section applies where—
   (a) a person believes that—
      (i) an adult holds funds;
      (ii) an adult is entitled to income or other payments or is likely to become so entitled; or
      (iii) a fundholder holds funds on behalf of an adult; but
   (b) the adult does not have a suitable account in the adult's sole name in which the funds, income or other payments can be placed for the purposes of intromitting with the adult's funds under this Part.

(2) Where this section applies, the person may apply to the Public Guardian for a certificate authorising the opening of an account in the adult's name for the purpose of intromitting with the adult's funds.

(3) Where the Public Guardian grants an application under subsection (2), the Public Guardian must issue the certificate to the applicant.

(4) The certificate issued under subsection (3) may specify the kind of account which may be opened by a fundholder.

(5) A fundholder presented with a certificate issued under subsection (3) may open an account in the adult's name.

(6) But, if the certificate specifies a kind of account, the fundholder may open only an account of the type specified.

(7) On an account being opened in pursuance of subsection (5), the applicant must notify prescribed particulars of the account to the Public Guardian.

*Authority to intromit*

### Authority to intromit

**25.**—(1) A person mentioned in subsection (2) may apply to the Public Guardian for a certificate authorising the person to intromit with an adult's funds.

(2) Those persons are—
   (a) an individual (other than an individual acting in his capacity as an officer of a local authority or other body established by or under an enactment);
   (b) two or more individuals who wish to act jointly; or
   (c) a body (other than a manager of an authorised establishment within the meaning of section 35(2)).

(3) An application under subsection (1) which is accompanied by an application under section 24D may only be granted if—
   (a) an account is opened in pursuance of section 24D(5); and
   (b) prescribed particulars of that account are notified to the Public Guardian in pursuance of section 24D(7).

(4) Where the Public Guardian grants an application under subsection (1), the Public Guardian must—

(a) enter prescribed particulars in the register maintained by the Public Guardian under section 6(2)(b)(iii); and

(b) issue a certificate of authority (a "withdrawal certificate") to the applicant.

(5) No application may be made under subsection (1) if a person is already authorised to intromit with the funds of the adult to whom the application relates (unless the application is made by that person).

(6) In this Act, an individual or a body who holds a valid withdrawal certificate issued under this Part is referred to as a "withdrawer".

**Authority to intromit: application**

**26.**—(1) An application under section 25(1) must—

(a) state the purposes of the proposed intromission with the adult's funds, setting out the specific sums relating to each purpose;

(b) specify an account held by a fundholder in the adult's sole name which the applicant wishes to use for the purpose of intromitting with the adult's funds (or be accompanied by an application under section 24D to open an account for that purpose);

(c) contain an undertaking that the applicant will open an account (the "designated account") solely for the purposes of—

(i) receiving funds transferred under the authority of any certificate granted; and

(ii) intromitting with those funds;

(2) The application may also specify another account held by a fundholder in the adult's sole name which the applicant also wishes to use for the purpose of intromitting with the adult's funds (or be accompanied by an application under section 24D to open an account for that purpose).

(3) In this Part—

(a) the account specified or, as the case may be, opened for the purposes of subsection (1)(b) is referred to as 5 the adult's current account.

(b) the account specified or, as the case may be, opened for the purposes of subsection (2) is referred to as the adult's second account.

*Withdrawal certificates*

**Withdrawal certificates**

**26A.**—(1) A withdrawal certificate may—

(a) authorise the transfer of funds—

(i) from the adult's current account to the designated account;

(ii) from the adult's current account to the adult's second account;

(iii) from the designated account to the adult's second account;

(b) authorise the continuance or making of arrangements for the regular or occasional payment of funds from the adult's current account for specified purposes (for example: by standing order or direct debit);

(c) authorise the withdrawal of funds from the designated account for specified purposes;

(d) place limits on the amount of funds that may be so transferred, paid or withdrawn.

(2) But such a certificate does not authorise a transfer of funds or payment that would cause—
  (a) the adult's current account;
  (b) the adult's second account; or
  (c) the designated account,
to become overdrawn.

(3) If any of the accounts mentioned in paragraphs (a) to (c) of subsection (2) is overdrawn, the fundholder of that account has a right of relief against the withdrawer.

(4) In subsection (1)(b), "specified" means specified in the certificate of appointment.

*Joint and reserve withdrawers*

**Addition of joint withdrawer**

**26B.**—(1) This section applies where an individual has or individuals have been appointed as a withdrawer in relation to an adult.

(2) Where this sections applies, another individual may apply to the Public Guardian for appointment as a joint withdrawer.

(3) An application under subsection (1) must be signed by the existing withdrawer.

(4) Where the Public Guardian grants an application under subsection (1), the Public Guardian must—
  (a) enter prescribed particulars in the register maintained by the Public Guardian under section 6(2)(b)(iii); and
  (b) issue a certificate of authority (a "withdrawal certificate") 5 to the existing withdrawer and the applicant.

(5) Subject to sections 31(2) and 31A, a certificate issued under subsection (4)(b) is valid until the date on which the withdrawal certificate held by the existing withdrawer would cease to be valid under section 31(1) or 31D(6), as the case may be (regardless of any subsequent extension, reduction, termination or suspension of the existing withdrawer's authority).

(6) In this section, "the existing withdrawer" means the individual or individuals mentioned in subsection (1).

(7) In this Part, where two or more individuals are appointed as withdrawers, each individual is referred to as a "joint withdrawer".

**Joint withdrawers: supplementary**

**26C.**—(1) Joint withdrawers may, subject to subsection (2), exercise their functions individually, and each joint withdrawer is liable for any loss incurred by the adult arising out of—
  (a) the joint withdrawer's own acts or omissions; or
  (b) the joint withdrawer's failure to take reasonable steps to ensure that another joint withdrawer does not breach any duty of care or fiduciary duty owed to the adult.

(2) Where more than one joint withdrawer is liable under subsection (1), they are liable jointly and severally.

(3) A joint withdrawer must, before exercising any function conferred on the joint withdrawer, consult the other joint withdrawers, unless—
  (a) consultation would be impracticable in the circumstances; or
  (b) the joint withdrawers agree that consultation is not necessary.

(4) Where joint withdrawers disagree as to the exercise of their functions, one or more of them may apply to the Public Guardian for directions.

(5) Directions given by the Public Guardian in pursuance of subsection (4) may be appealed to the sheriff, whose decision is final.

(6) Where there are joint withdrawers—
  (a) a third party in good faith is entitled to rely on the authority to act of any one or more of them; and
  (b) section 31A(4) (interim authority) only applies where the Public Guardian terminates the authority of all of the joint withdrawers.

### Reserve withdrawers: applications

**26D.**—(1) In any case where an individual is issued with a withdrawal certificate ("a main withdrawer"), the Public Guardian may, on an application by the main withdrawer, appoint another individual ("a reserve withdrawer") to act as a withdrawer in the event of the main withdrawer temporarily becoming unable to act.

(2) An application for appointment of a reserve withdrawer may be made at the time of the application under section 25 for a withdrawal certificate or at any later time.

(3) The application for appointment as a reserve withdrawer must be signed by the proposed reserve withdrawer.

(4) Where the Public Guardian grants the application, the Public Guardian must enter prescribed particulars in the register maintained by the Public Guardian under section 6(2)(b)(iii).

### Reserve withdrawers: authority to act

**26E.**—(1) Where—
  (a) a reserve withdrawer has been appointed under section 26D; and
  (b) the main withdrawer considers that the main withdrawer is or will be unable to carry out some or all of the main withdrawer's functions under this Part,
the main withdrawer may notify the Public Guardian that the main withdrawer wishes the Public Guardian to authorise the reserve withdrawer to intromit with the adult's funds for a specified period.

(2) Where a reserve withdrawer becomes aware that the main withdrawer is unable—
  (a) to carry out some or all of the main withdrawer's functions in relation to intromitting with the funds concerned; and
  (b) to notify the Public Guardian under subsection (1),
the reserve withdrawer may apply to the Public Guardian for a certificate authorising the reserve withdrawer to intromit with the adult's funds for a specified period.

(3) The Public Guardian, on being notified under subsection (1), must or, on an application under subsection (2), may—
  (a) enter prescribed particulars in the register maintained by him under section 6(2)(b)(iii);

   (b) issue a certificate of authority (a "withdrawal certificate") to the reserve withdrawer; and

   (c) notify the adult and the main withdrawer.

(4) The certificate issued under subsection (3)(b) is—

   (a) valid for the specified period, or such shorter period as the Public Guardian thinks fit, but does not extend beyond the date on which thevalidity of the withdrawal certificate issued to the main withdrawer would cease under section 31(1) or 31D(6), as the case may be;

   (b) suspended during any period when the authority of the main withdrawer is suspended;

   (c) terminated if the authority of the main withdrawer is terminated.

(5) The main withdrawer and the reserve withdrawer are liable (jointly and severally) for any loss incurred by the adult arising out of the reserve withdrawer's acts or omissions.

(6) In this section, "specified" means specified in the notice or, as the case may be, application.

*Variation of withdrawer's authority*

**Variation of withdrawal certificate**

**26F.**—(1) The Public Guardian may—

   (a) on the application of a withdrawer, or

   (b) if notified under section 30A,

vary the withdrawal certificate (the "existing certificate") issued to the withdrawer.

(2) But a withdrawal certificate may not be varied under this section so as to alter the period of validity of the certificate.

(3) Where the Public Guardian decides to vary the withdrawal certificate under subsection (1), the Public Guardian must—

   (a) enter prescribed particulars in the register maintained by the Public Guardian under section 6(2)(b)(iii); and

   (b) issue a varied withdrawal certificate to the withdrawer.

(4) The existing certificate ceases to be valid on the date the varied certificate is issued under subsection (3)(b).

*Authority to transfer funds*

**Authority to transfer specified sums**

**26G.**—(1) A person mentioned in subsection (2) may apply to the Public Guardian for a certificate authorising the transfer of a specified sum from a specified account ("the original account") in an adult's sole name to—

   (a) the designated account;

   (b) the adult's current account;

   (c) the adult's second account; or

   (d) such other account as may be specified.

(2) Those persons are—

   (a) a withdrawer;

   (b) a person who has applied for a withdrawal certificate under section 25;

(3) An application under subsection (1) may also seek authority—
  (a) to close the original account;
  (b) to terminate an arrangement for the payment of funds from the original account to another account (for example: a standing order or direct debit).

(4) Where the Public Guardian grants an application under subsection (1), the Public Guardian must—
  (a) enter prescribed particulars in the register maintained by the Public Guardian under section 6(2)(b)(iii); and
  (b) issue the certificate to the applicant.

(5) In this section, "specified" means specified in the application under subsection (1) or, as the case may be, in the certificate granted under subsection (4).

*Applications: general*

## Applications: general requirements

**27.** An application under section 24C, 24D, 25, 26B, 26D, 26F or 26G must—
  (a) be signed by the applicant;
  (b) contain the name and addresses of the nearest relative, named person and primary carer of the adult, if known;
  (c) be submitted to the Public Guardian no later than 14 days after—
    (i) where it is required to be countersigned under section 27A, the day the application is so countersigned, or
    (ii) in any other case, the day the application is signed by the applicant as mentioned in paragraph (a).

## Countersigning of applications

**27A.**—(1) An application under section 24C, 24D, 25, or 26B must be countersigned by a person who must declare in the application that—
  (a) the person knows the applicant and has known the applicant for at least one year prior to the date of the application;
  (b) the person is not any of the following—
    (i) a relative of or person residing with the applicant or the adult;
    (ii) a director or employee of the fundholder;
    (iii) a solicitor acting on behalf of the adult or any other person mentioned in this paragraph in relation to any matter under this Act;
    (iv) the medical practitioner who has issued the certificate under section 27B in connection with the application;
    (v) a guardian of the adult;
    (vi) a welfare or continuing attorney of the adult;
    (vii) a person who is authorised under an intervention order in relation to the adult;
  (c) the person believes the information contained in the application to be true; and
  (d) the person believes the applicant to be a fit and proper person to intromit with the adult's funds.

(2) An application under section 26D (reserve withdrawers) must be countersigned by a person who must declare in the application the matters set out in paragraphs (a) to (d) of subsection (1) but with references in those paragraphs to "applicant" read as references to the proposed reserve withdrawer.

(3) This section does not apply to an application made by a body.

### Medical certificates

**27B.** An application under section 24C, 24D, or 25 must be accompanied by a certificate in prescribed form from a medical practitioner that the adult is—

(a) incapable in relation to decisions about; or

(b) incapable of acting to safeguard or promote the adult's interests in,

the adult's funds.

### Intimation of applications

**27C.**—(1) On receipt of a competent application under section 24C, 24D, 25, 26B, 26D, 26F or 26G, the Public Guardian must intimate the application to—

(a) the adult;

(b) the adult's nearest relative;

(c) the adult's primary carer;

(d) the adult's named person;

(e) where the applicant is—

(i) the individual mentioned in both paragraph (b) and (c); or

(ii) a body other than a local authority,

the chief social work officer of the local authority; and

(f) any other person who the Public Guardian considers has an interest in the application.

(2) A competent application is an application which complies with section 27 and, where appropriate, sections 27A and 27B.

### Determination of applications: applicant to be fit and proper

**27D.**—(1) The Public Guardian may grant an application made under section 24C, 24D, 25, 26B or 26D only if satisfied that—

(a) the applicant in an application under section 24C, 24D, 25 or 26B, or

(b) the proposed reserve withdrawer in an application under section 26D,

is a fit and proper person to intromit with the funds of the adult.

(2) In deciding whether a person is fit and proper, the Public Guardian must have regard to any guidance issued in relation to that matter by the Scottish Ministers.

### Determination of applications: opportunity to make representations

**27E.**—(1) The Public Guardian must not grant an application 5 under section 24C, 24D, 25, 26B, 26D, 26F or 26G without affording to any person who receives intimation of the application under section 27C or any other person who wishes to object an opportunity to make representations.

(2) Where the Public Guardian proposes to refuse the application the Public Guardian must intimate the proposed decision to the applicant and advise the applicant of the prescribed period within which the applicant may object to the proposed refusal.

(3) The Public Guardian must not refuse an application without affording to the applicant, if the applicant objects, an opportunity to make representations.

### Referral of application to sheriff

**27F.**—(1) The Public Guardian may remit an application under section 24C, 24D, 25,26B, 26D, 26F or 26G for determination by the sheriff at the instance of—

(a) the Public Guardian;

(b) the applicant; or

(c) any person who objects to the granting of the application.

(2) The sheriff's decision on an application remitted under subsection (1) is final.

### Multiple applications etc.

**27G.**—(1) Where a person who has made an application under section 24C, 24D or 25 in respect of an adult makes another application under any of those sections in respect of the same adult, the Public Guardian may disapply any of the provisions in sections 27 to 27B to that application.

(2) Where the Public Guardian is to issue more than one certificate under this Part to the same person, the Public Guardian may instead issue a combined certificate to the person.

(3) References in this Part to a withdrawal certificate or other certificate issued under this Part include references to any combined certificate issued by the Public Guardian instead of the withdrawal or other certificate.

*Fundholders*

### Fundholders of adult's current account and adult's second account

**28.**—(1) The fundholder of an adult's current account may act on the instructions of a withdrawer to the extent authorised by the withdrawal certificate issued to the withdrawer.

(2) The fundholder of an adult's current account presented with a withdrawal certificate must not allow any operations to be carried out on that account other than those carried out in accordance with the certificate by the withdrawer.

(3) The fundholder of an adult's current account or an adult's second account presented with a withdrawal certificate may provide the withdrawer with a copy of any statement or other correspondence issued by the fundholder to the adult during the period when the withdrawal certificate is valid.

### Fundholder of original account

**28A.** The fundholder of an original account may act on the instructions of a withdrawer to the extent authorised by the certificate issued to the withdrawer under section 26G(4).

**Fundholder's liability**
**29.** The fundholder of an account mentioned in section 28 or 28A is liable to the adult for any funds removed from the account under that section at any time when it was aware that the withdrawer's authority had been terminated or suspended by the Public Guardian under section 31A but, on meeting such liability, the fundholder of the account has a right of relief against the withdrawer.

*Withdrawers*

**Use of funds by withdrawer**
**30.**—(1) Any funds used by the withdrawer must be applied only for the benefit of the adult.
(2) Despite subsection (1), where the withdrawer lives with the adult, the withdrawer may, to the extent authorised by the certificate, apply any funds withdrawn towards household expenses.

**Notification of change of address**
**30A.**—(1) A withdrawer must notify the Public Guardian—
    (a) of any change in the withdrawer's address; and
    (b) of any change in the address of the adult.
(2) A notice under subsection (1) must be given within 7 days of the date of the change to which it relates.

**Records and inquiries**
**30B.**—(1) A withdrawer must keep records of the exercise of the withdrawer's powers.
(2) The Public Guardian may make inquiries from time to time as to the manner in which a withdrawer has exercised the withdrawer's functions under this Part.

*Duration etc. of authority*

**Duration of withdrawal certificate**
**31.**—(1) Unless this Part provides otherwise, a withdrawal certificate issued under section 25 is valid for a period of 3 years commencing with the date of issue of the certificate.
(2) The Public Guardian may reduce or extend the period of validity of a withdrawal certificate; and an extension may be without limit of time.
(3) Subsections (1) and (2) are without prejudice to the right of the withdrawer to make subsequent applications under section 25 after the withdrawal certificate ceases to be valid or, as the case may be, a suspension 5 or termination of the withdrawer's authority.
(4) The validity of a withdrawal certificate ceases—
    (a) on the appointment of a guardian with powers relating to the funds or account in question;
    (b) on the granting of an intervention order relating to the funds or account in question; or
    (c) on a continuing attorney's acquiring authority to act in relation to the funds or account in question,

but no liability is incurred by any person who acts in good faith under this Part in ignorance of the withdrawal certificate ceasing to be valid under this subsection.

**Suspension and termination of authority**
**31A.**—(1) The Public Guardian may suspend or terminate the authority of a withdrawer under a withdrawal certificate.
(2) The Public Guardian must without delay intimate the suspension or termination to—
    (a) the withdrawer whose authority is suspended or terminated;
    (b) any other joint withdrawer;
    (c) any reserve withdrawer; and
    (d) the fundholder of the designated account; and
    (e) such other persons as the Public Guardian thinks fit.
(3) A suspension or termination under subsection (1) suspends or, as the case may be, terminates all operations on the designated account by the withdrawer whose authority is suspended or terminated.
(3A) The Public Guardian must on suspending or terminating the authority of the withdrawer enter prescribed particulars in the register maintained by the Public Guardian under section 6(2)(b)(iii).
(4) The Public Guardian may on terminating the authority of the withdrawer issue to the withdrawer an interim withdrawal certificate to continue to intromit with the adult's funds for a period not exceeding 4 weeks from the date of the termination.

**Renewal of authority to intromit**
**31B.**—(1) This section applies to an application under section 25 if condition A or B is satisfied.
(2) Condition A is that the application is made by a person holding an existing withdrawal certificate.
(3) Condition B is that—
    (a) the main withdrawer has died or become incapable or the main withdrawer's authority under this Part has been terminated; and
    (b) the application is made, without undue delay, by an individual who was the reserve withdrawer at the time of the 5 death, incapacity, or termination, as the case may be.
(4) Where this section applies, the Public Guardian may disapply any of the provisions in sections 26(1), 27A and 27B to an application to which this section applies (but may require the applicant to provide such other information as the Public Guardian requires to determine the application).
(5) Where condition A is satisfied in relation to an application under section 25, the existing withdrawal certificate will continue to be valid until the application is determined.
(6) Where an application to which this section applies is granted, the existing withdrawal certificate ceases to be valid.

**Duration of certificates issued under section 24C, 24D, and 26G etc.**
**31BB.**—(1) A certificate issued under section 24C, 24D or 26G is valid for such period as it may specify.

(2) But the Public Guardian may cancel the certificate at any time before the end of any period so specified.

(3) The Public Guardian must without delay intimate such a cancellation to—

    (a) the person to whom the certificate was issued,

    (b) where the certificate was issued under section 26G, the fund-holder of the original account, and

    (c) such other persons as the Public Guardian thinks fit.

*Appeals*

**Appeals**

**31C.**—(1) A decision of the Public Guardian—

    (a) to grant or refuse an application under section 24C, 24D, 25, 26B, 26D, 26E, 26F or 26G;

    (b) to refuse to remit an application to the sheriff under section 27F;

    (c) to reduce or extend the period of validity of a withdrawal certificate under section 31(2); or

    (d) to suspend or terminate the authority of a withdrawer under section 31A,

may be appealed to the sheriff.

(2) The sheriff's decision on an appeal under subsection (1) is final.

**Transition from guardianship**

**31D.**—(1) This section applies where—

    (a) there is a guardian with powers relating to the property or financial affairs of an adult; and

    (b) an application is made under section 25 in relation to the adult's funds.

(2) Section 27A does not apply to the application if it is made by the adult's guardian.

(3) The Public Guardian may disapply section 27B to the application.

(4) Where—

    (a) it appears to the Public Guardian that, if the application were granted, the adult's interests in the adult's property and affairs can be satisfactorily safeguarded or promoted otherwise than by the existing guardianship; and

    (b) the Public Guardian proposes to grant the application,

the Public Guardian must initiate the recall of the guardianship under section 73.

(5) The Public Guardian may not grant the application unless the guardianship is recalled.

(6) Where the Public Guardian grants the application, the withdrawal certificate issued to the withdrawer is valid for such period as the Public Guardian specifies at the time the Public Guardian grants the application.

(7) This section does not apply, and no application under this Part may be made, in the case of an adult if there is a person who is—

    (a) appointed or otherwise entitled under the law of any country other than Scotland to act as a guardian (however called) in relation to the adult's property and financial affairs during the adult's incapacity, and

(b) recognised by the law of Scotland as the adult's guardian.

(8) Despite subsection (7), no liability is incurred by any person who acts in good faith under this Part in ignorance of any guardian of the type mentioned in that subsection.

*Miscellaneous*

**Joint accounts**
**32.** Where an individual who along with one or more others is the holder of a joint account with a fundholder becomes incapable in relation to decisions about, or of safeguarding the individual's interests in, the funds in the account, any other joint account holder may continue to operate the account unless—

(a) the terms of the account provide otherwise; or
(b) the joint account holder is barred by an order of any court from so doing.

*Interpretation*

**Interpretation of Part 3**
**33.**—(1) In section 24B, 27A and 31 any reference to—

(a) a guardian includes a reference to a guardian (however called) appointed under the law of any country to, or entitled under 5 the law of any country to act for, an adult during his incapacity, if the guardianship is recognised by the law of Scotland;
(b) a continuing attorney includes a reference to a person granted, under a contract, grant or appointment governed by the law of any country, powers (however expressed) relating to the granter's property or financial affairs and having continuing effect notwithstanding the granter's incapacity.
(c) a welfare attorney includes a reference to a person granted, under a contract, grant or appointment governed by the law of any country, powers (however expressed) relating to the granter's personal welfare and having effect during the granter's incapacity.

(2) In this Part—

"fundholder" means a bank, building society or other similar body which holds funds on behalf of another person,

"withdrawal certificate" means a certificate issued under section 25, 26B, 26E, 26F or 31A.]

**Commentary**

As can be seen the whole of Pt 3 of the 2000 Act (ss.25 to 35) is replaced **12–26** and additional sections (s.24A to 33) are inserted into the 2000 Act.

This introduces a completely new statutory scheme to access and intromit with the funds of an incapable adult and the sorts of expenditure that can be authorised by the Public Guardian. The person who would like access to intromit with the funds will inevitably have to be somebody who cares deeply for the adult as although they can receive the Public Guardian's fees for processing the application any other expenses will not be met from the adult's estate.[54]

An application to intromit can only be made where an adult is incapable in relation to decisions about the funds actually concerned and if an adult already has a guardian, intervener or an attorney with powers relating to those funds an application cannot be made.[55]

One of the deficiencies of the 2000 Act scheme was that a certain amount of information was required in order to make the application and under data protection quite often the person wishing to help was unable to obtain such financial information from banks and building societies, etc. On application the Public Guardian may provide a certificate authorising a bank or other financial institution to provide information about the adult's account or accounts so that the application can be made for authority to intromit.[56]

The new legislation further allows for a certificate to be issued authorising the opening of an account in the adult's name for the purposes of intromitting with funds; previously an intervention order or guardianship order would have been required for this purpose. The Public Guardian can specify the kind of account which can be opened and as soon as the account is opened the applicant must notify the Public Guardian of the details of the account.

Under the 2000 Act only individuals could apply for authority to intromit with funds but under the new legislations applications can be made by individuals, joint individuals or bodies (other than managers of authorised establishments) under Pt 4 of the 2000 Act. A person who is given authority to open an account will subsequently receive a withdrawal certificate and will thereafter be referred to as the withdrawer on the account.[57] A withdrawal certificate may be conditional setting transfer limits, permitting the creation of standing orders or direct debits, etc. and authorising withdrawals for particular purposes but an overdraft is not permitted.[58]

A major practical problem as far as most families were concerned was that only one person could be given authority to intromit on an account, but it is now possible to have an additional withdrawer.[59] Joint withdrawers are obliged to consult with each other before exercising authority and if they cannot agree they can apply to the Public Guardian for directions with an appeal to the sheriff possible and indeed third parties who transact with joint withdrawers in good faith are protected in the event that the joint withdrawers have exceeded their authority.[60] It is also possible to have a

---

[54]   Adult Support and Protection (Scotland) Act 2007, s.24A.
[55]   Adult Support and Protection (Scotland) Act 2007, s.24B.
[56]   Adult Support and Protection (Scotland) Act 2007, s.24(4).
[57]   Adult Support and Protection (Scotland) Act 2007, s.25.
[58]   Adult Support and Protection (Scotland) Act 2007, s.26A.
[59]   Adult Support and Protection (Scotland) Act 2007, s.26B.
[60]   Adult Support and Protection (Scotland) Act 2007, s.26C.

substitute or reserve withdrawer to ensure continuity for an adult particularly where the original withdrawer may be elderly themselves.[61] The mechanics of the reserve withdrawer authority coming into force are set out in s.26E.

During the period of the withdrawal certificate it is possible now to make an application to the Public Guardian for a variation of the terms (but not the period).[62]

Greater flexibility is provided in that the adult's original account can be closed or standing orders or direct debits can be varied or ended or lump sums transferred if authorised by the Public Guardian. This is far more flexible than the original scheme.

The application procedure has changed altering the conditions of the counter-signature[63] whilst applications by organisations do not require a counter-signature.[64]

The terms of the medical certificate required to accompany an application have also altered and will specifically have to refer to the adults ability to manage funds.[65]

The Public Guardian must be satisfied that an applicant or a proposed reserve withdrawer is a fit and proper person to intromit with an incapable adult's funds before any application is granted[66] and is required to hear objectors in relation to all applications and refusals of applications. Any objection can be made either orally or in writing.[67] The Public Guardian may refer an application to the sheriff to be determined and the sheriff's decision is final.[68]

The application system is fairly streamlined in that the Public Guardian can dispense with the need for the same information to be provided on more than one occasion where there is a series of applications in respect of the same adult. For example an application supported by a counter-signature and a medical report may be made for an application for authority to get information and then once the information has been obtained an application is made to open an account and for authority to intromit in which case the Public Guardian can dispense with the need for the second application to be counter-signed or a second medical certificate produced. It is possible to apply for a number of authorities all in the same application and receive a combined certificate.[69]

---

[61] Adult Support and Protection (Scotland) Act 2007, s.26D.
[62] Adult Support and Protection (Scotland) Act 2007, s.26F.
[63] Adult Support and Protection (Scotland) Act 2007, s.27A(1).
[64] Adult Support and Protection (Scotland) Act 2007, s.27A(3).
[65] Adult Support and Protection (Scotland) Act 2007, s.27B.
[66] Adult Support and Protection (Scotland) Act 2007, s.27D.
[67] Adult Support and Protection (Scotland) Act 2007, s.27E.
[68] Adult Support and Protection (Scotland) Act 2007, s.27F.
[69] Adult Support and Protection (Scotland) Act 2007, s.27G(1) and (2).

The fund holders of the relevant account are bound by the terms of the authority in the withdrawal certificate and must not allow the account to be operated in any other way.[70] If a fund holder is aware that the withdrawer's authority has been terminated or suspended, if they allow any operation on the account they will be liable to reimburse the funds and then having done so can recover from the withdrawer who has acted after the authority has ceased.[71]

A grey area under the previous Act has been clarified so that whilst the adult's funds are supposed to be spent on the adult's own requirements, it may be used for shared household expenses as it is recognised that many withdrawers are the partners of the incapable adult and will live in the same accommodation. Withdrawers are required to keep records of the exercise of their authority and must inform the Public Guardian, within seven days, if either withdrawer or adult changes their permanent address. The Public Guardian has power to make enquiries into the exercise of the withdrawer's authority.[72]

Withdrawal certificates are made for a three-year period, but the Public Guardian can reduce or extend this if a guardianship order or intervention order is made or a continuing attorney appointed with powers in relation to the funds which are the subject of the withdrawal certificate, and the withdrawer's authority will end.[73]

In line with the focus on continuity of care for the adult there is a new system of application to renew authority or for a reserve withdrawer to come forward if the main withdrawer has died, become incapable or has had authority terminated. The Public Guardian has flexibility to dispense with the application requirements to speed up the renewal process. To clarify matters all the transitional provisions have been brought together under s.31D.

It has been recognised that often an adult will require a guardianship order and after the guardian has been in place for some time will have been able to simplify all the financial matters and perhaps will have spent quite a lot of the estate on care meaning that the financial guardianship is no longer necessary. The adult remains incapable of managing his or her finances and so does require assistance, and intromission with funds would be more appropriate in keeping with the principals of minimum intervention whilst providing benefits to the adult. The streamline transition from guardianship to intromission with funds is introduced under s.31(e).

As outlined in Ch.9, a joint account may be operated by a joint account holder where the other joint account holder no longer has capacity in relation to the account. Section 32 specifically enables joint accounts to continue to be so operated.

---

[70]  Adult Support and Protection (Scotland) Act 2007, s.28.
[71]  Adult Support and Protection (Scotland) Act 2007, s.29.
[72]  Adult Support and Protection (Scotland) Act 2007, ss.30, 30A and 30B.
[73]  Adult Support and Protection (Scotland) Act 2007, s.31.

## INTERVENTION ORDERS AND GUARDIANSHIP ORDERS

**Medical reports**

It has been recognised that obtaining the relevant medical reports and suitability report, all within 30 days prior to making the application to the court can be practically difficult and so the ends of justice are not always served. It can be difficult to co-ordinate the two doctors. A medical report more than 30 days old can be valid providing the sheriff is satisfied the adult's condition is unlikely to have improved since the examination. A person not living in Scotland but the subject of an application for an intervention order or guardianship order may be examined by a medical practitioner in the country where he or she lives if that person has the recognised qualifications, etc.[74]     **12–27**

**Discretion regarding caution**

The requirement for caution is now to be a matter of discretion for the sheriff in respect of intervention orders and guardianship orders relating to property and/or financial affairs.[75]     **12–28**

**Change of address**

Interveners are now to be under a similar requirement to guardians to notify the Public Guardian of an adult's change of address within seven days of such a change.[76]     **12–29**

**Tidying up provisions**

Renewal of guardianships is simplified such that it is now to be dealt with by the sheriff on the basis of an application form supported by medical reports completed not more than 30 days before the application and another report either from a mental health officer or the chief social work officer where the adult is unable to communicate, where the application relates to the adult's welfare or from the Public Guardian if it relates to the adult's property and/or financial affairs.     **12–30**

As for guardianship applications where the reason of the incapacity is mental disorder, the medical report or one of them must be carried out by a relevant medical practitioner.[77]

Interim guardianships can now be granted not just for the original three months but for a longer period up to a maximum of six months.[78] There are also various tidying up provisions of some unintended affects of the original drafting of the 2000 Act, e.g. s.60(11) provides that the Mental Welfare Commission may recall guardianships relating to personal welfare only in

---

[74]   Adult Support and Protection (Scotland) Act 2007, ss.59 and 60.
[75]   Adult Support and Protection (Scotland) Act 2007, ss.59 and 60.
[76]   Adult Support and Protection (Scotland) Act 2007, s.59(2).
[77]   Adult Support and Protection (Scotland) Act 2007, s.60.
[78]   Adult Support and Protection (Scotland) Act 2007, s.60(1)(d).

those cases where incapacity relates to a mental disorder and not as at present to all guardianships relating to personal welfare.

Where it is clear that a youth will become an adult with incapacity the guardianship order can be applied for in the three-month period prior to that individual's sixteenth birthday for the order to come into effect on the sixteenth birthday.[79]

All welfare and financial guardians who became such by virtue of having previously been *Curators Boni, tutors-dative* or *tutors-at-law* prior to the coming into effect of Pt 6 of the 2000 Act will cease unless there is an application for renewal within two years of the commencement of this subsection or within two years of the person becoming 16 if that is a longer period. Most *Curators Boni* will have already renewed or made other provisions following the guidance in the code of practice for welfare and financial guardians.[80]

## ADULT SUPPORT AND PROTECTION (SCOTLAND) ACT 2007 MISCELLANEOUS AMENDMENTS AND REPEALS

**12–31** Sections 42 and 43 of the National Assistance Act 1948 currently require a spouse or parent of a person resident in accommodation provided by or secured by a local authority under the Social Work (Scotland) Act 1968 are provided with accommodation under s.25 of the Mental Health (Care and Treatment) (Scotland) Act 2003 to contribute to the costs of the resident's care. Section 62 of this Act repeals the reference to liable relatives and simply makes law match the current guidance to councils.[81]

Where a person receiving community care services moves between local authority areas, the Scottish Executive policy is that the local authority in which a person is ordinarily resident is financially responsible for the community care services of that person and s.65 of the new Act clarifies and updates the legislation. This relates to cover direct payments and so when the local authority provides the accommodation they can recover the cost from the responsible authority, i.e. the authority in which the person would ordinarily be resident. It is particularly useful where there are certain accommodations suited to particular ailments, e.g. drink related dementia, which are situated only in one authority which is not the person's normal authority of residence.

The Public Guardian is given greater authority to aid the protection of adults.[82] The Public Guardian will be able to take part and initiate court proceedings where it appears necessary to him or her to safeguard the property or financial affairs of an adult with incapacity. Currently the Public Guardian can only enter into court proceedings if this is related to an

---

[79] Adult Support and Protection (Scotland) Act 2007, s.60(16).
[80] See Ch.8.
[81] See para.13–22.
[82] Adult Support and Protection (Scotland) Act 2007, s.67.

investigation he or she has carried out and it is now extended to any matter about which the Public Guardian is aware, particularly derived from prior dealings with the adult's affairs rather than from a particular investigation.

## MENTAL HEALTH MISCELLANEOUS AMENDMENTS AND REPEALS

A number of alterations are made to Mental Health (Care and Treatment) **12–32** (Scotland) Act 2003 which are outwith the scope of this book.

# Chapter 13

# CARE

## CARE AT HOME

13–01 Local authorities have a duty to prepare community care plans for their local area.[1] The bedrock of the community care system is the assessment of needs.[2] The local authority has a duty to assess needs formally and to record how it proposes those needs should be met. The record should also note the needs the local authority has noted but cannot meet. Where there are also health or housing needs, the assessment should be carried out in conjunction with health and housing services in accordance with the "Shared Assessment Guide".[3]

### Physical assistance at home

13–02 Not everyone who becomes infirm needs to live in a care home, and many may prefer to stay in their own home with some assistance. Having fallen ill the elderly client, the carer or any other interested person is entitled to request the local authority to arrange a care and needs assessment to identify how those physical needs can best be met in the home.

Small items of equipment are likely to be provided free of charge but larger items or adaptations will have to be contributed towards by the client although loans may be available. Some physical aids may be available on loan from British Red Cross, Age Concern, WRVS, etc. These would include rails and supports, alarm system and walkers.

Day care may be something the client would enjoy and this may be run by the local authority or by the local Age Concern. If some help with household tasks would be of benefit, ask what the local authority can supply or consider a private agency or employing someone and applying to the local authority for a direct payment to fund the cost.

Some local authorities will provide a laundry service. Each local authority will have its own policy on meals on wheels, respite care, etc.

The client's GP will be able to inform the client about community health services, such as district nurses and health visitors, chiropodists, physiotherapists, etc. Specialist nursing or care at home for those with a

---

[1] Social Work (Scotland) Act 1968, s.5A(1).
[2] Social Work (Scotland) Act 198, s.12A.
[3] *Guidance on single shared assessment of community care needs* (Scottish Executive circular, CCD8/2001).

terminal illness can be invaluable to the person's last few months. The GP can supply information about Macmillan nurses or local hospices.

### Charging for services

For services other than personal care at home, the local authority can **13–03** (and does) make a charge providing that it is reasonable to do so.[4] A person can appeal against any charges[5] upon which the local authority must examine the person's financial circumstances and must then assess a reasonable amount. If a person receives a service and later become unable or unwilling to pay for it, the service cannot be withdrawn but the local authority can pursue recovery of the unpaid amounts in the sheriff court.

The definition of "personal care" includes help with a variety of tasks such as bathing, personal hygiene, dressing, getting in and out of bed, continence management, assistance with eating and preparation of a special diet.

Those requiring personal care at home will need to be physically assessed in order to trigger the payment of free personal care. Nursing care is free to those who live at home as it is provided by the NHS and so payment of nursing care allowance is not relevant to those who live at home.

People aged over 65 who receive payment for free personal care will lose their entitlement to attendance allowance. Those who receive nursing care but not free personal care and pay all their own fees will receive attendance allowance.

### Direct payments

Following an assessment by the social work department a client deemed **13–04** to be in need of community care services to help them remain at home can choose to receive cash from the social work department rather than the actual service.[6] Direct payments allow a person to make arrangements for their own personal care and a person may choose to have some services provided and arranged by the social work department and use a direct payment to arrange to take control of provision of care for him or herself. Direct payments can be used to pay for respite care of up to four weeks in a year[7] and to purchase aids and equipment for the house. They cannot be used for residential accommodation nor to pay a spouse or close relative for care. These direct payments are made in lieu of services that the social work department assess the person as requiring, and the local authority deducts the client's financial contribution from the amount of the direct payment.

The local authority must be satisfied that the person will be able to manage the scheme either alone or with help from someone else. Attorneys can consent to the scheme if the person is unable to do so him or herself.[8]

---

4  Community Care and Health (Scotland) Act 2002.
5  Social Work (Scotland) Act 1968, s.87(1A).
6  Social Work (Scotland) Act 1968, s.12B.
7  Direct Payments Regulations, reg.6.
8  Social Work (Scotland) Act 1968, s.12B(1)(b).

### Privately employed care worker

**13–05**     Many clients will be financially secure and will have their mental faculties but simply be too frail to manage to cope in the house alone without some help. Those clients may simply wish to employ nurses or care workers direct perhaps via an agency or perhaps by advertising for an employee. The client should be advised that employing someone direct makes the elderly person an employer and so PAYE, contracts of employment and national insurance contributions and all other employer related responsibilities and potential liabilities should be carefully considered. If the local authority has assessed a person as needing physical assistance, they have a duty to arrange it even if the person will be fully funding it themselves.

### The right to social work services

**13–06**     Several pieces of legislation can apply to the same person and there are entitlements to assessments and consequent care under each of them.

If a client has a disability, is chronically sick or has a mental disorder[9] they are entitled to an assessment by the local authority and in addition the local authority has a duty[10] to any person who seems eligible for community care services to carry out an assessment of the need for these services.[11] Lack of resources is not a valid reason for failing to assess for community care[12] and excessive delay is not acceptable either. Under the Chronically Sick and Disabled Persons Act 1970, if the local authority deems that a person requires certain services, it must provide those services or must arrange to provide them if no one else is doing so. The two assessments may be carried out at the same time.

In addition, anyone with a mental illness, learning disability or personality disorder can insist on an assessment and if the local authority receives a written request from the person or his advocate, named person or primary carer it must respond within 14 days.[13]

The local authority must take into account the amount of care any carer provides and must so far as reasonable and practical take the views of the carer into account and must advise the carer of his right to request a carer's assessment of his or her ability to provide care or to continue to provide care in the future.[14]

After the assessment of needs, the local authority must make a formal decision about the services required and those it will provide.[15] Costs can be taken into consideration if there is more than one way to meet the needs.[16]

---

[9]   Chronically Sick and Disabled Persons Act 1970.
[10]   National Health Service and Community Care Act 1990, s.55.
[11]   Social Work (Scotland) Act 1968, s.12A(1)(a).
[12]   *R. v Bristol City Council Ex p. Penfold* (1998) 1 C.C.L.R. 315, QBD (English case on the English Act).
[13]   Mental Health (Care and Treatment) (Scotland) Act 2003, s.228.
[14]   Social Work (Scotland) Act, s.12.
[15]   Social Work (Scotland) Act 1968, s.12A(1)(b).
[16]   *R. v Lancashire County Council Ex p. RADAR* [1996] All E.R. 421.

However a person's ability to pay for those needs should not be taken into account; the assessment of need and the decision on provision are first and then the assessment of means is separate and comes second.[17]

The local authority will then write up its care plan and the person should be given a copy.

## Complaints

If a client disagrees with the assessment of needs he or she can ask for a **13–07** review and if still not satisfied, there is the local authority social work complaints procedure, and ultimately there is the Scottish Public Services Ombudsman and the Local Government Monitoring Officer and the Mental Welfare Commission for Scotland or even an appeal to Scottish ministers or an appeal through the courts.

## HOSPITAL DISCHARGE

### NHS continuing health care

Since April 1996[18] each local NHS board has been obliged to set out and **13–08** publish its policies, plans and criteria for meeting the continuing health care needs of people living in its area. In order to receive NHS continuing health care services you need to meet any criteria which the local NHS board has set out for that particular service; you do not necessarily need to be in hospital to receive the care.

### Discharge from hospital

If a person has been in hospital, any discharge decisions made by the **13–09** NHS or local authority should be given in writing to the patient and should set out which help will come from the local authority (and therefore will cost the client money) and which will be paid for by the NHS (and therefore will be free of charge). Each of the patient and his carer have a right to ask for an assessment; the carer being entitled to say that they are not able and willing to continue the caring which they had previously been giving.

### Free day care

Anyone aged 65 or over who requires home care after receiving NHS in- **13–10** patient care is now entitled to receive up to four weeks' free care, including home helps, shopping service and minor home adaptations.[19]

Local authorities should not ask for relatives or carers to contribute towards the cost of day care. However the situation regarding spouses can be different. Spouses have a legal duty to maintain each other and local authorities do have the right to recover residential day care costs from a spouse

[17] *Robertson v Fife Council* [2002] UKHL 35.
[18] NHS MEL (1996) 22, NHS *Responsibility for Continuing Health Care.*
[19] Scottish Executive Circular CCD2/2001.

who refuses to pay[20]; but there is no equivalent provision relating to day care in the home. COSLA guidance suggests the financial assessment should be on both spouses the argument being that these charges will be for services which are non-personal (given the introduction of free personal care) care, which by its very nature benefits both spouses and so the resources of both should be taken into account. If a spouse is asked to pay, he or she would need advice on the possibility of the local authority taking court action and the likelihood of a good outcome from the sheriff's decision, i.e. on whether spouse should pay and if so, how much is reasonable.

### Discharge of patients requiring intensive support—NHS care

**13–11**    In these circumstances, the discharge decision will be made by the consultant and he will decide whether continuing inpatient care is required and therefore funded by NHS, or whether a period of rehabilitation and recovery needs to be arranged and therefore funded by the NHS. The reasons for the decision should be included and there should be an explanation if the decision is that the patient does not meet the criteria for NHS funding. If the client is a NHS hospital patient and disagrees with the decision about meeting or not meeting criteria, this decision can be appealed. Information about the review procedure is available in the treating hospital, which is via the standard health service complaint system.

In England, the *Coughlan* judgment confirmed that nursing care for a chronically sick patient could, in appropriate cases, be provided by a local authority as a social service, rather than by the NHS, and the patient could, depending on his or her means, be liable to meet the cost of that care. However, if the needs of the patient were primarily health needs, the health authority is, as a matter of law, responsible.[21]

Even after the *Coughlan* case there has been no alteration to the Scottish guidance.[22] The lack of formalised process for assessment within MEL means there is a lack of clarity for the patient and this has led to a number of complaints where patients consider they have unfairly been refused NHS continuing care. These complaints have reached the Ombudsman and a recent judgment sets out the Ombudsman's views on the procedural difficulties and confusion arising from MEL.[23] This and other complaints have led to the Ombudsman reaching the conclusion that a review is urgently required of the guidance on NHS Funded Continuing Care which is now 11 years old. The Ombudsman intends to draw this matter to the attention of the Scottish Executive Health Department.

NHS care is paid for by NHS boards and the care offered will be either in hospital, an NHS care home or may be in a private or voluntary sector care home.

---

[20]    National Assistance Act 1948, s.43.
[21]    *R. v North and East Devon Health Authority Ex p. Coughlan*, July 1999.
[22]    NHS MEL (1996) 22, NHS *Responsibility for Continuing Health Care*.
[23]    Ombudsman, Scottish Parliament Region: Mid-Scotland and Fife Case 200501504: Fife NHS Board.

If the consultant's decision is that the patient does not meet the criteria for NHS continuing care then the local authority social work department will take over the decision making.

### Discharge of patients requiring intensive support—NHS care refused

There are two main ways the care may be met.                    **13–12**

- Placement in a care home funded by the local authority (means tested) or funded by the elderly person. All persons over 65 following a physical assessment are entitled to a payment for personal and/and or nursing care if judged as needing this; or
- Package of health and social care to allow a return to home or to live with family or to sheltered housing. This package may involve the NHS and local authority services working in tandem.

The client may be asked to pay for some of the social work services but should not be asked to pay for NHS continuing health care services.

### Right to refuse discharge to a care home

Where a person who has been assessed as not meeting the criteria for **13–13** NHS continuing in-patient care, they do not have the right to occupy an NHS bed forever and ever. In general they can refuse to be discharged to a care home so how does a person get out of this limbo? Normally the local authority social work department will work to explore alternative options which may result in discharge and the client paying for the care which they receive.

If the client is not in hospital he can still ask for his health needs to be assessed by any of the services being part of the NHS continuing health care services. This can be through the GP or social work department.

### Palliative health care

This can be given in a hospice, at home, a care home or an NHS hospital **13–14** and is not service which is chargeable.

### Respite health care

This can be provided by the local NHS board and the local authority. **13–15** Where the local authority provides it, it will be charged for depending on the level of care. It could be in the home, in a day centre, in hospital (free and now quite unusual unless someone has special nursing or medical needs which need a health setting), in a nursing home (if less than eight weeks this can be at a discounted rate) and if for more than eight weeks will be at the full rate.

### Specialist transport

This will be part of the NHS board's policies and the client can check to **13–16** see whether they qualify or not.

### Cross-border issues within the UK

13–17    Legislation for Wales, Scotland and Northern Ireland provides that the responsible authority for an individual's healthcare provision is the one where a person is usually resident and is not based on GP registration as provided by English legislation.

In the case of persons resident in Scotland but registered with a GP in England, Scotland is the responsible commissioner.[24] This applies from October 1, 2002 when the Functions Regulations came into force. From July 8, 2003 for patients who are resident in England but registered with a GP in Wales, Scotland or Northern Ireland the responsible commissioner is the English primary care trust in whose area the patient is resident.[25]

## CARE IN A CARE HOME

### Guidance and policies

13–18    Essential reading for all practitioners is the Scottish Executive Health Department circular "The Residential Charges Guidance".[26] The guidance covers assessments, personal expenses allowance, capital, treatment of property, income, income other than earnings, earnings, trust funds, liability of relatives, students, etc. The key word in relation to this is "guidance"; it is not a statement of the law and local authorities will set their own policies based on the guidance.

If a client disagrees with an assessment it is essential to ask the local authority for a copy of its current policy and to try and challenge the assessment as quite frequently a challenge on the application of the policy can be successful.

Ultimately a client may need or wish to move into a care home on a permanent basis. The local authority social work department has a duty[27] to provide or arrange permanent care in a home for a person if they have been assessed as requiring this care. If a person cannot arrange his own care the local authority has no power to oblige a friend or relative to do this, unless they are so willing.

### Non-means tested financial contributions

13–19    Free personal care allowance and/or free nursing care allowance will follow a physical assessment by the social worker and will be paid if so assessed as being required. These are not means tested.

---

[24]    See SI 2002/2375 where the definition of "practice patients" excludes residents in Scotland.
[25]    See SI 2003/1497, amendment to SI 2002/2375.
[26]    *Revised Guidance on Charging for Residential Accommodation*, CCD1/2006.
[27]    National Assistance Act 1948, s.21.

## Means tested financial contributions

Income and capital are taken into account in financial assessments. A **13–20** person in care is always left with some money per week to meet personal expenses. It is currently £19.60 per week. Most welfare benefits (excepting the mobility element of disability living allowance) are counted as income. If a person has a pension, 50 per cent of this will be ignored where there is a spouse or civil partner, providing the spouse or civil partner is actually given the money. Unmarried residents with partners of either sex can apply to the local authority to have some of the pension made available for the partner.

If a person has more than £20,000 in capital he will be expected to pay for living costs (the total cost less any payments made for free personal and free nursing care) until his capital is reduced to £20,000.

If there is capital between £12,250 and £20,000 both income and capital are taken into account in the means test. There is a sliding scale of an assumed income for every £250 or part thereof of capital between the limits will be assessed as providing an extra £1 per week of income. The limits of capital and income change annually in April, in line with inflation.

## Refusal to pay

If a person refuses to pay his own contribution to the care home fees the **13–21** local authority cannot force him or her to do so. However there is usually a contract with the care home under which somebody will be liable to the care home for the costs. This could be family or it could be the person in question and so avoidance of care home costs is not possible in that situation.

Local authorities can take the adult to court to recover the debt and they could apply to the court to have a guardian or an intervener appointed obliging that person to pay the debt or they could indeed threaten to bankrupt the adult. Ultimately, the debt of course can be recovered from a deceased person's estate and will therefore be the liability of the executors.

## Liability of spouse or civil partner

Spouses and civil partners (but not co-habitees or divorced coupes) were **13–22** previously legally obliged to maintain their other halves.[28] Local authorities could ask a spouse or partner to contribute towards a person's care but they did not have the power to make the spouse or partner give details of his or her income or savings. The spouse or partner could agree to pay what he or she feels is a reasonable amount and should not suffer hardship as a result of any contribution which is agreed. For example the local authority should not expect the person to be reduced to the level of income support but instead he or she should be able to continue with his or her usual quality of life. If a spouse or civil partner refuses to pay the local authority would previously have to consider going to court. The Scottish Government have

---

[28] National Assistance Act 1948, s.42 (now repealed under s.62 Adult Support and Protection (Scotland) Act 2007).

changed the rules on liability[29] and the liability to maintain a spouse or child in relation to accommodation charges has been removed.

The spouse in the care home could, as indeed could the spouse who remains at home, enforce the ongoing obligation of support (which exists until divorce, and is independent of divorce) to ensure an adequate lifestyle where there is disparity in income and wealth between the spouses. If the court is called upon to decide on the level of support, it will have regard to the needs, resources, earning capacities and "generally all the circumstances of the case".

### Deprivation of assets

**13–23**    A most frequent topic of advice lawyers are asked to provide is whether a person should give away assets, in particular the family home. Providing there are other reasons for the gift other than simply trying to avoid care costs, and the risks are fully explored and appreciated by the client, there is no reason why the gift should not take place. By the time the donor comes to be assessed the rules may well be different or indeed the reasons for the gift may be accepted in which case it was worth doing. The only certain advice is that if they do not make the gift at all then the asset will almost certainly be a target for care costs.

### Disregard of home

**13–24**    Claiming financial support towards care-home fees will lead to a financial assessment of all assets and property owned unless the stay is temporary. The local authority disregards the value of the home for 12 weeks after the resident's admission to permanent care. If the entry to the care home was on a temporary basis, but the care becomes permanent, the 12 weeks runs from the date of the decision of permanency. If the property is sold within the 12-week disregard period, the disregard ends on the date of sale. If one spouse moves to a care home, the disregard is applied. If the other one then enters care, the disregard is applied separately to him or her.

If the client's former home is occupied by:

- a partner or a relative who is aged over 60;
- a younger incapacitated (for which there is no definition) relative;
- a former partner who is divorced or estranged from them but who is a lone parent; or
- a child under 16 years who is maintained by the adult,

the property will be disregarded.[30]

The local authority also has discretion to disregard the property if it is the home of somebody other than the above groups.[31]

---

[29]    Adult Support and Protection (Scotland) Act, s.62
[30]    National Assistance (Assessment of Resources) Regulations 1992 (SI 1992/2977), as amended.
[31]    National Assistance (Assessment of Resources) Regulations 1992 (SI 1992/2977), as amended.

If the person has a low income and is trying to sell their property, its value will be ignored for up to 26 weeks or longer so that pension credit can be claimed.

**Valuation of property**

If the property is not being disregarded, its value will be assessed. Its value **13–25** is the market value less any mortgage or loan secured on it less 10 per cent of its value (a notional figure to represent expenses involved if it were to be sold). The 10 per cent rule is for calculating the value of a property prior to its sale and as logically once it has been realised it is the net free proceeds of sale which would form the capital.

**Ownership of capital**

The legal ownership of property may be in one person's name whilst the **13–26** beneficial ownership of it lies with another.

**Valuation of jointly owned capital**

The rule of thumb is that the capital will be valued by dividing the value **13–27** by the number of joint owners.

However in relation to pension credit and other social security benefits it is the person's interest that must be valued. The valuation should be by an expert valuer who looks at all the factors including whether there is actually a market for say one-third of a property and if there is a value what the valuation will be. As there are very few people who wish to purchase a percentage of a property the valuation may be low or even nil. However on sale it is the net free proceeds of sale which belong to the claimant which will form the capital.

The local authority must value the resident's interest in the property rather than the property itself.[32] If the joint owner is not willing to buy out the claimant's share then there must be unlimited or in fact no market for percentages of properties and so the value must be low.

**Deprivation of assets and notional capital**

In relation to pension credit, a gift of capital or income which brings a **13–28** person into the realms of being able to claim pension credit may be seen as notional capital and so the benefits simply would not be paid.

In relation to local authority assessment for nursing home fees, the claimant may be treated as still owning the property or still receiving the income. There are time rules in relation to this. If the gift was made within six months of the assessment the local authority can make the donee liable to contribute towards the accommodation charges.[33] If it is more than six

---

[32] National Assistance (Assessment of Resources) Regulations 1992 (SI 1992/2977), as amended.
[33] Health and Social Services and Social Security Adjudications Act 1983, s.21.

months the local authority will consider debt collection and bankruptcy of the claimant but cannot force the return of the asset.

The local authority may deem any transfer at any time as deliberate deprivation of capital, as there is no time limit on how far back they will look and, of course, in one sense a house is the worst asset to transfer as there is a permanent and public record of all house transfers in either the Register of Sasines or the Land Register. If the motive or a substantial part of the motive for the transfer was to avoid paying for residential care then it will be caught.[34]

### Occupant of the house wishes to move

13–29    The Scottish Government has given guidance that it would be unreasonable for local authorities to prevent the occupant of the house moving to another house and using the capital belonging to the care home resident to purchase the new home. Simply allowing one's spouse, e.g. to spend the money on another house should not be viewed as deliberate deprivation of assets. Unmarried partners and other relatives should ask the local authority to treat the property in the same manner as if for a spouse.

### Choosing a care home

13–30    Anyone moving into a care home has the right to choose it providing it is suitable and available.[35] The resident cannot insist that the local authority provides accommodation costing more than it normally expects to pay, but he or she can go into a dearer home if a relative or third party (but not the spouse) is prepared to pay the extra amount.[36] The local authority will only agree if satisfied the relative can afford this for so long as the resident will be in care.

### Deferred payments

13–31    Cost of care fees can be deferred indefinitely if the local authority is prepared to enter into an agreement with the resident, such agreement avoiding the need to sell the house. The method is for the local authority to take a standard security over the house and the charges are rolled up and not payable until 56 days after the date of death of the resident.[37] No interest accrues until the 56 days are up after which the local authority can charge a reasonable rate of interest until payment is made. In a situation where a house takes a while to sell the rate should not be punitive.[38]

All local authorities must give details of these schemes to those who might be eligible and the schemes should be made available to anyone whose capital (excluding the value of the home) is less than the lower capital limit for funding care (currently £12,500).

The schemes seem rarely to be used in practice.

---

[34]    *Yule v South Lanarkshire Council (No1)*, 1998 S.L.T. 490; *Yule v South Lanarkshire Council (No2)*, 2000 S.L.T. 1249.
[35]    Social Work (Scotland) Act 1968 (Choice of Accommodation) Directions 1993, para.3.
[36]    Social Work (Scotland) Act 1968 (Choice of Accommodation) Directions 1993, para.4.
[37]    Community Care and Health (Scotland) Act 2002, s.6.
[38]    Scottish Executive Health Department Letter HDL 2003/6.

# Chapter 14

# PRACTICAL ADVICE FOR THE ELDERLY CLIENT

## INTRODUCTION

Many elderly clients will not have any close relatives living nearby and, as **14–01** the geographic scattering of families continues, this trend is likely to increase. Many solicitors will look after the affairs of elderly clients whether acting as attorney or otherwise and will find that rather than legal questions it is often a matter of practicalities to be dealt with to ensure that the client is properly looked after. This chapter offers some lateral thinking and advice and deals with aspects out with the legal and financial jurisdictions.

## GAS AND ELECTRICITY

### Changing suppliers

Whilst money may be saved by changing suppliers it can happen that a **14–02** person may be unhappy about having been duped into a contract on the doorstep.

### The best deal

On looking at the most recent bills a householder can estimate annual **14–03** consumption and how much they are paying for that supply. The independent consumer watchdog, Energy Watch, can then be contacted[1] and they will supply price comparison material, based on consumption, for suppliers in the area where the client lives. This is preferable to checking and relying on the numerous private web sites doing comparisons. If the client has a very limited income, it might be prudent to check supplier's policies on debts and/or disconnection if either of these possibilities is a reality.

### Getting out of a bad deal

If a "sales rep" has called uninvited to the house then the householder has **14–04** seven days to change their mind about the contract which they have signed for the new supply. If the re-organisation was over the telephone there are seven days from the date written confirmation of the agreement is received in which to alter the decision.

---

[1] By telephone on 0845 906 0708 or web site *http://www.energywatch.org.uk* [accessed July 18, 2007].

**Additional services**

**14–05**    Pensioners, the disabled and the chronically sick are entitled to certain additional services from the energy supplier which include: large print or braille bills; free annual gas safety check; priority restoration of an interrupted supply; supply of temporary heating and cooking facilities; and notice of any anticipated interruption to the supply, if the supply is necessary for any medical equipment.

**Debt and disconnection**

**14–06**    As with any debt, the best advice is for the client to contact the creditor as soon as possible and try to negotiate a repayment plan. If the negotiations do not go well, approach Energy Watch. Disconnection should not be threatened by the supplier whilst the customer has agreed a repayment plan or is disputing or discussing the size of the bill.

Energy suppliers are not allowed to disconnect the supply to those of retirement age between October 1 and March 31. For those on pension credit it might be possible to request "fuel direct" from the energy company or through Energy Watch. An amount is deducted from the benefit payment each week and paid direct to the energy company. This limits the maximum level deducted per week towards fuel costs and the service is cheaper than paying for fuel through a prepayment meter. It also helps a person to budget when on a low income.

## SPECIALIST EQUIPMENT

**Daily living equipment**

**14–07**    Many lawyers carry out home visits and will have seen an elderly client struggling round the house and quite clearly having difficulties performing day-to-day tasks.

After seeking the client's permission, the social work department of the local authority can be contacted who will arrange for an assessment of the client in their own home by an occupational therapist. Anyone can instigate this; there does not have to be a doctor's referral to start this process.

The social work department has a duty to ensure provision of services to support disabled people.[2] Each council will have its own local eligibility criteria and if those criteria are met the client is entitled to have the services which will meet or address those needs. The situation varies from council to council as the council is entitled to take its own physical resources into account when preparing its eligibility criteria. However once the criteria are created and an assessment agrees that the criteria are met by an individual, lack of resources is thereafter not a valid reason for failing to provide those services.

---

[2]   Chronically Sick and Disabled Persons Act 1970.

Local authorities are allowed to charge for much of the equipment and many of alterations that they provide, although many do not do so. The current guidelines say that equipment and minor adaptations provided and required to support a person's discharge from hospital should be free if they are supplied and fitted within four weeks of discharge. If the lawyer feels that a client has been unfairly charged for this service then a copy of the local authority's policy and criteria should be sought and the matter followed up with the social work department.

Large expensive items may be classed as adaptations and so disabled facilities grants will be available to be pursued through the housing department of the local authority.

### Health related equipment

Such equipment might be hearing aids, low vision aids, commodes, health **14–08** and daily living and walking aids. Those on pension credit may not have to pay for such items. Those on a low income may be eligible for the NHS low income scheme.

### Wheelchairs

These are supplied via the NHS wheelchair service which will have its own **14–09** criteria to be used for assessing eligibility. Details are provided by the NHS on free long-term loan. Of course they may be quite basic rather than the latest models.

More advanced wheelchairs may be purchased with the help of charitable funding by contacting Charitable Search. The British Red Cross can lease or lend one on short-term loan if only required for a temporary period.

### Community alarms

Many elderly clients will answer the door wearing a community alarm **14–10** pendant. This is a comforting option for many, allowing freedom and independence with the knowledge that back up is there at the touch of a button or by telephone or pull cord to the central service.

### Funding

*Those in employment*

The employment service or Jobcentreplus may fund equipment which a **14–11** person requires to be able to work. The disability employment adviser at the local Jobcentreplus should be able to advise and assist.

*Value added tax*

Disabled people do not have to pay VAT when purchasing equipment **14–12** designed or adapted to help them with daily living. This VAT exemption also relates to the cost of servicing and maintaining the equipment.

## TELEVISION

### TV licence concessions

**14–13**     Many elderly clients are fully subscribed to satellite television and enjoy their sport and movie packages. However satellite fans or not, a television licence is necessary.[3] These are no longer available from the Post Office.

TV licences are free for individuals aged over 75. A person becomes eligible and will have to apply for a free licence from the start of the month in which they become 75. Refunds are available of any fee they have paid in error and there are ways to part-pay a licence for the period up until the qualifying birthday. On application TV Licensing ask for proof of the individual's national insurance number and date of birth. They then verify that this information is correct with the Department for Work and Pensions, who are authorised to disclose dates of birth and national insurance numbers to the BBC and its agents, to allow TV Licensing to check eligibility. Only one free licence is available to claim (one per principal property not TV set), and licences for second homes must be paid for in full. Short-term licences are available for those aged 74.

Those who registered blind can claim a 50 per cent discount on the cost of the TV licence.

Those who are disabled or retired aged over 60 and (1) do not work more than 15 hours per week; and (2) who live in a care home will be eligible for a residential care licence. This may also apply to sheltered housing and the application is made by the managing authority of the care home or sheltered home and offers a licence at a much reduced cost to each resident. There are very strict rules about this.

On death the free licence remains in force until its expiry date when the remaining householder, if aged under 75, will have to make arrangements for a paid licence.

### Digital switch over

**14–14**     This is programmed to happen in Scotland between 2008 and 2010 and clients should be advised to make arrangements for Freeview by cable, digibox or satellite sooner rather than later.

## GETTING OUT AND ABOUT

### Disability living allowance

**14–15**     If a person becomes disabled before 65 and makes a claim they will get disability living allowance containing a mobility component. This will be either at the higher or lower rate depending on the level of disability.

---

[3]  Communications Act 2003.

## Bus travel

From April 1, 2006 people aged over 60 and also disabled people are **14–16** entitled to a free bus pass and certain free off-peak bus travel. The generosity of the scheme varies from local authority to local authority and details of the scheme will be available from the local authority. A national entitlement card is required and can be applied for from Transport Scotland.[4]

## Rail travel

Senior rail cards are available to anyone aged 60 or over and cost £20 for **14–17** one whole year. This entitles various discounts and concessions.[5]

A disabled persons rail card is currently £14 per year and offers similar discounts but does allow a companion to come with the disabled person at the same reduced rate. Wheelchair users without rail cards can get discounts as can their travelling companion.

Registered blind or partially sighted people without rail cards can get discounts if they travel with a companion.

## Drivers and cars

### Mobility

The AA, RAC, Mobility Advice and Vehicle Information Service and the **14–18** Mobility Information Service can all advise on being a disabled driver. Motability has a scheme to help disabled people lease and buy new cars and also second-hand cars.

### Licence

All drivers must renew their driving licence on reaching the age of 70 and **14–19** every three years from then on. On the renewal form the driver must declare whether he or she is suffering from any of the notifiable medical conditions. On disclosing a medical condition a further form is sent to supply greater details of the condition and allowing DVLA to get a medical report from the doctor. This will lead to the licence being renewed, restricted or revoked.

### RoSPA

If the driver feels perfectly confident but family members are putting on **14–20** pressure to give up the car then the experienced drivers assessment by the Royal Society for the Prevention of Accidents might be a sensible way to resolve the issue.

### VAT

As with house adaptations, adaptations to a car may be VAT exempt and **14–21** this exemption may also apply to repairs, etc.

---

[4]  *http://www.transportscotland.gov.uk* [accessed July 18, 2007].
[5]  *http://www.senior-railcard.co.uk/* [accessed July 18, 2007].

*Vehicle excise duty*

**14–22**    For those who receive the higher rate of the mobility component of the DLA there should be no vehicle excise duty paid. For this exemption to apply the vehicle must be used either by the disabled person or directly for them, which means the person can be a passenger.

*Blue badge*

**14–23**    Full details of the Blue (formerly Orange) Badge Parking Scheme are issued by the Department for Transport. The person qualifies for the badge, which allows for on-street parking concessions enabling people with severe walking difficulties (either as drivers or passengers) to park as near as possible to their destinations.[6]

The Scheme is administered by local authorities that deal with applications and issue the Blue Badges.

Qualification is based on whether an individual:

- receives the higher rate of the mobility component of the disability living allowance;
- receives a war pensioners' mobility supplement;
- uses a motor vehicle supplied for disabled people by a government health department;
- is registered blind;
- has a severe disability in both upper limbs, regularly drives a motor vehicle but cannot turn the steering wheel of a motor vehicle by hand even if that wheel is fitted with a turning knob; or
- has a permanent and substantial disability which means that he or she is unable to walk or has very considerable difficulty in walking.

The local authority may also request information from the individual's doctor or ask the person to attend an assessment by a qualified medical professional, such as an occupational therapist.[7]

*Parking spaces*

**14–24**    Disabled drivers may be able to ask the local authority to provide them with a parking bay outside their home. These are not usually enforceable by the police and are not for the exclusive use of the applicant but for any disabled badge holder. It is possible to have a disabled bay provided via a traffic regulation order which would make it legally enforceable. The parking bay provided may be free of charge or there may be a charge depending on the local authority.

**Taxicard scheme**

**14–25**    Broadly speaking, a taxicard scheme allows disabled people to travel in licensed taxis at substantially reduced fares. Taxicard can effectively complement or provide an alternative to dial-a-ride (ring-and-ride) schemes

---

[6]    *http://www.dft.gov.uk/transportforyou/access/bluebadge/* [accessed July 18, 2007].
[7]    Department for Transport.

which, whilst providing a valuable service, are inappropriate for certain trips that cannot be scheduled. Taxicard draws on the availability of taxis as a pre-existing, flexible, on demand service.

The decision to introduce a taxicard scheme is down to individual local authorities and will depend on a number of factors such as the availability of funding and the number of accessible taxis within a given locality

### Electric scooters

Scooters and buggies can be driven on the pavement or the road but **14–26** surprisingly are not the subject of the Highway Code as they do not fit into any road user category. Perhaps more surprisingly in today's climate of public safety there is no requirement to undertake any basic training. They must not exceed four miles per hour on footpaths and there is no requirement to have insurance nor a driving licence or road tax disc. The prudent user would arrange insurance for a personal injury to self or others and would practice manoeuvres in a safe environment before venturing out amongst pedestrians and traffic.

Previously these scooters were free from not only VAT but also import duty. The EU in June 2007 changed the customs classification of these vehicles from "carriages for disabled persons" to "motor vehicles for the transport of persons". This means scooters on average costing £2,500 and imported mainly from China and Taiwan will now attract a 10 per cent import duty pushing up the price to the consumer.

### Volunteer transport

In some areas the WRVS will have volunteers who use their own cars to **14–27** drive people who cannot use public transport. The British Red Cross, St John Ambulance, Council for Voluntary Service or Rural Community Council may be able to help.

## CRIME PREVENTION

Many elderly people are vulnerable and are the target for criminals and their **14–28** nasty scams. Apart from the usual advice about having all windows and doors locked, a burglar alarm, only using a chain to answer the door, having a spy hole, etc. there are certain things that elderly people need to be more aware of. Psychologically speaking, as one ages, strangers start to look more and more similar and indeed to such a stage that a person never met before can look familiar. It is vital to advise clients always to ask for identification if somebody comes to the door and to make sure that the back door is locked before answering the front door as criminals often work in pairs.

### Mass marketing scams

**14–29**    Anything unsolicited, once in a lifetime, seems too good to be true, requires a quick response, is based overseas or asks for any personal or financial details, or asks the person to call a premium rate phone line is likely to be something the client should NOT be interested in.

### Identity theft

**14–30**    Another scourge of modern life is identity theft. All papers being "binned" should be carefully shredded or incinerated. Details of bank accounts should never be disclosed to anyone, and PIN numbers for cards should not be written down.

## EMPLOYMENT

**14–31**    Retirement age is set to rise to 68 and with many pensions forecasts being dismal; many pensioners are continuing to work. The law in the UK provides for protection against discrimination on the grounds of sex, race, disability, transgender status, marital status or civil partnership status, sexual orientation, religion or belief and most recently, age discrimination in respect of employment or vocational education for people of all ages.[8] Discrimination can be direct or indirect and may include harassment and victimisation.

The key provisions are removal of the upper age limit of 65 for unfair dismissal and redundancy claims, the right to request to continue working after employer suggests a retirement date, the right not to be forced to retire before age 65 unless this can be objectively justified by the employer and the right to protection against discrimination on the grounds of age generally.

## PLANNING FOR RETIREMENT

**14–32**    As a person approaches retirement and wishes to stop working it might be prudent first to reduce hours or responsibilities to make the transition to full retirement. Alternatively the employer may be willing to transfer the employee to a community organisation for a similar reason. Some people however do not wish to give up work and would like to continue working beyond normal retirement age. In these circumstances the advice of an independent financial adviser is essential to check the terms of any occupational pension or private pension to see whether the pension should be drawn or contributions should be continued (at existing level, increased or decreased) or discontinued.

State pension, pension credit, housing benefit and council tax benefit can all be claimed if a person is over state-pension age whether in or out of work. On reaching state-pension age clients should be advised to cease making national insurance contributions; this does not happen automatically.

---

[8]  Employment Equality (Age) Regulations 2006 (SI 2006/1031) (in force October 1, 2006).

## ROYAL TELEGRAMS

On reaching 100th, 105th and subsequent birthdays, and on 60th, 65th, 70th **14–33** wedding anniversaries and every year thereafter Buckingham Palace issue celebratory messages to individuals and couples. The centenarian section of the Department for Work and Pensions and the anniversaries office at Buckingham Palace arrange the messages.

Details of anniversary and birthday messages can be found on the website[9] under the section "Anniversary Messages". Copies of birth/marriage certificates should be sent along with application form not more than three weeks before the celebration date. The pension service notify Buckingham Palace of all forthcoming centenarians who are in receipt of state retirement pension and currently living in Scotland, England and Wales.

---

[9]  *http.//www.royal.gov.uk*. [accessed July 18, 2007].

CHAPTER 15

# DEATH

"The art of living well and dying well are one".[1]

## DYING TIDILY

**15–01** Sensible planning should ensure that lifetime planning complements death wishes. A holistic approach to organising a client's affairs should ensure that the desired results are achieved, with the minimum of fuss. Despite a magnitude of statistics on life expectancy and causes of death it is normally impossible to identify actually when death will occur. Therefore planning must be flexible, regularly reviewed and contain contingency plans relative to the person's circumstances at that time and to those of their family and selected beneficiaries. For example it is not necessary to know down to the last pence what the value of your estate will be, but good planning will ensure you strive for the best balance between financial security and tax efficiency. Similarly, the beneficiaries' positions must be accounted for—are you going to make their own inheritance tax position worse? Do they have difficulty dealing with money? Are they minor beneficiaries or those who could be under the age of 25 at the time of your death?

As Ch.2 identifies, making a will allows you to record your wishes and ensure that, as far as you can, these will be carried out on your death. As well as recording instructions on what you would like to happen to your estate, a will can be a useful opportunity to consider your funeral wishes. Death is undoubtedly an extremely stressful time for a family, regardless of the circumstances, and an expression of wishes can help to ease the stress and avoid family arguments on what one's wishes were. The majority of wills also provide for funeral costs being deducted from the estate and this will therefore ease the financial burden for the family. Additionally, funeral expenses are expressly detailed as deductible for inheritance tax purposes, and therefore can create an opportunity in themselves for limited tax planning.[2] Reasonable mourning expenses[3] and the cost of a tombstone or gravestone[4] are allowed for IHT purposes as well. Where assets are held abroad an allowance, not exceeding five per cent of the value of the

---

[1] Epicurus.
[2] Inheritance Tax Act 1984, s.172.
[3] Extra-Statutory Concessions F1 found at *http://www.hmrc.gov.uk/specialist/esc.pdf* [accessed August 30, 2007].
[4] SP 7/87.

property, is available for offsetting against the value of that property[5] to account for the extra administration.

Although it may be unusual for elderly clients to be acting as guardian or parent for minors, narrating wishes of who should take over the role of guardian in the will is very sensible.

The Presumption of Death (Scotland) Act 1977 and the Succession (Scotland) Act 1964 play important roles where the timing or order of death is unclear, e.g. a family calamity or where an individual has disappeared. The Acts provide clear rules on how the uncertainty can be addressed. This is vitally important for succession and the distribution of someone's estate. The rules are summarised below.[6]

In a common calamity where it is not possible to establish the order of death the younger person is deemed to have survived the older,[7] other than in the case of husband and wife, or civil partners where they are deemed neither to have survived the other.[8]

A court action may declare an individual dead if they have not been known to be alive for the last seven years or there is evidence that they are thought to have died.[9] For disappearance cases the date of death will be held as seven years after the person was last seen alive. This has significant impact on the distribution of an estate (see case study below).

**Case study**

Mr Jones died leaving a will dividing the whole of his estate between his **15–02** two sons. Following a family feud 10 years before one son had disappeared and no contact with the family or anyone else had been made. The executors of Mr Jones' will were unable to complete the administration as they could not distribute to the son who could not be located. The executors therefore raised an action to have the son presumed dead which was successful. The son was therefore deemed to have died seven years after the family feud which treated him as predeceasing the father, leaving the whole of the estate to the other brother. The costs of the action were significant and furthermore the family was then tasked with dealing with the intestate estate of the missing, presumed dead brother.

Prepaid funeral plans can be useful tools in recording wishes and taking part of the burden away from the family. However, the plans do carry certain risks that may not be immediately obvious—what if the individual's circumstances change, e.g. they remarry and no longer wish to be buried in the family plot, or their religious beliefs are different. Also the documentation can often be mislaid leaving the family with no knowledge of any plan and

---

[5] Inheritance Tax Act 1984, s.173.
[6] For an excellent fuller review of the Act see MacDonald, *Succession*.
[7] Succession (Scotland) Act 1964, s.31(1)(b).
[8] Succession (Scotland) Act 1964, s.31(1)(a).
[9] Presumption of Death (Scotland) Act, s.1(1).

the funeral is effectively paid for twice. The funeral directors may also cease trading or may not offer the flexibility for wishes to be changed.


## INTESTACY

**15–03**  Death without a will results in intestacy and the individual's estate must be wound up in accordance with the Succession (Scotland) Act 1964. This states that an estate should be divided firstly by deducting any outstanding debts, secondly payment of prior rights, thirdly payment of legal rights and finally distribution of the free estate.


### Prior rights

**15–04**    Spouses and civil partners are provided with prior rights over the estate which may or may not exhaust the estate, depending on the size. Prior rights allow for the spouse/civil partner receiving[10]:

(1) Where the deceased had an interest as owner or tenant in a dwelling house in which the surviving spouse/civil partner was ordinarily resident, the surviving spouse has a prior right—
    (a) where the value of the interest does not exceed £300,000, to the interest (or in certain cases to a sum equal to its value); or
    (b) in any other case, to the sum of £300,000.
(2) Where the deceased owned the furniture and plenishings of a dwelling house in which the surviving spouse was ordinarily resident, the surviving spouse has a prior right—
    (a) where the value of the furniture and plenishings does not exceed £24,000, to the whole furniture and plenishings; or
    (b) in any other case, to such part of the furniture and plenishings, to a value not exceeding £24,000, as the surviving spouse may choose.
(3) The surviving spouse has a prior right—
    (a) where the deceased left issue, to the sum of £42,000; or
    (b) where the deceased left no issue, to the sum of £75,000.


### Legal rights

**15–05**    In intestacy, after the prior rights allocation, children, including adopted children, or grandchildren (or remoter issue) of a predeceasing child by representation and the surviving spouse/civil partner then have the right to make a claim for legal rights.

- *Survived by spouse/civil partner and children*
  Surviving spouse/civil partner entitled to one-third of net moveable estate.
  Children (or their descendants by representation) entitled to one-third of net moveable estate.
- *Survived by spouse/civil partner only*

---

[10]  Succession (Scotland) Act 1964, ss.8, 9 and 9A as amended by The Prior Rights of Surviving Spouse (Scotland) Order 2005 (SSI 2005/252) (amounts with effect from 1st June 2005).

Surviving spouse/civil partner entitled to one-half of net moveable estate.
- *Survived by children (or their offspring) only*
  Children (or their offspring if children predeceased) entitled to one-half of net moveable estate.

Spouses/civil partners and children (or the offspring of predeceasing children) are also entitled to legal rights in testate cases, unless they have discharged their rights during lifetime (e.g. a separated spouse in a minute of agreement). Interest accrues on the legal rights entitlement from the date of death to the date of payment. If an individual claims their legal rights they forfeit any entitlement under the will.

If one claimant has received advances from the deceased during the deceased's lifetime the other claimants may insist on some of these advances being collated.

The period in which prior rights and legal rights must be claimed extends to 20 years, after which the rights are deemed to have prescribed.[11]

**The free estate**

In intestacy, after payment of the prior rights and legal rights, the remaining estate (the "free estate") is distributed to the following, in order of priority (subject to representation): **15–06**

(a) children;
(b) parents and brothers and sisters (divided equally between the classes if both classes alive);
(c) brothers and sisters (if no parents alive) (full blooded siblings take preference over half blood);
(d) parents (if no brothers or sisters);
(e) spouse;
(f) uncles and aunts;
(g) grandparents;
(h) grandparents' brothers and sisters; and
(i) remoter relatives in order of family tree closeness.

Where there are no surviving children (or their issue) or surviving spouses/civil partners the free estate will make up the whole of the net estate.

In cases where none of these family members survive the individual the estate falls to the Crown as *ultimus haeres*.

The Family Law (Scotland) Act 2006[12] introduced the right for a co-habitee, in the case of intestacy only, to raise an action for provision, from which the court may make an order for payment of a capital sum, transfer of property or an interim order as the court sees fit,[13] accounting for various factors such

---

[11] Prescription and Limitation (Scotland) Act 1973, s.7.
[12] Family Law (Scotland) Act 2006, s.29.
[13] Family Law (Scotland) Act 2006, s.29(2).

as the size and nature of the deceased's net estate.[14] There is a time limit of six months from the date of death for the application to be made.[15]

An intestate estate is normally more expensive to administer and the time-scales are greater. Furthermore an insurance policy, known as a bond of caution, is normally necessary to protect the executors who distribute the estate under the intestacy rules in case a valid will is later identified. The policy premium is dependent on the size of the estate, but tends to be significantly higher than the cost would have been to have instructed a solicitor to prepare a will.

## ADMINISTRATION ON DEATH

**15–07** The doctor recording the death will issue a medical certificate narrating the cause of death. This must be taken to the local registrar's office[16] within eight days of the death for registration.[17] Deaths occurring outside Scotland should be registered in that country and a translation can be obtained, if need be, by the British Consul in that country.

Registration of the death at the registrar's office can be done by any relative of the deceased, the deceased's executor, any person present at the death, a legal representative or any other person possessing the required information. The deceased's birth and marriage/civil partnership certificates should be produced at the time the death is registered along with the medical certificate. Once the death is registered the registrar will issue the formal death certificate.

Before any funeral plans are made the deceased's will and papers should be checked for any funeral wishes, funeral plans or insurance, and any record of their wishes for organ/body donation. The funeral can then be organised by a firm of funeral directors who along with the solicitor dealing with the estate will organise the death notices in the newspapers.[18]

Most wills expressly provide for the cost of the funeral being settled from the estate.[19] If insufficient funds exist the funeral directors will normally seek payment from the person who organised the funeral, although financial help can be obtained from the social fund.[20] Burial and cremation are the most popular options and the funeral directors will be able to assist with the entire funeral organisation.

---

[14] Family Law (Scotland) Act 2006, s.29(3).

[15] Family Law (Scotland) Act 2006, s.6.

[16] Telephone numbers and addresses can normally be found in the Phone Book.

[17] It is an offence to register a death outwith the eight day period and a fine may be due.

[18] Most newspapers will only publish a death notice on the instructions of the funeral directors or a solicitor.

[19] Such expenses are deductible for IHT purposes provided they are "reasonable", Inheritance Tax Act 1984, s.172.

[20] Available from local JobCentre Plus Office or website *http://www.jobcentreplus.gov.uk/ JCP/Customers/WorkingAgeBenefits/Dev_008260.xml.html* [accessed July 19, 2007].

Before an estate may be distributed all of the assets and debts must be identified and valued as at the date of death. Furthermore, lifetime transfers in the seven years before death must be considered for the purposes of inheritance tax together with the net death estate. It may be necessary to also account for transfers up to 14 years before death so good records should be kept where possible.

As with items in deposit boxes at banks, most organisations require confirmation (formal granting by the court allowing the executors to ingather the estate) to be obtained before they will distribute the asset to the executor for making over to the beneficiary. If the estate is relatively small, e.g. the funds in a bank account are under £15,000, confirmation may not be necessary. There are special rules for small estates that reduce the administration.

**Case study**

As is not unusual the solicitors were tasked with dealing with winding up **15–08** the affairs of an elderly person who had died without close family. During the review of papers at the deceased's house a bank safety deposit box was identified. Banks are not generally keen on releasing the contents of deposit boxes until confirmation has been obtained. However by the time access for review of the contents was granted six weeks had passed since the death. Unfortunately, the only document within the safety deposit box contained the funeral instructions, many weeks after the funeral had actually taken place. This is obviously not the right place to keep funeral instructions.

## CONFIRMATION PROCESS AND PAYMENT OF IHT

The confirmation process involves narrating the individual's details, the **15–09** executors and compiling a list and valuation of the assets.

In addition to the Form C1 the correct HMRC form must be completed. Form C5 may be used where the gross value of the estate is less than the excepted estate limit (the IHT threshold amount for that tax year apart from deaths occurring between April 6 and August 5 inclusive when the previous year's threshold is used) or is less than £1,000,000 and after deduction of liabilities and spouse and civil partner and/or charity only (taking account of no other relief) the estate is below the IHT threshold (£300,000 for 2007/08). In all other cases the lengthier and more detailed IHT200 must be completed. These forms provide HMRC with details of the estate and the executor must complete the declaration that the information recorded is accurate to the best of their knowledge and belief.

The IHT200 requires a greater amount of information to be reported and there are probing questions into lifetime transfers and pensions that could affect the IHT due.

Where the estate is taxable the inheritance tax must be paid before confirmation can be obtained. This proves difficult in that the assets cannot be released until the organisations have sight of the confirmation. The executors are then tasked with locating funds to be able to meet the IHT liability. This can be done by way of an executry loan or, if liquid funds are available, some banks, building societies and national savings will advance the funds to the Revenue for this purpose. An instalment option for paying the IHT is available for qualifying property including land, shares or an interest in a business.[21] Otherwise the deadline for IHT to be paid is the earlier of the delivery of the account and six months after the end of the month in which the death occurred (for chargeable lifetime transfers the due date is also six months after the end of the month in which the transfer occurred unless it took place after April 5 and before October 1, in which case the IHT is due at the end of April the next year).[22] The executors are responsible for paying the tax and delivering the accounts.[23] The penalties for failure to deliver the accounts[24] and pay the tax[25] are cumbersome encouraging fulfilment of the timescales.

The duties of an executor should not be taken lightly and every effort should be made to comply with HMRC's requirements. As with the C5, the C1 and IHT200 also contain declarations which rely on the executors reporting accurate information. The testator (or court in the cases of intestacy) has entrusted the executor to administer and distribute the estate and meet all obligations imposed on them. There are financial penalties and the risk of prosecution for concealing or falsifying information; a custodial sentence is not unheard of. In the first prosecution of a taxpayer for inheritance tax fraud the executor was found guilty of embezzlement and defrauding the Inland Revenue of IHT and sentenced to seven years in prison.[26]

HMRC have certain rights and timescales for investigating estates and requesting papers so the executors should ensure that papers are kept beyond the administration period, and ideally for a minimum of seven years.

Life assurance policies can be taken out specifically for paying the IHT liability on death and are common options for clients who do not wish family members to be burdened with meeting the liability, or if a client has made a potentially exempt transfer and recognises that a tax liability could become due depending on their date of death.

Life assurance policies, in general, if they have been successfully written in trust may be paid out on sight of the death certificate and funds are therefore more readily available. The insurance company should have recorded wishes on where the funds are to go, but they are entitled to use their discretion.

---

[21]  Inheritance Tax Act 1984, ss.227 & 228.
[22]  Inheritance Tax Act 1984, s.226.
[23]  Inheritance Tax Act 1984, s.216.
[24]  Inheritance Tax Act 1984, s.245.
[25]  Inheritance Tax Act 1984, s.233.
[26]  *R v John Gardner Braes Lamberton* (unreported).

Assets in the estate may qualify for agricultural property relief (APR), business property relief (BPR) or woodlands relief. It is important that these reliefs are claimed by the executors as they can result in a significant reduction in IHT (50 per cent or 100 per cent for APR and BPR, or a deferred relief for woodlands).

If an individual died in active service or as a result of a wound, accident or disease contracted at a time when he or she was a member of any of the armed forces and was on active service against an enemy or of a warlike nature, their estate shall not be subject to IHT.[27] The relief can be claimed even where the wound/disease was only a contributory factor resulting from an injury some time before. In the case of *Barty-King v Ministry of Defence*[28] the death was due to cancer but a wound incurred 20 years before was held to have been a contributory factor and therefore the estate was exempt.

## QUICK SUCCESSION RELIEF

HMRC recognise that where deaths occur in quick succession it would be **15–10** considered unfair to have the same assets subject to tax twice (or more) over a short period of time. The quick succession rules[29] therefore provide for relief where there are two or more transfers within five years. Chargeable lifetime and death transfers are both given relief on the second (and later if applicable) transfers by reducing the normal IHT charge by the percentage relevant to the length of time between the transfers. The same assets need not be retained for the relief to apply. The appropriate percentages are[30]:

| Time period between transfers | Relevant Percentage Reduction |
|---|---|
| One year and under | 100% |
| 1–2 years | 80% |
| 2–3 years | 60% |
| 3–4 years | 40% |
| 4–5 years | 20% |

The relief can provide a substantial reduction in IHT, particularly where, perhaps one sibling has inherited on the death of another and then dies within five years of the first. Given that the executors of the estate may well be different people and the estate dealt with by different administrators it is possible that opportunities for claiming relief may be missed.

---

[27] Inheritance Tax Act 1984, s.154.
[28] [1979] 2 All ER 80. See also the case reported in *Express and Echo*, Thursday May 31, 2007.
[29] Inheritance Tax Act 1984, s.141.
[30] Inheritance Tax Act 1984, s.141(3).

## DOUBLE TAXATION RELIEF

**15–11**  In addition to the common-sense approach of the quick succession relief, double taxation relief may be claimed where there is a convention in place with the UK and another jurisdiction where the transfer (lifetime or death) is liable to a tax of similar character.[31]

Unilateral relief is also available where there is no double tax agreement between the jurisdictions, provided again that the tax is of a similar character and the same property is being taxed.[32]

## TAPER RELIEF

**15–12**  Lifetime transfers (either potentially exempt transfers or chargeable lifetime transfers) which are brought into account following death and which trigger an IHT liability as a result of exceeding the IHT threshold can have the IHT charge tapered if the transfer took place more than three years before death.[33] It is only the death tax which is reduced after calculating the IHT on the transfers within seven years of the death. The rates are[34]:

| | |
|---|---|
| Transfer made more than 3 but less than 4 years before death | 80% chargeable |
| Transfer made more than 4 but less than 5 years before death | 60% chargeable |
| Transfer made more than 5 but less than 6 years before death | 40% chargeable |
| Transfer made more than 6 but less than 7 years before death | 20% chargeable |

## ACCESS TO INFORMATION

**15–13**  It is of concern to many individuals how much of their personal information, on death, will be accessible to the public. It is normal procedure on death for many wills to be registered with the Books of Council and Register, the public record keeping office, to ensure that the deed cannot go astray and that an extract may easily be obtained. Once registered, anybody may request an extract copy of the will. Furthermore, once the papers are lodged with the local sheriff court for confirmation they again become publicly available, and these papers record the assets in the estate and their date of death values. Fortunately, in Scotland (other than some English newspapers) it is no longer common to see a record of who has died and what their will and estate contained. However, the information is accessible and on occasions estranged family members, the press and others may seek specific details about an individual. Previously, an option for avoiding such information being brought into the public domain would be to execute a

---

[31]  Inheritance Tax Act 1984, s.158.
[32]  Inheritance Tax Act 1984, s.159.
[33]  Inheritance Tax Act 1984, s.7.
[34]  Inheritance Tax Act 1984, s.7(3).

trust deed during lifetime allowing oneself with a liferent interest in the whole estate which was transferred to the trust. As a result, on death the assets themselves need not be confirmed to as they are in the names of the trustees who may distribute them in accordance with the trust terms. IHT would still be due on values over the IHT threshold but privacy was maintained. As a result of the Finance Act 2006 this route is less attractive as a transfer to a liferent trust is treated as chargeable transfer and IHT is due as a result of the lifetime transfer on the value over the IHT threshold.

## SUMMARY

There are so many factors to take into consideration on death. Good **15–14** planning can allow for a sustainable succession plan that is tax efficient and flexible. Elderly clients, in particular, as they approach their twilight years should review their wills and ensure that all aspects are covered. Proper advice should be taken at all times. The different issues covered in this chapter are not intended to cause alarm but to identify the need for matters to be addressed during lifetime so that those left behind can cope with the death with the best set of circumstances during one of the most difficult times.

# CHAPTER 16

# DEEDS OF VARIATION

**16–01** There are occasions when an individual who inherits considers that they do not need use of the funds/assets bequeathed. A deed of variation offers the opportunity for an inheritance, or part of it, to be redirected elsewhere as if it was always part of the original will.

## WHEN TO CONSIDER A DEED OF VARIATION AND THE RULES

**16–02** A deed of variation is a particularly useful tool for the elderly person who may have planned their own finances well thus feeling financially comfortable and wishes another individual/group of people/a trust/a charity to benefit instead. Additionally, an unexpected inheritance can also jeopardise the IHT planning of the beneficiary; therefore a deed of variation can reinstate the status quo in relation to the assets in their estate without triggering potentially exempt or chargeable transfers.

A correctly executed deed[1] of variation enables the transfer to be treated as though it was originally made from the deceased's estate, and not from the intended beneficiary. It will not, therefore, be a potentially exempt transfer if made to an individual (no IHT would be due subject to the individual surviving seven years) or a chargeable transfer where made to a trust (other than a disabled or charitable trust). Furthermore, if required, the capital gains tax (CGT) position can be treated as though the new beneficiary inherited at the date of death value which would avoid a CGT liability where a taxable gain would otherwise exist. Depending on any rise/fall in value it may not be desirable for the CGT election to be made. The person varying the will may have their own annual capital gains tax allowance available and this may adequately cover the gain, thus allowing the new beneficiary to take over the asset at a higher base cost.

The rules for deeds to be valid are:

- the deed must be in writing[2];
- the deed must be executed not more than two years after the death[3];
- the deed must contain a statement that the deed is to be effective for IHT purposes as set out in s.142 (2) of the IHTA 1984[4];

---

[1] The legislation only requires an "instrument in writing", but a formally executed deed is considered to be best practice.
[2] Inheritance Tax Act 1984, s.142(1).
[3] Inheritance Tax Act 1984, s.142(1)(b).
[4] Inheritance Tax Act 1984, s.142(2).

- the deed is made for no consideration in money or money's worth[5];
- if intended to be effectual for CGT purposes to treat the new beneficiary inheriting at date of death values and not at the date of transfer value (which could trigger a CGT liability for the person transferring) the deed must contain a statement that s.62(6) of the Taxation of Chargeable Gains Act 1992 shall apply.[6]

Executors must be party to the deed where the deed of variation increases the IHT liability.[7] HMRC need not be notified about the deed unless the IHT position of the deceased is affected. Obviously any new trust will need to be reported in the usual way.[8] Where additional IHT is due the executors must notify HMRC within six months after the date of variation, pay the IHT and send a copy of the deed.

Items may only be subject to one instrument and will not validly be redirected further,[9] therefore careful thought must be put into the deed and the arrangement before execution.

Even where the intended beneficiary has died after the individual whose will bequeathed assets to them, the executors of the intended beneficiary have the opportunity of entering into a deed of variation, providing they do so within two years of the first deceased person's death. This can be particularly useful where spouse or civil partners have died within two years of each other and the first had bequeathed their whole estate to the other which aggregated at an amount over the IHT threshold.

Deeds of variation can also be used in cases of both testate estates and intestate estates allowing beneficiaries to redirect their entitlement as they see fit.

Perhaps the most common planning opportunities for an elderly person considering a deed of variation are as follows:

### CASE 1

One spouse dies bequeathing the whole estate to the surviving spouse. The **16–03** gross estate of the surviving spouse is now the total of the two (no IHT on the transfer as is to an exempt beneficiary). If the surviving spouse intends for their children to ultimately benefit by executing a deed of variation the first spouse's nil rate band could be utilised and if the joint net estates are in excess of £600,000, and the variation allows for the full nil rate band amount (£300,000 for 2007/08) to pass to the children £120,000 of IHT is potentially saved as those assets could otherwise be in the estate of the second spouse and taxable on their death. Before executing the deed of variation the surviving spouse should carefully evaluate whether they may in fact require use of the funds to be financially comfortable.

---

[5] Inheritance Tax Act 1984, s.142(3). This is interpreted broadly and HMRC may investigate whether any arrangements are in place.

[6] Taxation of Chargeable Gains Act 1992, s.62(6).

[7] Inheritance Tax Act 1984, s.142(2A)(b).

[8] See Ch.3.

[9] *Russell v IRC* [1998] S.T.C. 195.

## CASE 2

**16–04** Situation as with case 1 but if the surviving spouse wanted a more flexible position the will could be varied creating a discretionary trust with the nil rate band amount. The surviving spouse themselves could be a potential beneficiary, along with the children and any other beneficiaries. The choice of trustees should be made carefully to reflect an element of independence in relation to the trust decision making. If desired the power to loan, and for the trustees to accept an undertaking, can be included if the surviving spouse anticipates that he/she may wish the use of the funds but would like the position to be as tax efficient as possible in terms of any advance from the trust ultimately being a loan as detailed in para.2–11.

## CASE 3

**16–05** Again as with case 1 but the surviving spouse may already feel financially secure and recognise that their children are too. Therefore a trust for the grandchildren could be established with the nil rate band. As discussed in Ch.3 a trust has many advantages in terms of protection and yet the funds are ear marked for their benefit. As the nil rate band amount would be the maximum transferred under the deed of variation (to avoid an IHT charge), the trust should not incur any future IHT charges on exit or on the 10-year anniversary unless the funds had increased in excess of the nil rate band at the time of exit/10-year anniversary.

Obviously for the full nil rate band to be available there would need to be adequate assets in the estate and no other transfers on death, or lifetime chargeable transfers, or legal rights claims which would reduce the amount which could pass tax free.

## CASE 4

**16–06** Grown up children who inherit may wish to execute a deed of variation in favour of their own children. The deed can be effective for IHT (i.e. the transfer will be treated as coming from the deceased's estate) but if the new beneficiaries are under 18 (and unmarried/not in a civil partnership) their parent redirecting in their favour should be aware that for income tax and CGT purposes the variation will be considered to be a parental settlement. Such settlements deem any annual income over £100 to be treated as that of the parent and any disposal assessable to CGT against the parent.

## CASE 5

**16–07** Many elderly people are sadly left without any surviving family and often think of their friends when making their wills. On death the friend may feel that they do not require all of the funds. If the sum passing to the friend was in excess of the nil rate band there would IHT due. By executing a deed of variation redirecting the funds to a charity the IHT liability could be reduced or completely removed depending on the value redirected. A common and heart warming choice by friends in such circumstances is to create in the deed of variation a charitable trust in honour of the deceased (often naming it the "..................." Charitable Trust) with charitable purposes which were of importance to the deceased. Chapter 3 identifies the requirements for charitable status in Scotland to be achieved and the charitable purposes recognised.

If on the death of one spouse the surviving spouse wished a charity to benefit a deed of variation would not be necessary. The surviving spouse could inherit as per the will/intestacy and then make the transfers themselves. The transfer by the surviving spouse would be an exempt transfer and furthermore there would be the opportunity of claiming gift aid relief if he/she is a UK income tax payer which could reduce his/her income tax liability for that tax year.

Attorneys and guardians may have been granted the power to enter into instruments of variation or discharge any rights in whole or in part under a will or intestacy. The powers should be expressly provided for and the attorney/guardian should ensure that any action can justifiably be shown to be in the interests of the adult, or implements past or present wishes.

## CASE STUDY

Mr White died leaving a will which bequeathed the whole of his estate **16–08** (approximately £300,000) to his wife. Mrs White, at the time of her husband's death, was settled in a nursing home but had lost capacity and had not granted a power of attorney. Mrs White's estate comprised of assets in excess of £500,000. One of Mrs White's children raised an action for an intervention order allowing her as guardian to act on behalf of her mother and redirect her mother's entitlement under her father's will to her and her siblings. Actuarial evidence was provided that Mrs White was very unlikely to ever require funds beyond what was already in her estate. As sufficient evidence was presented that the IHT saving would be in Mrs White's interests the order was granted. Had Mrs White died within two years of her husband her executors could have entered into a deed of variation on Mr White's estate instead of applying for an intervention order. However the intervention order was considered to be the best option as the date Mrs White would pass away was indeterminate.

Although deeds of variation offer opportunities in terms of planning they are no substitute for well-drafted wills. Many beneficiaries often feel that regardless of the tax advantages in executing a deed of variation they wish to honour the deceased's wishes and accept their inheritance. Therefore careful thought should be put into any will and the will should be reviewed regularly. Furthermore, if it is anticipated that a beneficiary may wish to enter into a deed of variation a separate letter of wishes could be prepared recording their views and reassuring the beneficiary that they must do what they see fit.

APPENDIX 1

# USEFUL CONTACTS

**Age Concern Scotland**
113 Rose Street
Edinburgh
EH2 3DT
Tel: 0131 220 3345

**Alzheimer's Disease Society**
2nd Floor
Gordon House
10 Greencoat Place
London
SW11 1PH
Tel: 020 7306 0606
*http://www.alzheimers.org.uk*
[accessed August 21, 2007].

**Alzheimer's Scotland — Action on Dementia**
22 Drumsheugh Gardens
Edinburgh
EH3 7RN
Tel: 0131 243 1453

**Buckingham Palace** — The
Anniversaries Office
Buckingham Palace
London
SW1A 1AA
Tel: 020 7930 4832
*http://www.royal.gov.uk* [accessed
July 19, 2007].

**Care and Repair Forum Scotland**
236 Clyde Street,
Glasgow
G1 4JH
Tel: 0141 221 9879

**Carers National Association**
3rd Floor
162 Buchanan Street

Glasgow
G1 2LL
Tel: 0141 333 9495

**Citizens Advice Bureau (CAB)**
Address of local CAB in phone
book
*http://www.citizensadvice.org.uk*
[accessed July 19, 2007].

**Contact the Elderly in Scotland**
15 Henrietta Street
Covent Garden
London,
WC2E 8QG
Tel: 0800 7165 43
*http://www.contact-the-elderly.org/
scotland.html* [accessed July 19,
2007].

**The Dementia Services Development Centre**
Iris Murdoch Building
University of Stirling
Stirling
FK9 4LA
Tel: 01786 467740

**Department of Work and Pensions**
*http://www.dwp.gov.uk/* [accessed
July 19, 2007].

**The Pension Service**
Tel: 0845 60 60 265

**Eaga Partnership Limited**
1st Floor
Flat A
Richmond House
The Water Mark
Swalwell

NE11 9SZ
Tel: 0800 316 6011

**Elderly Accommodation Counsel**
3rd Floor
89 Albert Embankment
London
SE1 7TP
Tel: 020 7820 7867
*http://www.eac.org.uk* [accessed
August 21, 2007].

**Energy Efficient Advice Centres**
Tel: 0800 512 015
*http://www.saveenergy.co.uk*
[accessed July 19, 2007].

**Funeral Standards Council**
30 North Road
Cardiff
Wales
CF1 3DY
Tel: 029 2038 2046
*http://www.funeral-standards-council.co.uk* [accessed July 19,
2007].

**HMRC**
*http://www.hmrc.gov.uk* [accessed
July 19, 2007].
HMRC's Taxback Helpline on 0845
077 6543.

**National Association of Funeral Directors**
618 Warwick Road
Solihull
West Midlands
B91 1AA
Tel: 0845 230 1343
*http://www.nafd.org.uk* [accessed
July 19, 2007].

**Office of the Public Guardian**
The Office of the Public Guardian
Hadrian House
Callendar Business Park
Callendar Road
Falkirk
FK1 1XR
Tel: 01324 678300

*http://www.publicguardian-scotland.gov.uk* [accessed July 19,
2007].

**Office of the Scottish Charity Regulator**
Office of the Scottish Charity
Regulator (OSCR)
2nd Floor
Quadrant House
9 Riverside Drive
Dundee
DD1 4NY
Tel: 01382 220446
*http://www.oscr.org.uk/* [accessed
July 19, 2007].

**Royal National Institute of the Blind**
105 Judd Street
London
WC1H 9NE
Tel: 020 7388 1266
*http://www.rnib.org.uk* [accessed
July 19, 2007].

**Royal National Institute of the Deaf**
19-23 Featherstone Street
London
EC1Y 8SL
Telephone: 020 7296 8000
Textphone: 020 7296 8001
*http://www.rnid.org.uk* [accessed
July 19, 2007].

**Scottish Government**
Telephone Enquiry Line:
Tel: 08457 741 741
*http://www.scotland.gov.uk/Home*
[accessed July 19, 2007].

**Scottish Public Services Ombudsman**
23 Walker Street
Edinburgh
EH3 7HX
Tel: 0131 225 5300

**Shelter Scotland**
4th Floor, Scotiabank House
6 South Charlotte Street
Edinburgh
EH2 4AW

*http://www.scotland.shelter.org.uk/home/* [accessed July 19, 2007].

**Solicitors for the Elderly**
Room 17
Conbar House
Mead Lane
Hertford
Herts
SG13 7AP
Tel: 01992 471568

**Tax Help for Older People**
12 Upper Belgrave Street
London
SW1X 8BB
Tel: 0845 601 3321

**TV Licensing**
TV Licensing
Bristol
BS98 1TL
Tel: 0870 241 6468

**Veterans Agency**
Service Personnel and Veterans Agency
Norcross
Thornton Cleveleys
Lancashire
FY5 3WP

# COMMUNICATION

In assisting the elderly client it is vital to ensure that the most effective communication methods are adopted to enable the client to fully understand the matters being addressed and to feel comfortable with the situation. Each client's needs should be assessed separately and time should be spent ensuring that the client is happy with the proposed communication methods. For example, letters typewritten in large font require no extra work by the practitioner and can greatly assist the client if they have restricted sight and would prefer to have letters formatted in this way.

There have been a number of studies undertaken to analyse the medical aspects of old age, and the best practice for maximising effective two way communication has also been reviewed. The Dementia Services Development Centre of the University of Stirling has undertaken various creditable studies and their findings and published literature are invaluable to those wishing to ensure they communicate effectively. This book has highlighted the importance of being able to assess a client's capacity and take correct instructions. The findings and advice of the Centre are extremely useful in enabling the practitioner to fulfil their role, whether it be taking will or power of attorney instructions or ensuring that a guardianship or intervention order is established in the best interests of the adult.

The following extracts are taken, and kindly reproduced with permission, from The Dementia Services Development Centre publications.

It is important to appreciate that communication is influenced by:

- *time of day and whether the person is tired or not;*
- *place—in their own home for example rather than in a hospital or day centre;*
- *number of distractions—it is usually more difficult to communicate if the television or radio is on at the same time, or if there are several conversations taking place at the same time, like at a family gathering or in a day centre.*[1]

Each person with dementia has a diversity and richness of life experience, and it is important that they communicate this. Knowledge of likes and dislikes, past and present relationships, and their interests are just a few areas in the diagram that carers can make professionals aware of. Behaviour

---

[1] A. Innes, *Hearing the Voice of People with Dementia*, Alan Chapman (ed.), (University of Stirling: Dementia Services Development Centre, 1997), p.3.

can then be seen in ways that can be understood and responded to more appropriately.[2]

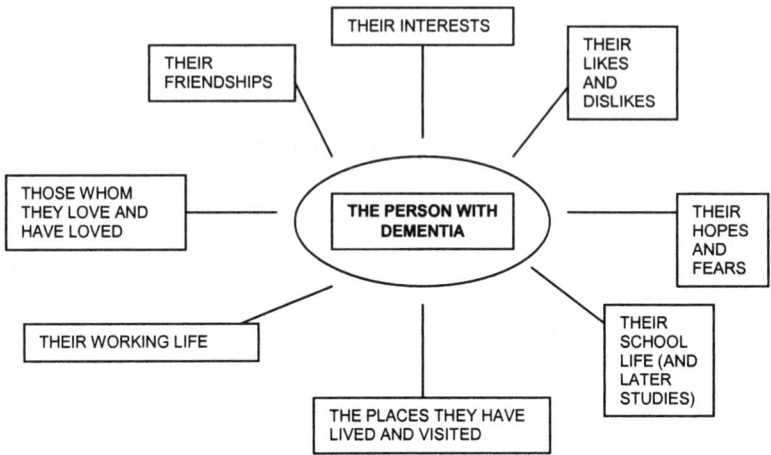

### Ten things to do to improve our communication[3]

- *Believe that communication with the person is possible.*
- *Try to focus on the non verbal signs as well as what is said.*
- *Avoid making assumptions: check things out with the person.*
- *Make your communication a two way process that engages the person with dementia.*
- *Avoid the use of jargon or complicated explanation. Keep your conversation as simple as possible without being patronising or sounding childish.*
- *Do not ask questions which have "why" in them. The person with dementia may find the reasoning involved in giving an answer too difficult and become annoyed with themselves.*
- *Be a good listener: give the person your full attention and resist the temptation to finish their sentences and talk at the person.*
- *Talk at a slow pace so that the person has an opportunity to grasp what is being said.*
- *Maintain a calm and unhurried approach.*
- *Discover the best time of day to spend time to talk with the person.*

[2]  A. Innes, *Hearing the Voice of People with Dementia*, p.13.
[3]  M. Goldsmith, M. Kindred and A. Innes, *Hearing the Voice of People with Dementia — A Study Guide* (University of Stirling: Dementia Services Development Centre), p.26.

# INDEX